An Insider's Critique of
THE KAZAKH NATION

An Insider's Critique of

THE KAZAKH NATION

Reflections on the Writings of Abai Kunanbai-uhli (1845-1904)

Garifolla Yesim

Translated and edited by R. Charles Weller,
with assistance from Tatyana Galkina, Zhuldyz Zhumashova and Sheri Six

Asia Research Associates
Boston, MA USA

Printed in the United States of America

First Edition
First Print Release, July 2020

Asia Research Associates
P.O. Box 95002
Newton, MA 02458-9998 USA
Telephone: (814) 327-7955
Email: ara@world-hcrc.com
Website: www.world-hcrc.com

ISBN: 978-0979495793 (hardcover edition)
Library of Congress Control Number (LCCN): 2020941704

In honor of the 175th Anniversary of Abai
1845-2020

In honor of the 175th Anniversary of Abai
1845-2020

Table of Contents

— Section One —
From Anacharsis to Abai:
The Intellectual Heritage in Historical Perspective
1 – 45

Anacharsis the Scythian

Yollug Tigin

Yusuf Balasaguni

Koja Ahmad Yasawi

Abai Qunanbayev

— Section Two —
'Concepts about Concepts' in the Songs & Poems of Abai
47 – 170

"Both God and His Word Exist"

"There Were Many Messages from the Creator, Especially Four of Them…"

"Do People Know Iskander?"

"The Times, They are a' Changin'"

"He Created Humankind in Love"

"Love for Three Things is Like Fragrant Flowers in Your Heart"

"God is Perfect and the Prophet Brings the Light of Truth"

"Old Age Approaches, No Hope Remains"

"The Past Errors of Those Who Stray Lead Them Down the Right Path"

"Lyrical Song is the King of Words, Their Highest Heights"

"Nature is Temporal, Humans Eternal"

"Earthly Life Is Like a River of Water"

"When the Number One is Gone, What Will Become of the Old Number Zero?"

"Poor Satan, the Spirit Banished by God"

"Tangri, Who Decorated the Earth, is the Master"

"Anxiety is a Person's Safeguard, A Sign of Their Thoughtfulness"

"Livestock – the Beauty of Humanity"?

"The One Who is Friends with Livestock Will Think Only about Livestock"

Review Statements

"Abai Kunanbai is one of the most renowned Kazakh intellectuals of the nineteenth century. Unlike so many of his contemporaries, his reputation as a poet and writer, a social and cultural leader, survived the Soviet era, albeit in a somewhat subdued form. He lived during an era of Russian expansion and colonization of the steppe, severe economic and social dislocation, but his works reflected a reformer's optimism and, equally, harsh social and cultural critiques. Charles Weller's new translation makes Abai's "words" available to an English-reading audience, accompanied by Garifolla Yesim's keen analysis and insight. It is a valuable contribution for scholars and others interested in Abai's life and work as well as Central Asian history."

Steven Sabol
Professor of History, University of North Carolina (Charlotte)
Author, *Russian Colonization and the Genesis of Kazakh National Consciousness* (2003)
and *"The Touch of Civilization": Comparing American and Russian Internal Colonization* (2017)

"Abai Kunanbaiuhli reminds me of George Sarton's profound observation... The author of the voluminous *Introduction to the History of Science* says that, "throughout the course of history, in every period, and in almost every country, we find a small number of saints, of great artists, of men of science." The 'Words' of the sage Abai presented by Garifolla Esim, a proficient witness of Kazakh society, demonstrate the harmonious place of the Kazakh people within the human family. I thoroughly enjoyed reading the book. I am sure it will capture the attention of many..."

Abdullah al-Ahsan
Professor of Comparative Civilization
Department of Political Science and International Relations
Istanbul Sehir University (Turkey)

About the Author

Garifolla Yesim (b. 1947) is a professor of historical, social and political philosophy. He has served as Dean of the Faculty of Philosophy and Political Science at both Almaty State University (1992-98) and Kazakh National University (2001-10) in Almaty, Kazakhstan. He now teaches at Eurasian University in Astana while serving as a Senate deputy in the Kazakhstani government. He is an academic of top national honors who contributes regularly to national television and radio programs as well as newspaper and magazine publications. He has written numerous books and journal articles in both Kazakh and Russian, including *The Elite Scholar Abai* (1994), *The Essence of Mind: Reflections on Politics and Culture* (1995-2007, 10 vols), *A History of Islamic Philosophy* (2000 and 2004), *Human-ity* (2001), *Kazakh Philosophy* (2005), *Kazakh Renaissance* (2006), *Political Philosophy* (2009), *The Philosophy of Independence* (2011) and *The Agony of Socialism* (2012, English edition 2017).

About the Book

Making a unique contribution to the study of Eastern philosophy and Muslim reform movements within the context of Kazakh and broader Central Asian history, *An Insider's Critique of the Kazakh Nation* offers "a window on the Kazakh world" through the eyes of one of the most prominent and treasured national philosopher-reformers to have appeared in their history: Abai Kunanbai-uhli (1845-1904).

Abai lived and wrote in the northeastern part of Kazakhstan from the latter part of the 19th to early 20th century serving as a pioneering and central figure in the Kazakh branch of the pan-Turkic, pan-Islamic 'Jadid' (i.e. 'new method') reform movement among the Muslims of Russia spearheaded by the Crimean Tatar Ismail Bey Gaspirali (aka Gasprinsky, 1851-1914). This situates Abai's work in its broader world historical setting among the parallel reform movements taking place across Asia among the Turks and Arabs of the Ottoman Empire, the Hindus and Indian nationalists of India, the Chinese nationalists and the Japanese Meiji reformers.

Abai's writings, particularly his *Book of Words*, have received international recognition, with translations into Russian, French, German, Chinese, English and other world languages. In the second half of his *Book of Words* Abai offered various reflections – all recorded in the latter part of his life – on the entire range of Kazakh religious, cultural, social and political lifeways and institutions addressed against the backdrop of late Tsarist Russian imperial rule in Central

Asia. He assesses what he considers to be the main obstacles to the advancement of Kazakh society in the face of Russian 'superiority' and domination, criticizing and praising both the Kazakhs and Russians in turn, offering suggestions for how the challenges facing his people might be overcome laced with lamentations for their failure to recognize and resolve these matters for themselves. He sets forth his reflections in a series of forty-five 'Words', each addressing a particular set of interrelated issues.

While at least two translations of Abai's writings have been made into English (albeit through Russian), what makes the present volume unique is that instead of providing a simple translation, Abai's late 19th-century reflections are interpreted through the commentary of a top national Kazakh scholar looking back across the 20th century and lifting out their meaning and significance for the Kazakh world in the early post-Soviet era, at a time when the newly independent nation of Kazakhstan was just emerging from some 150 to 200 years of Russian domination. It represents an important contribution to the earliest stages of their search to re-define themselves and their future by looking back to one of the central pioneers to embark on that quest until it was interrupted by the long Soviet intermission. We are thus offered the critique of two insiders – Abai and Yesim – each standing at crucial crossroads in Kazakh and, indeed, world history.

The multiple issues which both of these Kazakh insiders reflect upon carry plenty of relevance for peoples far and wide around the globe today, at both individual as well as community, national and even international levels. The latter is particularly true in their approach to Kazakh Muslim attitudes toward peoples of other ethnic and religious persuasions, with both Abai and Yesim calling for mutual friendship, embrace and dialogue with the non-Muslim world.

Translator's Preface

This book is an English translation of an original Kazakh work titled *Hakim Abai (The Elite Scholar Abai)* by Garifolla Yesim (1994). The author himself also produced a Russian version of the same work under the same title. The Russian version is not a mere rote translation of the Kazakh, it is a free rendering of its essential message which the author himself slightly condensed and modified for a Russian-speaking audience.

Making use of both the original Kazakh and the modified Russian versions, my approach to translating and producing the present English version has been eclectic. First, using their highly developed English skills together with their own personal commitment to precision and excellence, Zhuldyz Zhumashova and Tatyana Galkina of Kazakhstan translated their respective assigned sections of the book into English using the Kazakh and Russian versions respectively. Both worked quite tediously, with Galkina checking the Russian against the Kazakh at points and consulting with myself as well as other Kazakh and Russian scholars, including Yesim himself, to ascertain as precisely as possible the intended meaning and sense of original work(s).

I then took their translations and did two things: *One*: Sheri Six and I each edited designated sections of the English translations to achieve native-level accuracy and style, clarifying whatever was necessary by way of the original Kazakh version, the translators and the author. *Two*: using Galkina's English translation of section three as my starting point, I (re)translated entire select 'Words' and significant portions of others from the original Kazakh.

A good deal of Kazakh literature has fortunately yet unfortunately come to us via the medium of Russian translation, including several English versions of Abai's *Book of Words*,[1] Mukhtar Auezov's classic novel *Abai zholi* (*The Way of Abai*, with an abridged translation into English as *Abai: a novel*), Ilias Yesenberlin's classic novel *Koshpendiler*, that is, *The Nomads* (which became the basis for the 2005 Hollywood movie by the same title) and others. All of these compositions and a number of others which have been translated into English via Russian were originally composed in Kazakh, not Russian, and then translated by a separate, independent party into the latter language. This has definitely 'colored' the English-speaking world's perception of the Kazakh world, delivering it to us via a Russian filter which most assuredly has eclipsed and even at times distorted that world in significant ways.[2] Needless to say, all such translations, while retaining a great deal of value, need to be 'taken with a grain of salt'.

The present case should be clearly distinguished from such materials, however, since the Russian version employed herein is *not* a translation, but a version of the author's original work which has been produced afresh by the author himself and intentionally condensed as well as adapted by him for a Russian-speaking audience.[3] This translation, therefore, whether based upon the Russian or Kazakh versions, comprises a direct translation representing the author's own original message. In the end, the reader holds in their hands an eclectic, but highly reliable dynamic translation of the original *message* of the Kazakh author which comes with the full knowledge, confidence and approval of the author himself.

I have taken liberty to supply in the main text – typically without the use of distracting brackets or the like – important cultural and/or historical information which is implicit in the original work, things the average Kazakh or even Russian reader would know and understand, but which may be in need of clarification for the English reader. Where deemed appropriate, I have attempted to note and explain such clarifications via endnotes, particularly in section three. I have, likewise, taken liberty to produce a translation which remains as faithful as possible to the original, yet which departs from 'wooden literalism' when necessary in order to fully and faithfully communicate the intended sense of the original in a vocabulary and style natural to English.

I have not always followed the same paragraph formatting as occurs in the original Kazakh version, but have attempted, however arbitrarily, to create paragraph breaks where they seemed most natural in English. Somewhat relatedly, the English reader should take care not to pass judgment too quickly on the language or style which the original Kazakh author employs – albeit filtered via translation – to accomplish his aims. Though I was tempted at points to edit out or transpose the location of certain sections which did not seem, to my own mind, to necessarily flow or fit within the overall context, I have chosen to leave the original text in-tact on cultural grounds since it is extremely difficult for a foreigner, however fluent in the native language, to make judgments about such subtle cultural matters as communication and teaching/learning styles. The personal dimension, that is, Yesim's own style, would also be involved, with again both being left in-tact as much as possible, in balance with the need to achieve sufficient natural flow and clarity in English. I might also apologize here for the minor inconsistency in use of footnotes instead of endnotes in section two, and not providing an index, as admittedly preferred as the latter in particular would have been.

The Kazakhs value 'reflection' from scholars, elders and other respected figures, even in simple narrative form. Whatever influence might still be lingering from the deep oral tradition inherited from thousands of years of nomadic steppe culture would be a fascinating study in itself. Islamic traditions might also be playing some part. Regardless of sources however, if one is searching for a detailed analysis of written texts and the entire range of scholarly opinions attached thereto, marked by multiple endnotes and references to original as well as secondary sources, they will not find it here. But this does not detract from the quality or importance of the present work. Its value lies in its nature as well as the historical-cultural context in which and for which it was produced.

What the reader holds in their hands is not a line-by-line critical analysis of the text of Abai, but 'reflections' from a nationally recognized *post*-Soviet Kazakh scholar on the premier *pre*-Soviet representative of Kazakh national development and identity. Yesim wrote these 'reflections on reflections' as Kazakhstan was embarking on its second attempt in history to regain independence amid the breakdown of Russian imperial power. It was 'déjà vu' for the Kazakhs as they looked back on the late eve of the Tsarist Empire in Abai's day from the immediate aftermath of the Soviet Empire in their own. Ideas of *glasnost* were not yet a decade old and their expression within the newly independent republic of Kazakhstan were, in 1994, barely budding yet three years on the vine when Yesim penned this piece. In this light, Yesim's work must be viewed as part of a bold experiment to begin digging up national treasures of their past and attempting to re-interpret and re-apply them in their new opportunity for independence, a chance previously snatched from them just 70 years prior, soon after Abai lived and wrote.

The philosophical 'reflections' which lie at the heart of this work represent the very approach of Abai which Yesim intentionally sets out to model, in hopes of reviving and advancing this form of socio-political critique which did so much to impact the development of Kazakh national and international ideals in Abai's own day. In considering these 'reflections on reflections', it is not a matter of whether we feel these two Kazakh intellectuals, or any others for that matter, in critiquing their own historical and cultural context, are 'right' or 'wrong'. It is that they provide us with *An Insider's Critique* which offers us an important "window on the Kazakh world" of both Abai's and his post-Soviet interpreter's day.

The reader should also note, if they have not already, that I have intentionally chosen to break English grammatical rules by using plural referents for singular subjects in certain cases. My reason for this is that I am entirely sympathetic to the issue of inclusive language, that is, addressing both male and female readers as well as allowing for both male and female interpretations. But I am entirely unsympathetic to the cumbersome manner in which English works have become burdened with multiple variations of 'he/she', 'he or she', '(s)he', 's/he', etc.

The only exception to this are referents to 'God'. It would not bother me personally to allow for both male and female referents to 'God', in fact I would prefer it. I might even have gotten away with it since the Kazakh language resolves the whole matter for us by making no distinction between male and female in its third person pronouns, whether singular or plural. One word is used for both and the same. (Perhaps Kazakh, not English, should function as the international language!) But referring to 'God' as 'she' is not yet a widely accepted practice among the broader Muslim world. I thus leave the matter for feminist and other Islamic scholars writing in English to take up, as some are in fact already doing.

As for the term 'God', Kazakh has several, one of which is borrowed from the Arabic, namely 'Allah'. There has been some debate about whether or not this latter term should be translated as 'God' in English and I am among those advocating that this is, indeed, its normal, natural sense in the English language.[4]

Such discussion gives rise to one final point: Namely, the Western reader might be struck by how freely the author speaks about faith in God, love for God, service to God, etc, in a book which was written by a scholar within a 'secular' academic setting. Perhaps it is precisely there that we stumble, however, in our Western dichotomy of 'secular' and 'sacred', something which remains predominantly foreign to the Muslim mind. The historical context must also be borne in mind, namely the post-atheistic context of a predominantly Muslim nation which was (and still is) undergoing religious revival, including experimentation with just how issues of 'faith and scholarship' should be worked out within their own unique setting. Besides, it is impossible to reflect upon Abai's writings without addressing such matters at length, lest the bulk of Abai's work be passed over in the process. The book, on all these grounds and more, was and remains entirely welcome within their educational curriculum.

One thing is certain: Abai is clearly a proponent of Muslim devotion among the Kazakhs as an important, even essential foundation for healthy cultural, social and political practices and he therefore deals at length with issues of Muslim, as well as broader religious, devotion among his people. Yesim follows suit. What is refreshing about this in an age when, at least in the West, a more radical message of Islamic devotion seems to dominate the media and, thus, correspondingly our attention is that both Abai and Yesim insist on a form which is ultimately grounded in simple, genuine and non-violent love for God and others. They insist that

> …what we mean by faith (*iman*), that is, what we mean by being 'a servant of God', is to pay one's debt of love. … Abai sets forth the idea that all children of humanity are friends one with another, and if that be the case, then they are all guests one of

another in this fleeting life and guests themselves, likewise, in the world. ...When we speak of Abai's idea of being Muslim, it reveals a thinker who goes beyond the mere sphere of religious orthodoxy. ...He depends upon the central Muslim doctrine that 'people are friends one of another', be they Muslim or not.[5]

In like manner elsewhere – indeed at the very pinnacle and climax of the book – Abai's great word, "Love all humanity, calling them your brothers and sisters," is cited.

Yesim insists with respect to Abai's "abiding relevance" for the broader world community that "values common to all humankind form the basis of Abai's humanistic poetry."[6] "Abai [thus] remains a contemporary both for us and for future generations."[7] Indeed, Abai has bequeathed to his people as well as the world a rich heritage of critical, philosophical and poetic reflection. As Seisenbaev notes: "He was extraordinarily well-read and knew thousands of lines by heart. He read books in Arabic, Farsi, old Chagatay, and Russian."[8] He acquainted himself with the works of the great Greek classical philosophers such as Socrates, Plato and Aristotle, with well-known Islamic poets and scholars such as the Persian Muslim historian and theologian Al-Tabari (838-923), the Persian Muslim scholar Rashid ad-Din (1247-1318), the Persian Muslim poet of the 15th century Zhami (or Jami, 1414-1492), and the medieval Naqshbandian Sufi writer of Turkic Central Asia Ali Shar Nawai (1441-1501). He was likewise familiar with the most highly esteemed Russian writers such as A.S. Pushkin (1799-1837), L.N. Tolstoi (1828-1910) and F.M. Dostoevskii (1821-1881), and with well-noted Western figures such as B. Spinoza (1632-1677) and H. Spencer (1820-1903). To this list could be added many others.[9]

It is hoped that the translation and publishing of this book in English will only add to the rich heritage of Abai Studies which, since the beginning of the 20th century, has formed into its own unique tradition over the last 100 or more years. It is the heart and aim of Asia Research Associates (ARA) in making this work available to the broader international community to help further that endeavor as an integral part of our valued world cultural and human heritage. It is likewise hoped that the publication of this volume will contribute in some small way to genuine ongoing intercultural and interreligious dialogue, promoting mutual understanding, respect and cooperation among not only the broader Central Asian and Western worlds, but even other ethnic, religious, national-political and cultural-civilizational groups across the globe. It is a clear vision for true *inter*national peace and friendship, the only good and rightful alternative to the war, violence and hatred which cast their long shadows across "the centuries-long 'trot' of society's development," even regrettably down to our own day.

With Abai and his interpreter, we continue to work toward the day, however distant and sometimes unachievable it seems, when "all children of humanity are friends one with another."

R. Charles Weller
Washington State University and
Al-Farabi Kazakh National University

Author's Preface [10]

Delving deep into the heritage of Abai, going deep into the caverns of the great poet-sage's thought is an 'event', an undertaking that will continue on from generation to generation. Abai provides a wonderous, integrated world of reflection and insight which requires mastery through an ever-deepening understanding of the entire width and breadth and depth and height of humanity's existence. In the centuries-long trot of society's development, [11] the seeds of thought which he expressed in accordance with the circumstances of his own time regarding the great figures who, "never perishing, left behind their words" are lucid. Because of his abiding relevance, Abai remains a contemporary both for us and for future generations. Therefore, delving deep into the depths of his heart and mind, studying and learning about the poet-sage by way of thoughtful inquiry [12] and an observant mind – this is our solemn duty.

In the Soviet era, the spirit of Abai was studied from a perspective that reflected a narrow field of thought, an exacting, restrictive understanding in which shackles were placed upon the spiritual-cultural heritage of our nation. Those precious Kazakh companions who were among the first to express a breath of heart-love and offer a quality representation of Abai – namely Akmet Baitursinuhli (1873-1938), Magzhan Zhumabaev (1893-1938) [13] and Zhusipbek Aimauituhli (1889-1931) as well as Alihan Bukeihanuhli (1866-1937), who was the honorary veteran member of the early 20th century Kazakh political movement known as *Alash* and the first to introduce our great poet-sage to Russian readers – all of these ran headlong into persecution, becoming seared by the Red Affliction's flames of fire. After the society of "clear, precise thought" was established – that is, the Soviet ideology spoken of by one of Abai's most celebrated disciples, Shakirim Kudaiberdi-uhli (1851-1931) – the true spirit of Abai became twisted and, in the course of the effort to bequeath the heritage of the poet-sage's writings to the heart and soul of generations to come, false understandings began to gain a foothold.

Within the bounds of the narrow pastureland of exacting, restrictive totalitarian ideology, the brilliant writer Mukhtar Auezov, who dedicated his entire thought life and literary service to researching the heritage of Abai in all its riches of exceeding complexity and delicate mystery, left worthy works for future generations in accordance with the essence of his own restricted time. Auezov, in writing the epic 2-volume novel *The Way of Abai*, which is ranked among the classic pieces of Kazakh literature, [14] laid the foundation for the scholarly discipline of the study of Abai and was, through that endeavor, able to raise that scholarly discipline to a remarkable point of elevation.

The places in Abai's writings where he criticizes Kazakh lifeways and scorns the dogmatic mullahs as well as the cases in which he censures inconsistencies in Kazakh society – these were well-liked by the exacting and restrictive ideology of the Soviets. Thus the poet-sage was 'lassoed' by the reputation of "enlightener." This understanding, of course, sprang up in a place which proved burdensome and oppressive, along a path previously untrodden. It lacked the power and ability to fully lift out the keen insight of the poet-sage, who alone was set apart among a thousand. They subjected him to intensive reflection and research concerning his worldview.

Abai's decisive thoughts regarding human beings and their nature, that is, their mysteries and various qualities, require research from a perspective based in truth. According to Abai's explanation, the Creator of humankind is God Most High. The humaneness and intelligence of human beings is to be observed, first and foremost, in their sense of love for God. The recognition of God and the sense of his wisdom and knowledge turns out to be the source-spring of self-understanding for humanity. The space of Abai's worldview is located between God and humanity. Prophets are the respresentatives of the unchanging eternal world, though they also are human as much as the rest of us. That is why even prophets are unable to fully answer the question 'what is truth'? The one who gives a clear, straight answer to that question is God. But as for humanity, Abai offers an explanation of truth's essence in his 38th Word, "Life Itself is Truth." Among the treasures of that Word, Abai asks what kind of truth can possibly flow forth from human life? Only where there is life can there be a word observed, a thought spoken, a book written. Without human life, the essence of our existence would be meaningless. For, if there were no one to speak of the existence or non-existence of life, then who would be left to prove the true essence of one or the other?

For these and the other kinds of ideas which he expressed, we call Abai *hakim*, that is, an 'elite' scholar, one of special knowledge and insight. *Hakims* clarify, they help make plain the significance of and reason for life's phenomena. They seek to place humankind upon a straight path to follow. This is the perspective of the scholar Abai. As for us, we have dedicated this book to offering an interpretation of select ideas and thoughts from the great poet-sage's writings.

Notes:

---

[1] Two different online translations can be found at: URL: http://www.leneshmidt-translations.com/book_of_words_abai_kunanbaev_english/index.htm and URL: https://adebiportal.kz/kz/translation/view/595

[2] Proof of this is to be found, e.g., in comparing the English translation of Yesenberlin, *The Nomads* (translated by Oleg Chorakaev; Almaty: The Ilias Yesenberlin Foundation, 1999, Book 1, Part 2:1, pp. 103-105), with the original Kazakh (*Көшпенділер*, Алматы: БПКА, [1971] 2015). The English translation is based upon the Russian. The deviations between the English and Russian and the respective impressions as well as information received from the English and Russian versus the Kazakh significantly differ, particularly in their representations of Islam and Muslim-Christian relations.

[3] We should also take care to distinguish the present English translation's use of two versions of the same work from the problems encountered in the science of textual criticism when multiple manuscripts, including translations, of classical and other historical writings are involved, such as those of Homer, Herodotus, Plato, the Judeo-Christian scriptures, the writings of Al-Farabi, Zhusip Balasaguni (that is, Yusuf Khass Hajib), etc.

[4] This problem has been noted, for example, in connection with ongoing tensions between Christians and Muslims in Indonesia. While important distinctions between the world's various religious traditions certainly exist, the idea that we cannot or should not share certain vocabulary is extreme in my opinion. I am in essential agreement with S.H. Nasr (2003:4), *Islam: Religion, History and Civilization*, on this point, who notes that: "Arab Christians and Arabized Jews in fact refer to God as Allah, as do Muslims. The Arabic word 'Allah' is therefore translatable as God, provided this term is understood to include the Godhead and not identified solely with Christian trinitarian doctrines." The same basic argument for 'non-exclusivism' could be applied, both historically and presently, to the use of the term 'Allah' in Arabic and even other languages around the world, such as Kazakh, where the Arabic term has been absorbed into the local-national vocabulary.

[5] Words Thirty-Eight and Thirty-Four respectively.

[6] See commentary on 'Word Thirty-Six' below.

[7] From the first paragraph of author's 'Introduction' to the present volume immediately below.

[8] Rollan Seisenbaev, ed. *Abai: Book of Words* (Almaty, KZ: El Bureau, 1995), p. 7.

[9] Akmetov, Nisanbaev, and Shanbai, "Abai," pp. 9, 12.

[10] The 'Introduction' here actually occurs as a 'Conclusion' or final 'Afterword' of sorts in the original Kazakh version (pp 194-95), where it is marked off as a separate section following the author's commentary on Abai's final Word (i.e. Word Forty-Five).

[11] 'Centuries-long trot' employs a clear Eurasian nomadic perspective on the movement and flow of history, one thoroughly embedded within and saturated with at least 3000 successive years of the greatest nomadic empires and civilizations known in human history, including the Scythian-Saka, the Huns, the Turks, the Kipchak and, of course, the Kazakhs, Kirgiz and others. Even after intentional socio-political efforts to 'wean' the Kazakhs away from their nomadic lifestyle, including Stalin's "collectivization" campaign in the early 1930s, strong vestiges of Kazakh semi-nomadic life and culture remain clearly visible at the dawn of the 21st century in Kazakhstan.

[12] 'Wise insight' might be a more 'literal' rendering, but the context favors 'thoughtful inquiry'.

[13] The endings *uhli* and *ev/ov* which appear on the end of Kazakh names are Kazakh and Russian forms respectively, both meaning essentially 'son of' and typically appended to the end of Kazakh names in this fashion. (The female forms would be *kizi* and *eva/ova* respectively.) As indicated by the Russian form, this ending was most commonly appended to the end of the family name, a tradition which seems to have come to the Kazakhs via Russian influence. More traditionally and historically, the Kazakhs, like many Middle Easterners (cf. *ibn*) among others, used their father's names as the 'family' name, meaning that the 'family' name would change with each new generation. In cases where two or more people might wind up with the same name and it became necessary to clarify exactly who was who, they would simply repeat the custom back another generation with respect to the grandfather, the great grandfather, and so on. This custom was connected with the tradition of *zheti ata*, that is, 'seven (fore)fathers', which each Kazakh was expected to know and be able to recite in various social situations when required, including marriage. There has been a trend toward revival of this custom using the father's name in the post-Soviet era. Thus, one encounters Kazakhs who use their father's name along with the ending *uhli* ('son of') or *kizi* ('daughter of') as their middle name, so to speak, while retaining the Russian-style family name. Others simply replace the Russian ending with the Kazakh ending on their Russian-style family name. As for my choice of usage here, why I have replaced the Russian endings with Kazakh ones in most cases, yet retained the Russian endings in some cases is not entirely an arbitrary matter. Generally, I have tried to follow the Kazakh trend in restoring the Kazakh forms of names in cases of historical personages. Based on my own admittedly limited knowledge, Magzhan Zhumabaev's family name has typically been left in its Russian form *in Kazakh*. The same would go for Mukhtar Auezov's name which appears in the following paragraph (above in the main text). There is, however, Kazakh precedence for restoration of the family names of the other figures.

[14] An English translation has been published as: Mukhtar Auezov (1975), *Abai: A novel* (New York: Progress Publishers).

Section One
FROM ANACHARSIS TO ABAI

About 2500 years, or twenty-five centuries, passed between Anacharsis and Abai. In my view, this period is the historical space of the Kazakh nation's culture. It is complex. Several renaissances took place during those twenty-five centuries. It is a general rule that a renaissance usually consists of two components. One is to aspire for new qualitative transformations in civilization, and the other is to revive and innovate old traditions. Hence, during a renaissance, cultural tradition does not completely disappear; instead, it evolves. Revolutionary transformation is not typical for the nature of a renaissance. A renaissance is both innovation within as well as revival of a culture itself, according to internal cultural dynamics. It is common for renaissances in historical times to appear in transitional epochs, with such epochs giving birth to renaissance figures. By suggesting a historical-cultural concept spanning "from Anacharsis to Abai," I delineate a renaissance period, and thus, all the figures and works I analyze will be from a renaissance period, specifically those of: Anacharsis the Scythian, Yollug Tigin, who bequeathed to humanity the Orkhon inscriptions during the Turk khaganate (eighth century CE), Yusuf Balasaguni, author of the *Wisdom of Royal Glory (Kutadgu Bilig): A Turko-Islamic Mirror for Princes* among the Turkic Karakhanid khanate (eleventh century CE), Ahmad Yasawi, Maiqy bi (d. 1225 CE), an advisor to Chinghis Khan and one of the sources of the the Kazakh legal codes, and Abai. Some readers will no doubt disagree with my opinion, and they would add other figures to this list. And they might be right to do so depending on their argument. Here, though, I use language as the basis of my historical-cultural concept. Language gives rich insight into culture. It is the means to approach and understand history, the precise facts of that history. Ancestral words reach us through the language. The Turkic language is a commonly shared language for all the figures mentioned above. Needless to say, I mean the Turkic language conditionally, meaning that "all words have the same sources."

Anacharsis the Scythian

I intend to mark the genesis of Kazakh culture with Anacharsis, since it is already known that Scythians, Huns, Turks, and Kipchaks are offspring of the same "ancestors," at least culturally speaking in terms of the nomadic peoples of the Central Asian steppe. Therefore, there is nothing wrong with starting Kazakh history from the Scythian philosopher Anacharsis.

Most data about the time in which Anacharsis lived and the information specifically about him was known in oral form. Only a few written items have been uncovered, the earliest of which is Herodotus. Indeed, who can know the exact truth about people who lived 2500 years before? Much of the information is based on assumptions and hearsay. This is true not only for Anacharsis but for Thales of Miletus and Solon of Athens as well.

Nonetheless, there are many facts and legends about Anacharsis the Scythian, a famous philosopher among the Scythian-Saka peoples who inhabited the ancient Central Asian steppelands from approximately 3000 BCE down to the first century CE. According to Herodotus, Anacharsis lived and interacted with the Greek world between the seventh and sixth centuries BCE.

Anacharsis proved his viability in his own time and has since become known throughout the generations. I assume that if he had been born in Palestine or in any country of the Near East, as opposed to Scythia, he would most likely be among the prophets listed in the Bible or Qur'an. I say that because, if I compare Anacharsis with other figures from history, I can equate him with Jesus Christ. They have many similarities. It is likely true that he was killed at a young age. Similarly, Jesus was killed when he was thirty-three. And both men offered new life for humankind, that is, they were both advocates of democracy, in modern terms.

Of course, they also have differences. First, Anacharsis lived five centuries before Jesus Christ. Therefore, their eras are different. Second, their cultural settings were far removed. In the world of the Scythians, military skill was more important than art and education. All neighbors were enemies. The main concern for Scythians, who were nomadic and did not construct cities, was survival. Third, their worldviews were different. According to Jesus's followers, Jesus taught that knowledge of the world was possible through God, whereas Anacharsis was doubtful about such knowledge of the world. In European terms, he was a skeptic. Skepticism is considered a philosophical orientation formed when science is developed and when its results can be questioned. Of course, there were no scientific and educational developments that we know of among the Scythians. However, in Jesus's time, science and education had been developed to a significant level. Therefore, Jesus, rather than Anacharsis, could have been a skeptic.

But Jesus's worldview was based on faith; Anacharsis's worldview was based on doubt. A worldview based on faith is limited: it is necessary for the masses. But Anacharsis was not a slave to faith. We can even find doubts about faith in Abai's worldview. Great figures are arguably destroyers of faith rather than slaves to it. The thoughts of great figures endure through the ages.

A worldview based on faith requires an ideological form, that is, an orthodoxy. There was neither Christianity nor Islam in Anacharsis's time. Buddhism was also not widely spread in Scythian territory. World religions were not yet established when the philosopher was alive. However, there could have been an understanding of Tangri, the 'sky god' of the steppe peoples. To worship Tangri is not to follow a faith or a religion; it is accepting the harmony between humans and nature. Belief in Tangri does not require a doctrinal understanding which can be opposed. Tangrism is a concept derived from nature, and can be considered a synonym of the word "nature." A person's worshipping of nature can be viewed as a naturalistic conception, on the one hand, and as a searching for an outer spirit, on the other, and to conceive of it as a subject is the result of thinking abstractly.

To perceive of Tangri as an objective idea required great wisdom. In my view, only thinkers such as Anacharsis could think of Tangri in that way. It is logical that the idea of Tangri should have an author. For example, the famous Greek philosopher Plato (AD 427–347), who wrote many books intending to prove objective ideas in philosophy, lived several hundred years after Anacharsis. Plato, in fact, highly valued the great Scythian thinker. I think there were several reasons for this: First, Anacharsis was a close friend of Solon, who was a political reformer in Athens. Moreover, Solon was related to Plato's mother. Hence, Anacharsis was likely a topic of conversation in Plato's family. Second, it is suggested by some that Plato's objective ideas were influenced by Persian Zoroastrianism, so is it possible that Plato formed his ideas based on a Scythian worldview? It is a definite historical fact that Plato knew perfectly well who the Scythian thinker Anacharsis was.

Articles about Anacharsis have recently been published in Kazakhstan, but let me briefly comment on the ancient Scythian thinker. You will not be able to find Anacharsis's name in the five-volume philosophical encyclopedia, in a philosophical encyclopedic dictionary, in philosophical history textbooks, or in a history encyclopedia published in Kazakhstan. Only one who is acquainted with the works of ancient writers, whose works were the basis for philosophy and history, can find that there was a philosopher named Anacharsis.

Anacharsis's name can be found in Plato's works. In his tenth book, *The Republic*, he referred to Homer the historian, Thales the philosopher, and Anacharsis the Scythian. Later in the same book, he made the following comment: "Anacharsis is a legendary Scythian. When he traveled to Greece, he met Solon; he became famous for his wisdom through Solon's teachings. Herodotus wrote about this."[1] The Greeks called the peoples of the later Kazakh regions Scythians, whereas the Persians called them Saks.

However, we need to start the story with Herodotus, "the father of history," who wrote that: "In the countries of Darius, there were strange tribes, not to mention the Scythian tribes on the shores of the Black Sea. There is no cultural heritage on the northern coast of Pontus, except for the famous Scythian Anacharsis."[2] Thus, Anacharsis belonged to one of the tribes residing on the Northern part of the Black Sea.

It appears that Herodotus had heard many of the legends about Anacharsis. He revealed who Anacharsis was, how he came to Greece, and his father's name. According to Herodotus, Anacharsis was a paternal uncle to the Scythian king Idanthyrsus, who fought against Darius, the king of Persia. Idanthyrsus is a well-known name in history. There is no clear answer to the question of whether Idanthyrsus's father, Savlius, was Anacharsis's older or younger brother. Anacharsis was killed by his own brother. Their father was Gnurus, who was also a Scythian king. His father was Lycus, and his father was the son of Spargapithes, king of his people. In Plato's time, it was difficult to verify whether Thales or Anacharsis were mere legends.

Plato also wrote about what was known in his times. It is hard to say if Plato had access to any writings by Thales or Anacharsis. He could have had some. We know about them mostly through myths and legends. However, these were probably not simply fabricated. It is reasonable that Plato could have heard about Anacharsis, since Plato's mother was a descendant of the famed Solon. According to Diogenes Laërtius, Solon and Anacharsis were friends. There is a legend about him:

> The Greek historian Sosicrates of Rhodes (c. 180 BCE) has him coming to Athens around the time of the 47th Olympiad during the rule of Eucrates. Hermippus relates that on his arrival at the house of Solon, he told one of the servants to announce that Anacharsis had come and was desirous of seeing him and, if possible, of becoming his guest. The servant delivered his message and was ordered by Solon to tell him that men as a rule choose their guests from among their own compatriots. Then Anacharsis said that he was now in his own country and had a right to be entertained as a guest. And Solon, struck with his ready wit, admitted him into his house and made him his greatest friend.

Undoubtedly, this is the legend about the first meeting between Solon and Anacharsis. It is an ancient tale. Indeed, Solon and Anacharsis highly respected each other. Aristotle also made mention of this. According to Lucian, the main reason for Anacharsis's return to his homeland was Solon's death.[3]

Plato also highly valued Thales's and Anacharsis's inventive abilities. Thales's contribution to science was well known. He was similar to a modern hydro-engineer, and he studied the reasons for the sun's eclipse. It was also known that Anacharsis created the anchor used by ships.[4] Plato's opinion of Anacharsis was very high. In his work *Protagoras*, he considered him one of the "seven sages."

Anacharsis's name can also be found in Aristotle's works. In *Prior Analytics*, Aristotle stated the difference between knowledge of the fact and knowledge of the reasoned fact and continues with this example: "as in Anacharsis's account of why the Scythians have no flute-players: namely, because they have no vines."[5]

Anacharsis said that Scythians do not have flute players, because they do not grow grapes. No grapes, no vines. Hence, there was no need for flutes. To know that something exists and to know why it exists are not the same thing. To prove his logical assumptions, Aristotle used Anacharsis's quote, which was widespread in those times. In the tenth book of *Nicomachean Ethics*, Aristotle again relied on opinions from Anacharsis. "But to amuse oneself in order that one may exert oneself, as Anacharsis puts it, seems right; for amusement is a sort of relaxation, and we need relaxation because we cannot work continuously. Relaxation, then, is not an end, for it is taken for the sake of activity."[6]

It is hard to analyze Anacharsis's own worldview since we lack a sufficient written legacy. That said, I consider Thales a materialist, but list Anacharsis among the skeptics. The proof for that is in a work by the physician, ancient Greek philosopher, and skeptic Sextus Empiricus (ca. second or third century CE). Sextus specifically mentioned and analyzed Anacharsis's works. Sextus Empiricus is known as a thinker who systematized earlier ideas of skepticism in the history of philosophy. Let us refer to one of his statements: "There are many ideas and doctrines changing rapidly, but none systematically. However, today we can come to this conclusion...we might notice three directions devoted to the history of theories on the criterion [of epistemology]: Views on the criterion are as follows: there is no criterion; the criterion is in logos [or rationality], the criterion is in energeia [or action]; the criterion is in logos and enargeia. Those who say there is no criterion are Xenophanes, Xeniades, Anacharsis, Protagoras, and others."[7]

Sextus Empiricus also conducted a significant analysis of Anacharsis. According to him, Anacharsis is a skeptic because he is among those who say there is no criterion. Regardless of whether a discussion involves specialists of one direction or specialists from diverse spheres, it is impossible to come to one conclusion, because the one who is a specialist is a dilettante, and those who are in the same sphere of expertise usually cannot come to agreement. This is because they need a jury. The one who gets involved in such debates is both accuser and accused at the same time. Each of his statements can be true or false at the same time. Hence, there is no measure for truth. The existence of such discussions in the fifth-sixth centuries BCE was due to attempts at reasoning related to the issue of faith. If Anacharsis concluded there was no measure for truth, then he was not among the mystic thinkers.

In ancient times, searching for the reasons behind a phenomenon and thinking about it critically could be regarded as a sign of progressive thinking. The German scholar Hermann Diels wrote one of the most valuable works about Anacharsis, Socrates, and other earlier Greek philosophers, but this work has not yet been translated into Russian so as to enable those of us for whom Russian functions as a lingua franca to read it.

One of the philosophers who wrote about Anacharsis was Lucianus, whom the social philosopher Friedrich Engels considered the "Voltaire of classic antiquity." During his visit to Macedonia, Lucianus gave a speech for the people of the city of Philippo, a speech that is reminiscent of modern lectures. He used words such as "Scythian," "Herodotus," and "Zeuxis." There are many unknown ideas within those words, particularly Scythian. According to Lucianus, Anacharsis was not the first Scythian to arrive in Athens; before him, was a Scythian healer named Toksaris. There is a legend about Toksaris among the Greek people. According to Lucianus, Toksaris was the first person Anacharsis met when he arrived in Athens. Toksaris introduced the young Anacharsis to Solon, who was in his old age at that time. With Solon's support, Anacharsis then became a famous scholar among the Greek people.[8]

Anacharsis's image is described in the work of Plutarch (ca. 40–120/125 CE), *The Dinner of the Seven Wise Men*. This work has some historical inaccuracies and Plutarch added some people who did not exist into the plot; it should therefore be considered a work of historical fiction. The seven wise men were Thales, Solon, Periander, Pittacus, Bias, Chilon, and Cleobulus. Anacharsis was also at this dinner.

Periander was the one who organized the dinner. Even though he was rich and had authority, he organized a very simple gathering. His wife did not even wear jewelry; instead, she wore very simple clothes, since the invited guests were not people who cared for luxury. They were thinkers. When they happened to meet, they shared their opinions and engaged in dialogues. This was a way to not only compare knowledge, but improve social opinion. The seven wise men gave seven pieces of "advice" to King Amasis as follows:

> Solon started first: "In my opinion either a king, or a despot, would best gain repute if out of a monarchy he should organize a democracy for his people."
>
> Next Bias said: "If he should be the very first to conform to his country's laws."
>
> Following him Thales said that he accounted it happiness for a ruler to reach old age and die a natural death.
>
> Fourth, Anacharsis said: "If only he had sound sense."
>
> Fifth, Cleobulus: "If he trusts none of his associates."
>
> Sixth, Pittacus, "If the ruler should manage to make his subjects fear, not him, but for him."
>
> Chilon followed by saying that a ruler's thoughts should never be the thoughts of a mortal, but of an immortal always.
>
> When these sentiments had been expressed, we insisted that Periander himself should also say something. And he, not very cheerful, but with a hard set face said: "Well, I may add my view, that the opinions expressed, taken as a whole, practically divorce any man possessed of sense from being a ruler."[9]

Several dialogues are given in Plutarch's work. Anacharsis took part in all of them. It is not surprising that Anacharsis was mentioned in the *Seven Wise Men*. According to Plutarch, Thales, the famous ancient materialist scholar, had a high opinion of Anacharsis. Although it is hard to consider Plutarch's work as an accurate historical document, *The Dinner of the Seven Wise Men* helps one feel the spirit of those times, and the environment Anacharsis lived in is depicted in those essays. We cannot consider Anacharsis as one of the seven wise men, but it is impossible to learn about him without the *Seven Wise Men*.

For those who research Anacharsis, there might still be unknown facts to find about him. I think there could be some valuable data in the works of Greek authors that have not yet been translated into Russian. Among the translated works available, Michel de Montaigne mentioned the name of the Scythian thinker twice in his first work in the *Essays of Michel de Montaigne*.[10] His work about the philosopher from the Scythian tribe was first translated into Russian and published in 1979. There is also a good deal of coverage of Anacharsis in Diogenes Laërtius's *Lives and Opinions of Eminent Philosophers*, including mention of the friendship between Anacharsis and Solon. Diogenes Laërtius also participated in the endless disagreements concerning the list of the seven wise men. According to him, the names of four philosophers are obvious. They are Thales, Bias, Pittacus, and Solon. The other three should be chosen from among these six: Aristodemus, Pamphilius, Chilon, Cleobulus, Anacharsis, and Periander.

The well-known soviet philosopher A. F. Losev offers his own comments about the list of seven wise men in the preface to Laërtius's book, but he does not include Anacharsis. The point is not the fact that Anacharsis was or was not in the list of seven wise men but that he is always mentioned along with ancient philosophers. It reveals the significant role Anacharsis played in the history of philosophy.

Of course, most of the seven wise men left no written heritage. Their well-known sayings reach us as oral legends. One of these legends is about oratory art. There is a monument to Anacharsis in Greece. The words inscribed on it say that all disasters are from our tongues. Diogenes Laërtius details some of Anacharsis's sayings in his book:

> Being asked how one could avoid becoming a toper, he answered, "By keeping before your eyes the disgraceful exhibition made by the drunkard." Again, he expressed surprise that the Greek lawgivers should impose penalties on wanton outrage, while they honor athletes for bruising one another. After ascertaining that the ship's side was four fingers' breadth in thickness, he remarked that the passengers were just so far from death.
>
> When someone inquired which were more in number, the living or the dead, he rejoined, "In which category, then, do you place those who are on the seas?" When some Athenian reproached him with being a Scythian, he replied, "Well, granted that my country is a disgrace to me, you are a disgrace to your country."

Many similar sayings have been attributed to Anacharsis. There is even a proverb "to talk like a Scythian," which means to have the oratory skills of Anacharsis in Ellada.

According to Diogenes Laërtius, Anacharsis produced a poem of 800 lines. Some excerpts from his verses can be found in the collection of ancient Greek poets called *Greek Anthology*. This anthology spans from the second century BCE to the Byzantine epochs. It was shortened and translated into Russian in

1985 as *Greek Epigrams*, and it does not include the name of the poet Anacharsis. Hence, the authentic text rather than the translation must be studied, since it includes some fragments related to the lifestyle of the Scythians. Laërtius tells us the following: "After a while Anacharsis returned to Scythia, where, owing to his enthusiasm for everything Greek, he was supposed to be subverting the national institutions, and was killed."[11] Based on this passage, we might conclude that there were not only trade and state relations between Greece and Scythia but also spiritual-cultural interrelations. The death of Anacharsis was known among the Greek people and a legend was spread about it. Unfortunately, the poems dedicated to the spiritual-cultural history of interrelations between Scythia and Greek have still not been thoroughly studied.

Anacharsis traveled from Greece to Scythia after Solon's death. According to Lucius, Anacharsis might not have returned to his homeland if Solon had lived. But he probably faced some hardships in Ellada after Solon died. Happiness, however, was not waiting for him in his own country either. According to Herodotus, his brother, King Savlius, killed him because he followed Greek traditions. It is hard to agree with Herodotus on that issue, since the reason for his death had deeper meaning. The reason was not only Greek traditions; that was just a pretext.

Since Anacharsis was a friend of Solon, a famous Greek law reformer, it is clear that Solon could have attempted to introduce his philosophical ideas into the Scythian's lifestyle. Anacharsis must have been aware that he had seen, studied, and learned Greek ideas. Such reformations could have changed or even destroyed the ruling system established in Scythia. Would a Scythian king agree with that? We assume that the main reason for his death was his life experience, his intelligence, and his wisdom. His death is similar to Ulugh Bek's (or Ulugh Beg's). It is logical that he died in his homeland. It would be more surprising if he had returned to his homeland, lived a long life, and died a natural death. Anacharsis started practicing his Greek ideas in Scythia on his own. But those practices were not allowed in Scythian cities. Hence, the reason for Anacharsis's death is clear. His relatives (the king's family) not only killed him but also prohibited his name from being spoken. His name was preserved in history only thanks to his contemporaries in Greece. Herodotus wrote, "If we were to ask Scythians about Anacharsis, they would say, 'We do not know this man.'"

Thus, it is most likely that Anacharsis was big trouble for the Scythians. It is known from history that vivid thinkers can usually be serious threats to 'the ruling class.' Anacharsis the Scythian, an ancient philosopher, was one such person, and he has therefore not yet found his place in history, nor in textbooks on philosophy.

When Anacharsis was fatally injured by an arrow shot by his relative, he said: "When I was in Hellas, my wisdom was my protection, but in my homeland, I was a victim of envy."

I published my article "Seven Geniuses and Anacharsis" in *Almaty Aqshamy* in 1992. There the philosopher known in history as Anacharsis the Scythian found his followers, and his name was revived again in Kazakhstan. The article received a warm welcome by most people. However, the Kazakh intelligentsia still hesitates to "turn him into a Kazakh." Primordialism is not scientific; nor is it sufficient to offer only mere speculation for a theory. There must be evidence, concrete facts. While there is no concrete evidence, I did not simply speculate that Anacharsis might be of Kazakh origins. The fact that Anacharsis's name was "the Scythian" and that he was a citizen of Scythia should be evidence enough. It is evident that Scythians were ancestors of the Kazakhs (at least culturally, if not also to some degree ethnically). It is historical fact that a philosopher, who was recognized by such philosophers as Plato and Aristotle, was therefore a Kazakh ancestor.

Maiqy bi called him "Anarys," which could well be his real name. It is very likely that "Anacharsis" was his Latinized name. The word "Anaris" in Turkic is composed of two components: *ang-arys* (animal-support). Animal images had a significant place in Scythian art. Hence, the word "Anaris" does not sound strange to Kazakh ears. This is a hypothesis. However, linguists would have to do the research to determine whether the Anaris mentioned by Maiqy bi was Anacharsis. What I can state is that the Kazakh pronunciation of Anacharsis could be Anarys. There is no counter argument to our ancestor Maiqy bi's statement. Hence, Anacharsis—Anaris—our ancestor, only became recognized among his offspring two and a half thousand years later. We must prize his spirit and take action to serve to his name. The novel *Anacharsis's Stories* was published in the Middle Ages in Europe. Translation of that work into Kazakh is urgently needed.

In sum, it is desirable to study Anacharsis systematically. Today one cannot find his name in any encyclopedias, in any philosophical dictionaries. The names of his contemporaries such as Solon the Athenian and Thales of Miletus are mentioned, but not his name. Most likely, this was the result of one single statement by Karl Marx: "There was a Scythian philosopher Anacharsis, but referring to him does not mean we can assume there was a civilization in Scythia." If, as Marx stated, there was no civilization in Scythia, then where did a philosopher such as Anacharsis come from? Is it possible to make anything grow in a desert? Thus, Marx contradicted himself. Apparently, he had reasons for doing so. History makes it clear that Scythians invaded and destroyed. It is also known that they put great pressure on the followers of prophets as well. I am confident that Marx took these facts into account. Otherwise, it would be a surprising thing if a famous philosopher emerged from savage people.

Yollug Tigin

The next thinker of the Turkic world whom I will discuss is Yollug Tigin. One of the sources of Kazakh ethnic culture comes from the Turkic Orkhon inscriptions (seventh-eighth centuries). This collection includes the Kul Tigin steles and Tonyukuk inscriptions. Yollug Tigin (also known as Yollug Khagan) was the author of the Kul Tigin inscriptions. Certainly it is not easy to identify the author of a work written in the eighth century. However, the last statement at the end of "Kul Tigin" (the first poem) says, "The one who inscribed these inscriptions is his (that is, Kul Tigin's) nephew Yollug Tigin." There are no counter arguments that deny the inscriptions on the stone. Thus, Yollug Tigin is believed to be the author of the poem "Kul Tigin."

The following can be concluded from these assumptions. The Kazakh ancestors who lived in the seventh-eighth centuries had a culture of writing (they referred to authors). It takes its rightful place in world civilization. The foundation of a writing culture is its alphabet. Thus, the alphabet used on the steles is considered to be the highest achievement of those people's aesthetic and mathematical development and their understanding of the universe. Those nations with poor mathematics are unable to develop alphabets. Only when the essence of a calculation system is acquired can one create the concept of symbols. Alphabetical symbols are founded in the results of accurateness in thinking and spiritual heights. Two types of reasoning are typical for human beings: imaginary thinking and mathematical thinking.

Only a few nations in human civilization are known to have had their own original alphabet. None of the current modern European nations have their own alphabets. As for the Turkic alphabet, there are diverse arguments concerning its origins and history, but it would be fair to claim that it originated with the Turks. I do not intend to claim that the Turks invented the alphabet living in cultural isolation. Culture is never developed in isolation; it is a result of synthesis.

I mentioned earlier that the author of "Kul Tigin" was Yollug Tigin; that poem proves that there was a culture of author's rights in the Turkic Khaganate (empire) in the seventh-eighth centuries. The existence of copyright tradition is typical for a cultured country. It proves the existence of a moral education system that has respect for personality traits, which leads to being humane. The fact that Yollug Tigin sealed his authorship on stone and left his heritage to his offspring is the evidence for that.

When talking about copyrights, two issues should be considered. The first is the concept of objectivity, the truth of that time (the history of the Turkic Khaganate, the "Kul Tigin" poem, etc.), and the second is the subjectivity of the author, in this case, the personal perceptions of Yollug Tigin.

According to the inscription, the Turkic Khaganate was founded in 552 and collapsed in 745. What can be eternal under heaven? Obviously, the Turkic Khaganate is no exception, but the khaganate, which existed for two centuries, left its words inscribed in stone. The most vivid among them being "Kul Tigin."

In the poem, Kul Tigin is the ruler of the khaganate Bilge Kaghan's brother. Yollug Tigin is Bilge Kaghan's son. They are the descendants of the great ones. The name Yollug means heir to the throne, a comparable word in Russian would be *Tsarevich*. Hence, he is not only a poet and a thinker but also an heir to the throne and a political figure.

According to scholars of the Turkic culture, Yollug Tigin died a natural death in 739, and the poem was written in 732. Although, it was in the period of a mighty Turkic Khaganate, it was apparent that the empire had begun to decline. This is probably what made the politician Yollug Tigin write that poem in commemoration of Kul Tigin's death. Brave Kul Tigin was born in 684 and died in 731 at the age of 47. His death was especially hard for Bilge Kaghan, who mourned for him. This is probably why the poem was written as being narrated by Bilge Kaghan.

Indeed, the death of the famous military commander Kul Tigin was a serious loss to the Turkic Khaganate. The poem describes Kul Tigin's place in the life of the Khaganate. However, one can ask why Bilge Kaghan was the narrator. First, this is probably because, as already stated, Kul Tigin's death was a great loss for Bilge Kaghan. Kul Tigin, his younger brother, was the one who supported him in taking the throne. He was not only a close relative but also a military commander and the person he trusted most. Second, Bilge Kaghan was Yollug Tigin's father, so making him the narrator could have been Yollug Tigin's way of showing reverence to his father. Third, the poem is not merely mournful words about Kul Tigin; it is a poem about the khan of the Turkic Khaganate, the leader of the country; it is an expression of the mood of the people who had lost a hero like Kul Tigin.

We cannot refer to Yollug Tigin, who inscribed words on stone as if they came from his father, as merely a chronicler. He did not simply list historical events; he also wrote his own opinions about his age and society. His background, status, and education all gave him the right to do so, since he was not just a passive viewer of the events from the outside but also one of the personages involved.

Yollug Tigin was fully aware of the great khaganate's historical path, why it was weakened and how it revived again during Bilge Tigin's reign, with Kul Tigin by his side. Yollug Tigin was a thinker who could identify causes and consequences; he was an ancient philosopher who told us about events in the eighth century. I state this because the poem was written in 732 and that the Turkic Khaganate collapsed thirteen years later in 745. Hence, that was the period in which the decay and disease of the khaganate started. Who could distinguish and identify that disease? Such people existed in the khaganate, and one of them was Yollug Tigin.

One reason he wrote the poem was to leave a heritage for future generations. Only Tangri knows what will happen in the future. Yollug Tigin wrote about coming threats with this statement: "Oh, Turkic people, you are so full. You do not think of hunger and abundance. Having been full once, you never think of being hungry." Yollug Tigin's worldview was shaped based on a khaganate (imperial) mentality. It had an objective basis. One border of the Turkic Khaganate neighbored Kerch (Bosporus), while another side bordered Amu Darya, Iran, and Rome. It is not surprising that an imperial way of reasoning was typical in such an enormous state.

That reasoning played a crucial role in politics while the khaganate existed as a Eurasian state. Therefore, it is understandable that Yollug Tigin wrote these lines about those who disobeyed: "Those who had knees were made to genuflect their knees and those who had heads—to bow them."

Khaganate (imperial) consciousness was a solid basis for the development of Turkic peoples. In my opinion, that very Turkic Khaganate essence served as an origin, one that initiated the scholarly and cultural achievements in Central Asia and Kazakhstan in the tenth-eleventh centuries. There is a reason I state that. Russian scholars of the Orkhon monuments write that the Turks were introduced to history as iron makers. They rebelled against the Zhuzhans' invasion in Ergenekon (in the Altai Mountains), and in 552, Bumin declared himself kaghan, and thus, the Turkic state was founded.

One reason for their victories was that the Turkic peoples were professional blacksmiths, and they had mastered iron. Sergei Kiselev, a scholar on the Turkic Khaganate, wrote, "Early Turks produced iron, gold, and silver, tin and copper. They found iron ore and boiled it by adding carbon monoxide. They called it a "steel."[12]

Nikita Bichurin, another scholar on Turkic people, also supported this opinion and wrote that Turkic people made knives, iron armor, whistling bullets, long, curved swords, heavy, sharp, two-sided swords, sharp spears about a meter long, warrior masks with horns, and iron helmets with velvet inside—all from steel.

Mastering iron (metal) working skills requires a great deal of knowledge, sophistication, and courage. A detailed knowledge of metals creates a mathematically thinking system. Therefore, it is not surprising that these people created their own unique alphabet—the creation of tools and weapons from metal is directly related to a symbolic system. Weapons are the abstract form of all things in the world. The recognition of the properties of metals advanced the Turkic thinking system. Hence, Yollug Tigin wrote, "Above is blessed Tangri. Turkic beks and Turkic people were without suffering and grief."

As one can see, Yollug Tigin did not give way to arrogance. He is thankful to the sky-god Tangri and reveres the earth. He revered these two concepts. These spiritual powers were the basis of the religious beliefs of ancient Turks. Hence, Yollug Tigin's khanate consciousness has its own dimensions. The name of the dimension is Tangri. The Kazakh people still remember Tangri. They use the phrase "May Tangri bless you" (*Tangir zharilqasyn*) as a synonym for the phrase "May God's mercy rain on you" (*Allaning rahimi zhausyn*).

The phrase "khanate (imperial) consciousness" must, therefore, also be considered from a language perspective. It is logical that the khanate ideology must have one commonly shared language. Having a common language was one method of existence in imperial (khanate) life. And in the Turkic Khaganate, that common language was Turkic. The Turkic language existed for over two centuries as the state language. As such, over the years, the Turkic language became common to the customs, traditions, and worldviews of all ethnic groups residing within the khaganate.

Studying the function of a language in people's world perception is a common task for linguists and philosophers. Readers of "Kul Tigin" will undoubtedly recognize the worldview of the Turkic language through Yollug Tigin's words. For example, one can find the following words, which demonstrate the social status and conditions of people in the society: *bai* (rich), *bek* (aristocrat), *kedei* (poor), *qul* (male slave), *kung* (female slave), *kaghan* (ruler), and so on. These words still have these meanings. The word *bek* later became a thoroughly Kazakh notion. It is similar to the Russian word *aristokrat*, and it implies nobleness in Kazakh.

The words "sultan" (ruler) and *mirza* (master, mister) are not found in "Kul Tigin" or in the Tonyukuk inscriptions. They were introduced to the language later. Our unique concept is *bek*. Kazakhs must show tribute to this word, which is a legacy of the seventh-eighth centuries, and as heirs of Turkic culture, we must revive this concept both in language and in daily life, because the term *bek* was formed in line with the terms *Tangri* and *Turk*.

The Danish scholar Vilhelm Thomsen, the first scholar to decipher "Kul Tigin" (published in November 1893), distinguished the words *Tangri* and *Turk*. Thus, when the ancient culture started being revived, Kazakhs encountered those words, which were already familiar to them from their own language: *Tangri*, *Turk*, *bek*, *bai*. This is a sign of the continuity between Turkic and Kazakh culture.

There is no great difference between belief in Tangri and belief in God in Islam. If earlier nomads prayed to Tangri, then they started praying to the God of Islam and used 'Allah' instead of Tangri, or Tangri instead of 'Allah,' easily interchanging them. This was because the basis of both beliefs was the same. "Kul Tigin" starts in the following way:

> When the blue sky above and the reddish-brown earth below were
> created, the two human beings were created in between.

This truth is not too different from those given in the four holy books that were revealed by God (the Tarot revealed to Prophet Moses, the Zabur revealed to Prophet David, the Bible revealed to Jesus Christ, the Qur'an revealed to Prophet Muhammad; see section two below). When Tangri and God are explained, they are described not as creators but as givers of blessings. Tangri is not described as a creator in the poem, but that role is suggested with the phrase "When the blue sky above and the reddish-brown earth below were created." Tangri is perceived as mysterious and isolated in the Turkic world perception. The reason why the epistemological nature of Tangri was not revealed is related to the realities of that time. The concept of God is as mysterious and isolated as Tangri, but He is not only a ruler and giver of blessings, He is also a creator.

It is important to know and explore the worldview of Yollug Tigin because the tenth-eleventh centuries are considered the period when the Turkic and Arab-Persian cultures encountered each other. In this exchange, the Arabic-Persian culture undoubtedly dominated and the Turkish culture gradually collapsed. When it comes to Turkic and Arab cultures, it is not correct to put them in opposition to each other. I say this because Kazakh people (I cannot say the same about other Turkic ethnic cultures) did not completely lose their Turkic identity, but at the same time, they accepted the Arab culture in a specific way, one that was not from a religious perspective. As a result, it was the rise of a new ethnos, one that could think about the world in a Kazakh way. We call it a national identity (a uniqueness).

When talking about the culture of that era, Yollug Tigin stands out as a thinker and representative of the Turkic culture. So also does the contemporary Kazakh poet Qadyr Myrzaliyev, who says: "A person is born crying and people try to comfort them. A person passes away weeping and makes others cry." Kazakhs consider these statements as philosophical assumptions. They were the conclusions made by the Kazakh poet Abai Qunanbayev in the early twentieth century. When Abai said, "People come into this world crying and depart it in sorrow," Kazakhs respected this saying as wisdom (see section two). He was the best example of Kazakh thinking in the first half of the twentieth century.

What can be said about Yollug Tigin's saying, "All humans came to life to pass away in the end?" Will you wonder, or not? Will you bow your head before his spirit, or not? It is astonishing that philosophical thought about the meaning of this life was mentioned in the eighth century. Thus, we find the genesis of problems discussed in the West in the nineteenth and twentieth centuries such as the "philosophy of life," "philosophy of living a life," and "existentialist philosophy" in Yollug Tigin's worldview. The principle that "the value of a person is determined by his death" is widely accepted in civilized European countries. And it was also the basis for the philosophical contributions of the wise men Plutarch wrote about.

I would like to raise a question about the meaning of life according to Yollug Tigin and to explain the content of his thought as a solution. From the existential thought Yollug Tigin raised, two types of world perception can be distinguished. First is a pessimistic approach, which states that people are born to die; hence, it is useless to live an active life. The mysteries of death and a pessimistic outlook are reasons to act as one wants with no concern for others. The second view is an optimistic outlook, which says that even though all human beings are going to die, people must live to leave a message after their death and they must die bravely to protect their people.

Both these worldviews existed in the ancient Turkic epochs. Yollug Tigin preferred the latter approach. This claim is clearly supported by the eternal message he left in stone about the foundation of the Turkic ethnos. And his poem about the national liberation movement organized by Elteris, the founder of the Second Turkic Khaganate, is clear proof of his worldview.

Yollug Tigin understood clearly that this national liberation movement was significant, not for foreign people, but for the descendants of Turks. Therefore, he inscribed the poem on a stone. He did not write about the shadowed part of human beings; instead, he wrote about his aspirations for liberation and freedom. The basis for this is a Turkic concept, according to which Tangri is in the high heavens. Their heavenly Tangri is eternity, which gives them imagination, the wings to reach their dreams, and the energy to go further. Worshipping height, longing for height, makes a person strive for a high philosophy. Striving for height is the philosophy of heroism and courage. If there is such a supporter in the heavens as Tangri, then why not face challenges and take risks? Height and slavery are contradictory perceptions. Therefore, protest against the Zhuzhans (oppressors) is ordered by Tangri. It is destiny. "It is Tangri who determines destiny," according to Yollug Tigin.

Along with Tangri, Turkic people have their motherland. However, according to Yollug Tigin's assumption, humans were created in-between the blue Tangri and the earth; hence, humans are not only children of the earth (among Kazakhs, this concept was formed later) but children of Tangri as well. People belong to both of them, so the earth for a Turkic person is a source of strength, whereas Tangri gives one spiritual power.

Thus, Yollug Tigin explained the philosophy of liberation. He stated that the human body is created of spirit. The body is created on earth, and it will return to the earth, whereas his spirit will fly to the sky. Rather than using the word "dead," he used the phrase "flew away" to describe the death of Elteris. Therefore, his soul flew away. This is Tangri's will. The spirit of Elteris will not die. His son, who took his throne, advanced the Turkic people. "He made the poor people rich and the few people numerous."

I would therefore like to suggest my own aspirations regarding Yollug Tigin and Turkic culture:

1. In his book *As i Ya (Azia and Me)*, Olzhas Suleimenov proposed making 25 November Turkic Culture Day. Unfortunately, his proposal was not accepted. As mentioned previously, Thomsen published the Turkic version of the poem "Kul Tigin" on that date in 1893. Thus, 25 November should function as a holiday that celebrates Turkic culture, including organizing gatherings dedicated to Yollug Tigin.

2. The Kazakh Ministry of Culture could create a special complex of monuments to the rulers of the Turkic Khaganate and a monument

devoted to the Turkic Khaganate itself, which made valuable contributions to the development of numerous nations in Eurasia, along with a special museum devoted to Turkic culture.

3. Finally, streets, places, and educational institutions should be named after Kul Tigin, Yollug Tigin, and other leaders, heroes, and thinkers of the Turkic Khanate.

The past territory of the Turkic Khaganate is now located in the current territory of modern Kazakhstan. As the poet Maghzhan Zhumabaiev said, we Kazakhs are the main heirs of the Turkic Khaganate. Therefore, it would be right for us to have textbooks that introduce Yollug Tigin as a cultural activist and thinker of our nation.

Yusuf Balasaguni

The philosopher Yusuf Balasaguni (d. 1070) has a special place in the history of Turkic culture. Even though there are five centuries between these two individuals – Tigin and Balasaguni – there is a spiritual continuity between them. In terms of spiritual continuity, one can say that these two are the true sons of the Turkic culture, but their difference is in the epochs in which they lived.

Yusuf Balasaguni was a wise man who lived in the "transitional period." Turkic tribes began to adopt the Arabic-Persian culture in the eleventh century, and there were objective reasons for that. One is that when the Turkic Khaganate collapsed and it was being replaced by new states and ethnos, they needed another new cultural worldview. If there had been no such necessity, the Arabic-Persian culture would not be so widely spread throughout the Turkic world.

When Islam started spreading among the nations in Central Asia and the current Kazakhstan territory, it was a time when the teaching of Islam was not as intense as it had been in the beginning. If, initially, the first Arab occupiers spread Islam forcibly, then this attitude had changed. Now, there were missionaries who spread Islam. They started propagating Islam peacefully. Among Kazakhs, Islam was gradually spread in that peaceful way. One of the main reasons why Islam spread without bloodshed in Kazakh lands is related to the power of the Arab-Persian culture, which was introduced together with Islam.

It is not a coincidence that Yusuf Balasaguni, as a representative of the Turkic people, became a propagandist of Islamic ideology. But one who thoroughly reads Yusuf's poetic work *Kutadgu Bilik (Blessed Wisdom or Knowledge)* will understand that his purpose in writing this book was not to disseminate a religion but to introduce his ideas on how to unite people, how to build a society, and how to achieve justice and happiness. According to academician Andrey Kononov, the four main principles mentioned in the *Kutadgu Bilik* manuscript found in Namangan, are as follows: (1) *Adil* (justice); (2) *Devlet* (wealth); (3) *Akil* (wisdom); (4) *Kanaat* (gratefulness).

Two things must be taken into consideration in this case. First, *Kutadgu Bilik* is a Turkic-language work written in the Arabic alphabet. This means that the Turkic script was no longer used in the eleventh century. The culture of writing had shifted to an Arabic base. One might conclude that the two cultures of writing competed and were later integrated with each other (synthesized). Because of these processes, the Turkic writing culture (i.e., its script) was eventually lost, but the Turkic lexicon was preserved.

For example, the words *toreh* (leader) and *qut* (blessing) are Turkic words. Their meanings are deep. For instance, Turks used to say *törü* to imply right law. And there is a Kazakh social class concept called *tore*, which implies a person who judges and rules. Consequently, the term *törü* is preserved in the Kazakh lexicon. The conclusion is that, although Yusuf Balasaguni's book was written in Arabic, he used notions expressing a Turkic worldview. Hence, Yusuf is a great thinker of the Turkic people.

Second, the influence of Arab philosophy in *Kutadgu Bilik* is undeniable. For example, the principles of justice, wealth, wisdom, and gratefulness mentioned above, which are found in the manuscript from Namangan, reflect of the impact of Islam. These concepts (words) are Turkic loan words from the Arabic-Persian culture. They are the key concepts of Sufism. After the word *adil* was borrowed from Arabic, the Turkic word *törü* received another connotation. In the modern Kazakh language, *tore* refers to a social class. Similarly, because of the Arabic loan word "wealth," the word *qut* changed its connotation.

Thus, *Kutadgu Bilik* is a work that was created because of a synthesis of the Turkic and Arab-Persian cultures. It was a unique piece of work in its time. In times that saw an absence of manuscripts on humanity, society, and essence of life, this book turned into a favorite work of the country's leaders, scholars, and intellectuals.

There are many symbols in the book. For example, the sun is the symbol of justice; the moon is a symbol of wealth. These are not concepts borrowed from Arabs. Most likely, these are the symbols of people who worshipped Tangri. As Yusuf Balasaguni stated, "A clever person understands, an educated person knows." And a person who reads *Kutadgu Bilik* will experience diverse thoughts. One can notice in it the influences of Turkic, Arabic, Persian, and other cultures. Undoubtedly, Yusuf is a philosopher who is familiar with the culture of the ancient world. His statement "all illiterate people are sick" is proof of that.

Even though Yusuf suggested optimistic thoughts about life, he was also familiar with how pious people perceived the world. Thus, he stated, "Won't you see that a man is born and buried naked, then why should a man gather wealth?"[13]

However, Yusuf did not accept pious people's worldview. He did not reason only about death but also about life. He considered the statement that "all those alive are born to embrace death once" to be a warning: a reasoning man, who knows that death exists, will be wise. Then how should a wise man act?

The thinker Yusuf's advice was to become educated. A knowledgeable person can distinguish "well-being" from "wealth." A wise person needs well-being. A foolish, unreasoning person becomes a slave of wealth. What, then, does "wealth" imply? Well-being is not only being wealthy, but it requires knowledge and accountability. Well-being is the opportunity to live and to take care of the life in the other world. A person with well-being is a person who has belief in a creator. In my opinion, there is a difference between *qut* (blessing) and well-being. Consequently, Turks understood the birth of a child as a *qut*. Then *qut* is existence itself. For Turks, the one who gives *qut* is Tangri; for Arabs, the master of existence is God.

Yusuf was able to distinguish "well-being" and "wealth." Well-being is undoubtedly wealth, but wealth is not always well-being. In *Kutadgu Bilik*, Ogdulmish said to Elik:

> You managed to gather gold. You knew how to spend it.
> This gold is your definite enemy. Why don't you give it out? [14]

Hence, if one knows how to gather gold and how to spend it and if one does not get greedy, this is well-being. If you cannot spend gold as a means of wealth, then it is an assault on yourself. There is also a Kazakh proverb with the same meaning. It states the first wealth is health, the second wealth is *aq zhaulyq* (a wife), and the third wealth is *on saulyq* (a cattle herd). Kazakhs name these things wealth; it is fair to identify this type of wealth as well-being.

Koja Ahmad Yasawi

The eleventh century was a transitional period for Turkic people. It was a time of great cultural exchange and synthesis. A new worldview began to be established on the Turkic steppe, and it was the worshiping of God. People who worshipped Tangri accepted God, and in most cases, they used both concepts as synonyms and equally interchanged and worshipped them. Even today's Kazakhs do not distinguish a difference between Tangri and God. Most consider them as one concept.

Generally, transitional periods give birth to great personalities. One such individual is Koja Ahmad Yasawi. The time difference between Yusuf Balasaguni and Ahmad Yasawi is only 70–80 years, but Yasawi's worldview is different.

Ahmad Yasawi also wrote his *Dīvān-i Ḥikmet* (The Book of Wisdom) in Turkic using the Arabic alphabet, which is once again evidence of the synthesis of Arab and Turkic cultures. However, he brought an innovation to the nomadic way of life. This was the philosophy of Sufism, a pious worldview.

Arabs, and later Persians, introduced Sufi literature. The strongest supporters of Sufi literature are Arabian and Persian poets, who created excellent examples of Sufi literature. Though the phrase "Sufi-mystical" is wrong, mysticism is the philosophical orientation of Sufi literature. So how should one understand it?

For many years, people have been using the concept of mystery as a negative idea. But mysticism is not a pure irrationalism; it is a worldview. The worldview of mystics has deep meaning. The main concepts of mystic poets are God and an individual, with the latter's endless love for the former. Yasawi was a man who was truly in love. His poem is about affection. The subject of his affection is the one God.

Not everyone can fall in love with God. Such lovers reject the world and dedicate themselves to a pious life. Ahmad Yasawi was a pious man.

There were other saints before Yasawi who announced their love for God and lived a pious life. Mother Rābiʿa al-ʿAdawiyya al-Qaysiyya (713–801) is one example. I call her Mother Rabia in a figurative sense because she is usually considered the founder of such mystical love. There are many legends about her in Arabic literature and culture. She was a person who never married, who never had intercourse with a man, and who had special qualities.

Mystic love, which started as a worldview in the eighth century, reached Yasawi in the twelfth century. Numerous teachings were created about people's love of God during that period. This worldview essentially became a main gnoseological concept of one of the Islamic philosophies—Sufism. Since there are special works dedicated to this issue, I will not discuss the gnoseology of Sufism. Here, I intend to answer the question of whether Yasawi was only a pious proprietor of Sufism or whether he was a philosopher who had his own creative style.

There is no doubt that Yasawi was a mystical thinker. He was an acknowledger and fulfiller of the conditions of Islam. He never questioned the trueness of the Prophet. The evidence for that is his pious life. Scholars of his life claim that when he reached the Prophet's age, he rejected the world and lived the rest of his life underground. This is a recognition of the Last Prophet. Consequently, though he was a thinker, he did not oppose the basic principles of Islam. At first, it might seem illogical to accept one religion yet to propose humanistic thoughts. However, Yasawi found a solution for this issue. He stated, "The will given by God is an enemy to man." Two thoughts converge in this verse: God gives people free will, and that free will is their enemy. I will consider each of these separately.

Why did God give free will to people? Why did He not initially limit people's free will? There is a mystery here. This is the Creator's secret.

However, it seems that God gave free will to humans for specific purposes. If people did not voluntarily pray to God but were instead obliged to do it, they would be unable to recognize the power of God. In that case, there would be belief instead of thinking, and this belief in God would undoubtedly turn into an accepted axiom or truth. That is contrary to God's command. God wants His servants to recognize Him. For belief in God does not serve people's prosperity on earth. God is not merely a Creator of human beings; He is the Creator of the whole universe; He is the Controller.

People who are limited by having only a belief in God will never recognize God's artistry. If people have free will, they will be able to recognize God's miracle. God gave people free will to let them recognize His miracles. But feelings are the connection between people and God. We recognize God's miracle through reasoning, and we long for him through feelings. Feelings cannot convey God's image, but they confirm His existence. What we feel is the truth. The mind is not created from feeling but from thinking. Thought is not the truth but its logic. Truth is revealed through feelings. Truth's name is God. Hence, thinking and reasoning about the truth is a discussion about God. People are free to talk about God. God gives free will to people. The Creator gave people a choice along with free will. The pleasures of two worlds were created for people. These are the false and the eternal lives. This false life is short and comes first. Human beings are born into this "false" world. They grow and develop here. Since this life comes first, it is significant. The concept of everlasting life is unclear to people because they cannot experience or feel it. They can only imagine it. However, as I stated before, the idea is not the truth, but it is the system of the truth. Therefore, the eternal life mostly remains a mystery to those whose hearts have not been touched by it, and suspicion about God arises in the hearts of such people. This is called atheism in academic terms.

Thus, a person with free will has two choices. One is to believe in God, to recognize Him, and the second is to deny Him. As mentioned above, Yasawi was in the first group. However, there is a principle in Islam according to which people worship God to be able to go to paradise. However, Rābiʿa al-ʿAdawiyya was against making such a bargain with God. When she fell in love with God, she did not ask for anything from Him. Her only dream was to see the face of God. She had no other thoughts. Yasawi also followed this direction.

People are free to love the One who created them. Those who use their free will this way and took actions accordingly are called pious. The pious ones are those who recognize God with their hearts and fall in love with Him. Piety is a true worldview. They are mystics. However, they are not ones who reach piety as a result of ideological propaganda but ones who feel the will of the absolute truth on their own will. Undoubtedly, they are people who have unique qualities. This is the mystery of such people. The mystery of such people is the mystery of God. There are dimensions and limitations for people who want to go deeper into this mystery. And there is no "permission" needed to cross over into it. However, only people whose minds are not stable can claim that they utterly mastered the entire mystery of humankind.

The mystery of humankind is similar to people's free will: it is a phenomenon that comes from their minds. Society has come up with many false claims in the history of "a person with free will." People have speculated conclusions from those claims and called them theories. If you were to look at the foundation of the question of free will, you would find that the mystery of it is beyond of our understanding. In fact, people are not owners of their own free will. It seems that Arthur Schopenhauer's saying accords with the reality. I also support the idea that the will of humankind depends on the will of the universe. People have made the free will of a person much easier. They have even sometimes claimed that people can give another free will. In my opinion, God gives a person their free will. God is referred to as the concrete truth, as some absoluteness, or as nature. Humankind's will is not the product of one's own "possession" or the result of the society in which one lives; it is an expression of the world's "will" (the world's idea).

Regarding the question of why humankind needs a will, I can provide a brief answer: it is necessary for recognizing God. Other explanations are not needed. For knowing God is the path to humanity. Yasawi was of the same opinion concerning a person's will. In *Dīvān-i Ḥikmet*, he concludes, "Man's love for God is necessary for the purification of the world. It is not a thing needed only for one religion, but it is the truth needed for all humanity." This is the depth of Yasawi's thoughts.

I have said that free will is needed to recognize God, but why is recognizing God necessary? According to the worldview of the mystical thinker Yasawi, recognizing God is necessary for recognizing oneself. Yasawi's humanism was decorated with such conclusions. He deepened the humanism of Islam, cleaned it from orthodoxical excesses, and organized it into a system.

One's will is one's treasure. Yasawi knew that mastering one's will, taking required actions and inactions, is not something that everyone would be able to do, so he lived his own life as a brilliant example of this (demonstrating the use of free will). This is how we should understand the meaning of Yasawi's piety. The life of Yasawi is a life of brilliant example: his rejection of the world's pleasures, his living a pious life, his care for others, and his way of being a real example for them. This is not similar to the idea of sacrifice as exemplified by Jesus Christ in Christianity. According to the Bible, Jesus Christ sacrificed himself for the sake of humanity. There is no sacrifice in Yasawi's acts, but he is an exemplary model of how people should master their will.

The Sufi outlook is a spiritual force that has greatly influenced Kazakh folklore and culture. Since the Kazakh people preserved their nomadic traditions, they also had the opportunity to select some ideas from Islam. Kazakhs liked the idea of loving God but not the belief. However, the nomadic tradition made its own religion, and it understood love specifically. According to Yasawi, people desire to see the face of God. But in the Kazakh culture and worldview, this concept was transformed into love between a man and a woman. This type of love was considered piety in the name of love. In Yasawi's words, "The one who is in love loses his soul. He can sacrifice his soul in the name of love."

Kazakh lovers also followed this rule. In love stories, lovers would sacrifice their lives for each other if they could not be together. The vivid proof of this is a poem about Qozy Korpesh and Bayan Sulu, a traditional Kazakh poem about a tragic love. The worldview that having a beloved person should lead to self-sacrifice is typical only in Eastern poetry. It is the influence of Sufi philosophy.

Abai Qunanbayev

Abai Qunanbayev was born in 1845, 679 years after Ahmad Yasawi. He was born in the nineteenth century during a tragic time for the Kazakh people. Unfortunately, in the age of the Russian kings, the Kazakh khanates disappeared forever. People lost their right to self-government and became prisoners of colonizing policies. Instead of khans and *bis* (lawyers, prosecutors, courts), Russian rulers governed the people. They were divided into several provinces that were directly subordinate to the king. The only thing left for Kazakhs was to be a *bolis* (district head). People had to be thankful even for that, and they had to compete for that position.

Indeed, Abai Qunanbayev's identity in the spiritual realm of the Kazakh people has not yet been fully revealed. There is no doubt that philosophers are an inexhaustible treasure, and the value of that treasure is identified according to the historical period of each generation. History's recognition deepens with time. Social consciousness finds its specific uniqueness based on political claims and subjective concepts and notions of the past. Therefore, while there was no thinker like Abai Qunanbayev before him in the second half of the nineteenth century, the existence of such a thinker was a historical necessity.

Coincidence is a kind of reflection of necessity. Therefore, it is not an overstatement to claim that Abai's works identify the need for the development of people's spiritual culture. It is understandable that Abai's role in culture and his image as a thinker in the minds of people stand higher than his poetry. However, this topic has not yet been studied.

The secret of Abai's being perceived as a public figure and thinker is in the fact that his creativity is the result of social contradictions. Abai did not write his poems just to provide elegant aesthetic meaning through them; he also wanted to be an exemplar for youth who have a "sensible heart and skills of oratory." He did not conceal that he aimed to influence the people's consciousness and intensify its development. Abai's mission as a poet and as a social figure was to try to make transformations in the consciousness of all people. To this point, I provide an excerpt from Mukhtar Auezov's monograph "Abai" (Ibrahim Qunanbayev):

> In fact, one is most likely to find poetic power similar to Abai's poetry in the works of earlier poets. Probably, some of them were not famous.

Hence, if Abai had remained at the level of poetic consciousness and at the level of culture with themes based on class groups, he would not have turned into the classic Abai. If there were 100 poets before him, he would have just become the 101st poet; if there were 1000 poets before, he would have been merely the 1001st poet, and no more than this.

Abai was evaluated differently because he was the Abai who absorbed qualities and examples of Russian culture, and he agitated it, and he was the one who made new dreams and aims for the people of a new age. He was recognized as the greatest classic of all Kazakh people, who reached the highest achievement, who revealed the golden treasury, and who is truly invaluable.[15]

This approach has not yet been taken into account in studies of Abai's legacy. It is unlikely that literature scholars can study this problem in depth, but the public science sphere has not yet been able to reveal the patterns of transformation in the social economic forms of Kazakhstan. In short, the methodological foundations that can explain Auezov's words in depth and that can identify Abai's personality in the history of the Kazakh culture have not yet been revealed.

It is well-known fact that Abai was a thinker who lived in the second half of the nineteenth century. The main signs of that time were people shifting from a nomadic life to a stable way of life with places to stay for the winter and spring. Nomadic life was disappearing. Cities had been built in the Kazakh land, and these ancient cities intensively flourished. Urban culture began on the Kazakh steppe. Kazakh people were on the path to becoming a bourgeois nation. Other ideas also spread to the Kazakh steppes. Their content was diverse: religious ideology, ideology of Russian immigrants from the political-democratic intelligentsia. Kazakhs who were literate started to become acquainted with models of Western and Russian cultures. The revival period of the Kazakh steppe began.

Some literature scholars consider Abai as a poet who lived during the feudal society. I cannot completely agree with that. Abai was born into a society where the state's unity was lost and people lived under colonization. His formation as a poet accords to the second half of the nineteenth century, when people were experiencing hardships. This "transitional society's" contradictions not only raised Abai to the level of a poet but also made him a thinker and a humanist.

It is a mistake to try to find images of the proletariat and the factory worker in his poems, images that reflect "pure" bourgeois relationships. Change is in consciousness, in understanding. It is not enough to understand capitalism only as a factory. The capitalist management system of Kazakhstan was completed in the second half of the nineteenth century. Although the senior sultans and *bis* continued their existence as societal remnants that were similar to the Tsarist autocracy, the government of the Russian national minorities followed a bourgeois style. Settlements had to be officially registered and their authorities were taken over by legislative bodies.

Qualitative differences in the economy and the basis of the society have had a profound effect on Kazakhs' spiritual life. At that time, the artistic culture of our people, particularly oral literature and poetry, was in a high stage of development. As the concept of "urban culture" was forming, the people who lived a nomadic life were in need of new dimensions for spiritual culture, folklore, and artistic consciousness. This was set by the requirements of the time.

Abai Qunanbayev was the one who performed this task. First, Abai analyzed the *bis'* works. In those analyses, he found that pragmatism was more dominant than artistry. Poetry was subordinate to practical necessity in the works of *bis*. *Bi*, in modern terms, is a lawyer, prosecutor, and a court of the nomadic people.

Bis' creativity and oratory cultures developed simultaneously, as the practical activity of *bis* was based on ingenuity and oratories. Their oratory skills required artistry, including poetry. The main reason for this is that poetry played a significant role in people's consciousness. Therefore, generations that were brought up with a plentitude of poetry related everyday life's complex solutions to poetry. A *bi* was a person who was convenient for the nomadic way of life and its social essence, but when class antagonism became complicated, *bis'* words and *bis* themselves became archaisms. Therefore, oratory art also required a new dimension. When social tensions grew and bourgeois relations began to be established, the creativity of *bis* lost its democratic characteristic and they turned into the tools of Russian governors. As such, they lost their authority. Abai criticized the tautological characteristics of *bis*:

> *If I look to the past bis*
> *I can notice that they speak very skillfully, adding proverbs to their*
> *speech*

In Abai's time, *bis'* creativity lost its activity in society, and they preserved only some features of their oratory skills. Furthermore, the spiritual development of the society of the nomadic ages experienced significant changes. People changed to a sedentary style of life. More and more unknown social phenomena started being spread among the people. A new type of government was formed, and *bis* lost their functions as a decisive power. Thinking about *bis* and their heritage was a significant topic of that time. It had to be considered. Abai performed this task. His statement that "I will not utter useless speeches with proverbs, as *bis* do" is not only a criticism of *bis* but also a new requirement for the principle and development of spiritual culture. Although *bis'* creativity was directly related to poetry, they were not a source for nourishing poetry, but they did gain power from poetry.

Poetry (Kazakh folklore) is mainly based on ancient Turkic and Persian poetry. Ancient Turkic poetry reached Abai mainly through oral literature. Kazakh people developed as one direction and branch of the ancient Turkic people, but they were "heir" only to the oral literature, not to the written literature. This has a historical reason.

The Kazakh people were a nation of nomads. Their comfortable form of migratory culture developed folklore in a unique way. The people lost the alphabet and thus totally relied on poetry. Poems, *zhyrs* (legends), and epos were passed orally from generation to generation. This method of artistic imagination and outlook greatly enriched people's abstract thinking. It was a common practice to recite poems. However, in the oral literature, the acts of its vibrant representatives and the tendencies of societal development contradicted each other. In addition, this contradiction had become very apparent in the second half of the eighteenth century, and it had turned into a significant problem for the spiritual and cultural development of Kazakhs. It is therefore understandable that Abai was not only a critic of the *bis'* poetry but also a critic of poetry in the oral tradition.

Usually, when analyzing Abai's works, scholars refer to three sources: oral literature, Eastern poetry, and European and Russian literature. This choice needs to be reconsidered, especially with regard to the problem of the oral literature before Abai. Nowadays, there is the notion of "Old Turkic writing culture." The oral folklore of the Kazakh people, one of the nations of Turkic-speaking people residing in the territory of Central Asia and Kazakhstan, is one branch of the ancient Turkic written culture. Hence, Kazakh oral literature is the lawful heir to the ancient Turkic written culture.

The transition of ancient and earlier Turkic people's cultures to oral literature was controversial. Thus, it is difficult to say if the transition from written culture to folklore was a success or failure. On the one hand, it is a defeat in the development of spiritual culture. We lost our alphabet. Our famous scientists, poets, and historians were forgotten. Historically true events were erased from memories, became vague, and were turned into legends and myths.

With the disappearance of cities in Kazakhstan, the culture of writing did not completely disappear and the culture was not erased. It was transformed from one state into another. Thus, the spirit of the people was not eradicated in the era of historical transformation, but it was preserved in the special form of

28

art of consciousness that is folklore. The subsequent social function of folklore became a factor of national and ethnic consolidation. It was especially evident in the preservation and advancement of the literary language. The language preserved its purity. People raised the culture of language to a high level, and the spiritual culture was developed into many genres. *Bis'* words, oratory words, proverbs, riddles, epic poems, poems of rites, and so on, were all different literary types.

Thus, when stating that one of the sources of Abai's poetry was oral literature, one needs to take into account all these different types. The creativity of the poet advanced because of oral literature. Abai's criticisms of Shortanbai's, Dulat's, and Bukhar's creativity were not restricted only to these elder poets; his critiques applied to oral folk literature in general. It is obvious that when folklore lasts into written literature, it loses its uniqueness that was typical for the nomadic life and receives new content. Abai's demand for the earlier poets was a requirement of his time. The issue was related to tradition. The creative tradition used in Shortanbai's poetry contradicts that used in Abai's poetry. Abai offered a new principle for poetry. He was not critical of Shortanbai per se but of the poetic traditions and imitational poetry of Shortanbai's time. At issue was the contradiction between the nomadic culture and the sedentary culture.

Social contradictions were complicated in Abai's time, and thus, the dimensions of social consciousness clearly reflected those qualitative characteristics. New dimensions and new qualities were needed for poems in that situation. Abai aimed to recognize the creativity of Kazakh poets in comparison to the best examples in world poetry. Undoubtedly, the works of Shortanbai, Dulat, and Bukhar, who followed the traditions of folklore, could not be compatible with such requirements.

He suggested a demanding program for Kazakh poetry, one that would make it comparable to the world poetry. Abai—a great figure living in the transitional period between earlier literature and written literature—proved by his own example how such a program could be implemented. Hence, it is logical that he wrote to following:

> *Shortanbai, Dulat, and Bukhar Zhyrau, their poetry is like a patchwork.*
> *Oh, if there were a person who knows the value of a word, he would see their faults!*

These were not just words about a coincidence. This was a reflection on the dialectic of a transitional period in our spiritual culture. This was Abai's wisdom that he stated with his whole consciousness and intention. These were words born from his empathy for his people's culture, these were his intentions to innovate that culture, and these were words of wisdom that came from the heart of his heart.

Abai mastered the writing of good poetry. He reached such depth not only by absorbing the national heritage but also by sensing the poetry of European masters such as Goethe, Byron, Pushkin, and Lermontov and by perceiving their qualities as qualities peculiar to him.

Abai's strong criticisms of earlier poets were aimed at improving Kazakh poetry. According to the law of dialectics, his criticisms were a rejection of the negation between the old and the new—not a metaphysical rejection but a dialectical rejection, that is, rejecting the old but not destroying its characteristics, instead continuing and developing them. Thus, Abai came to national heritage and to earlier poets through a dialectical rejection.

When I claim that Abai brought a new dimension to poetry, I mean that he intended to enrich and advance poetry, not only with modern and Western poetry, but with Eastern poetry as well. Abai's main principles were innovation and the preservation of traditions. The fact that Abai prayed to poets whom he admired with the following verses is not a coincidence:

> *Fuzuli, Shamsi, Seihali,*
> *Navoi, Saghdi, Firdowsi,*
> *Hozha Hafiz—all of you,*
> *Oh, please give me strength, you most honored poets.*

These are all Eastern poets. In addition, Navoi, Fuzuli, and Seihali are representatives of Turkic culture; these are not figures common to Arabs or Persians, but they are common for Turkic nations.

Therefore, the age of Abai can be identified as the Renaissance era—the Kazakh Renaissance. Its essence was the revival of the traditions of the Turkic written culture in the Kazakh land. The Turkic-speaking Kazakh people returned to their native written language.

It is a demand of contemporary times to accept Abai as a poet, as an heir of Turkic written culture who gave it a new dimension and who, as a thinker, gave birth to oral literature. But it is also important to study all poets in their complexity. Similarly, continuity in the transformation of oral culture into written culture is an issue that has not been fully discussed.

It is impossible to say final, concluding statements about great renaissance figures such as Abai. As the people's consciousness will advance and be fulfilled, so our understanding of Abai will widen; each generation will have its own concept on Abai, and they will have their own Abais. Therefore, the recognition of Abai is the recognition of our nation and its spiritual wealth.

In fact, we are only now reaching out to the spiritual development of our people. Since the 1920s, Kazakhs studied their spiritual treasures, but they did not give them their real value. "Rude sociology" dominated in the social consciousness. Most scholars of Abai's philosophical and social views were promoters of this "rude sociology." They attempted to separate Abai from his people, his land, and to separate the people from this authentic poet. Such abuses were committed against not only Abai but also Dulat; Shortanbai; the whole literary, cultural heritage; and the people's consciousness.

How could the truth be told about Abai in the times when the "rude sociological" view was in full swing? It is natural that the great thinker had contradictions, but there must be higher thinking and perfect knowledge in order to understand them. There was no such knowledge among "rude sociologists." They were just concerned with certain points of controversy, and they could not reach the depth of Abai's ideas. That is why they portrayed Abai as wealth loving, as too religious, and as a regressive person. If you read the publications from those years, you will find plenty of metaphors with such meanings. There is a common proverb that says, "The dog barks and the caravan goes." Abai's caravan is passing from generation to generation. Therefore, instead of discussing some individuals' negative claims about him, I would rather briefly review the most important aspect of Abai's creative work, his philosophical views.

When considering Abai's philosophical views, one must take into account that he was not a thinker who created a philosophical system, nor did he write a philosophical treatise. Therefore, there is no need to seek gnoseological principles, which would systemize his world outlook and philosophical concepts based on one foundation about the universe, one world-centered worldview. Since Abai did not write purely philosophical works, it is useless to try to refer to him as a representative of a group on materialism or idealism. Abai scholars have described his philosophical views as either deism or theism, and they continue to do so today. But it is unreasonable to support any of those ideas. In fact, it would be more reasonable to study his creativity rather than trying to forcefully push his worldview into the world's philosophical systems and conceptions. The main reason for this is that Abai is first and foremost a poet. His wisdom is reflected through his poetry. Thus, there are two ways of mastering the issues in his creative work. One is through an artistic expressive (poetic art) method, and the other is through a logical or philosophical (dialectical) approach. Abai's worldview should be constructed by synthesizing these two approaches.

Although Abai is definitely acknowledged as a poet, it is impossible to distinguish which consciousness (philosophical or artistic consciousness) dominates in his worldview. Abai never considered life only as a poet or only as a philosopher. His worldview was constructed on the acceptance of his environment in unity. Abai was a person who accepted the contradictions of the social essence of his time as a whole and "who [bore] heavy thoughts."

Abai did not make philosophical conclusions, so it is difficult to find him among representatives of materialism, idealism, or dualism. He had no singular monastic philosophical view; his world outlook was beautifully decorated with artistic images. This is a phenomenon typical of earlier Kazakh poets. However, Abai was not only a poet who had mastered the artistic consciousness of his people (the *termes* (epic songs), *zhyrs*, poems, etc.); he was not only a poet who brought new concepts into the transitional period from feudalism to capitalism; he was also a thinker who intended to bring qualitative transformations to the spiritual life of a society.

As such, he fairly criticizes the *bis* and old-time poets whose age was passing away. Because Abai realized that spiritual development requires a radical change in society. That is why, in his fifth and twenty-ninth Words (pieces from his "Words of Wisdom"), he criticizes some meaningless Kazakh proverbs, and in the second, ninth, and twenty-third Words and in other poems such as "My nation, my Kazakhs, poor people," he calls on people to get rid of negative habits. In poems such as "Do not be proud until you find knowledge," "Children are studying in the boarding schools," and "Finally hard work will give its fruit" and in his thirty-second Word, he encourages youth to acquire knowledge, to work honestly, and to learn the Russian language and culture.

Eastern cultures and his own culture played significant roles in Abai's formation as a humanist and as a thinker. Abai grew up learning about humanitarians such as the poets Fuzuli, Shamsi, Saihali, Navoi, Ferdowsi, and Khoja Hafiz from a young age. He learned about the philosophical concepts and systems that existed in India, China, Greece, Egypt, and other countries through these works. Abai learned about philosophers such as Plato, Aristotle, Luqpan, and Socrates through Sufi philosophy and later from Plutarch's writings.

He also thoroughly studied the works of the Western European philosophers Herbert Spencer and Auguste Comte, which had been translated into Russian and delivered to Semey Library. These great thinkers founded positivism, the most important trend of the nineteenth century. These Western thinkers are the great figures who rejected traditional views to philosophy and attempted to turn it into a positive science and who developed new conclusions based on their approaches. They taught that science, including philosophy, must not remain a mere abstract consequence of the mind, but it must be applicable to life. Abai also speaks about the direct benefits of science to real people. He was familiar with Draper's encyclopedia-like book *History of the Intellectual Development of Europe*. There is no systematic philosophical principle in this book, but there is a great deal of information. Abai must have used this work as a "textbook" in the word's modern interpretation.

It is not difficult for Kazakhs to be acquainted with the books Abai read in Russian. The works of the mentioned authors are stored in libraries. What Kazakh's cannot find are the books Abai read in Arabic, Persian, and Turkic. In particular, we often do not know about Sufi literature.

Sufism is a religious philosophy developed and renewed in the framework of Islam. During the years that Kazakhs had a negative view toward religion, we refused to acknowledge Sufism as a philosophical direction. As a result, we did not understand the meaning of many of the concepts and terms that reflected Abai's philosophical views.

It is true that in addition to Sufism, Abai was acquainted with world philosophical trends and directions, and he thoroughly studied Russian philosophy. Abai scholars have often noted this. However, it is also a fact that Abai was an Eastern poet, a figure of Eastern culture. To say it more clearly, he is one of the most prominent thinkers of the Islamic East. As Yevgeni Bertels, a scholar on Sufism opined, "It is impossible to understand the cultural life of the East in the Middle Ages unless you study the Sufi literature. His classics kept influencing the Eastern literature into the early twentieth century."[16]

Abai glorified Fuzuli, Shamsi, Saihali, Navoi, Saghdi, Firdowsi, and Khoja Hafiz, whose worldviews were formed under the influence of prominent Sufi thinkers such as al-Ansari, al-Khalaj, al-Harkany, al-Ghazali, al-Hamadani, Sanasi, Attar of Nishappur, and Rumi. That means that Abai recognized Sufism first through these great poets and then as theory through the works of the great Sufi philosopher Ahmad Yasawi. He raised the question of learning Arabic, Persian, and Turkic languages in his twenty-fifth Word. Abai himself was fluent in the Turkic language. Yasawi, who was one of the most influential figures in Turkic culture, also wrote his works in the Turkic language, not in Arabic.

Abai both supported and disagreed with Sufism in his work. In fact, it is worth considering the poet's view on Sufism separately: "Sufism and Abai" is a new topic for research. However, any such study must first begin with Ahmad Yasawi.

As stated previously, Yasawi was a major figure in the formation of the religious philosophy of Sufism, so much so that a new sect of Sufism, Yasawism, was developed based on his life and teachings. Without looking at Sufism, it is hard to reveal Abai's view on religion. Abai claims that we are on the path of God and the Prophet, but the poet's opinion about God often does not coincide with the basic principles of Islam. This is a point of contention. In the context of the Islamic religion, there is religious ideology and religious philosophy. Abai avoids religious ideology, so one must look for his views in religious philosophy.

Ideological religious leaders tortured and executed Mansur al-Hallaj, a great thinker in Sufism, because he said that he becomes one with God and he is united with God. When al-Hallaj was joined to God, he said, "I am myself the truth." In Islamic ideology, even the Prophet himself contacts God via angels, to say nothing about man's contact with God. But there is a very complex philosophical concept about God in Sufism, which Abai explored. And in doing so, he was modernizing Sufism.

The word "God" is mentioned often in the Abai's poems. But this does not mean he was a religious fanatic. He is the first thinker who strongly criticized Islam and its ideological character in Kazakh society. In Abai's works, the word "God" has three meanings:

1. An ontological meaning: God is the truth, the truth that describes the truth and existence of the universe, the truth that is the objective reality beyond the will and consciousness of a human being. One cannot deny obvious truth. Abai stated, "Both God and His words exist." In addition, "the substance cannot be a lie" is Abai's acceptance of God as the truth. However, it is impossible to understand this truth through reason. Thus, Abai comes to an agnostic conclusion: "God is almighty, but our powers are finite."

   He proved his view in his thirty-eighth Word as follows: "It is impossible to measure the infinite with the finite. Eager to fix the idea of Him in our minds, we repeat, 'There is no god but God, God is one and unique.' Yet, the very notions of 'is' and 'one' cannot express the essence of God, which is beyond human understanding, for no phenomenon in real life can escape the measure 'one.'" This theory reached the Kazakh steppe through the philosophy of the Sufis. One can also clearly see the impact of Plato's and his successor Plotinus's conviction that it is impossible to recognize God with intellect.

2. A cosmogonical meaning: God is the Almighty Creator of the universe. "Humankind was created with love, so you too love God, who is sweeter than your own soul." If one must love God because humankind was created with love, then God must be the Creator. Hence, one's love must also be devoted to the Creator only. That is why Abai said, "The mind is the source of power for the heart when a man has love for Tangri." In calling for the love of God, Abai did not follow the mysticism in Sufi philosophy but kept a humanistic thinking. Unlike the Sufis, Abai was against rejecting the pleasures of life for the sake of worshipping God. He categorically opposed dividing people according to their religion, race, and nationality, saying, "Love all mankind as a good brother and consider that way as the just way of the True One." To make such a highly humanistic conclusion during a time when Islamic ideology was dominant in the society was a clear criticism of religion.

3. A gnoseological meaning: In Islam, recognition of God can be achieved through His messenger. It is not permitted to accept God directly without His messenger on earth. At the same time, there is no higher sin in Islam than not accepting the Prophet. However, Abai was a poet who did not propagate the Prophet; he did not call on people to recognize the Prophet. He stated that "Times and people, their morals and occupations are changed; prophets change one another in turn." By this, he regards prophecy as a common thing and calls on people to respect others in order to feel the wisdom of God. He also openly criticized Islam in his thirty-eighth Word.

A careful reader of Abai's poems will find that he was acquainted with Buddhism, Zoroastrianism, and philosophical principles in Christianity. Research has not yet been conducted on Abai's direct involvement with Buddhism. However, Mukhtar Auezov noted the following:

> According to his own words, he started reading Russian thinkers in his thirties, and up until his forties, his own world was turned upside down. He said, "My east became my west, my west became my east." Undoubtedly, his west in this case is Russia, from which he learned language and art. Abai had a habit of going deep into each of his readings, when he found any worthy readings. For example, after reading the Buddha,

he said, "How deep are the words of Buddha, how sad that I did not come up with his words when I was younger!"

Even though Sufism and Buddhism are not strongly emphasized in Abai's thoughts about humankind, one can notice their influence in his words. The poet not only places people on a level with God, but he even removes limits on their self-development and raises them too high. According to Abai, God is the Creator, God is the Truth, but the driving force of life and the universe is humankind. Such humanism is typical of Buddhism. One principle in this religion is that if a person can become Buddha, then they are superior to God. Apparently, this conclusion seems to have been borrowed from Buddhism and then developed by Sufi scholars. This Buddhist-Sufi view about people became the core of Abai's creative work. Love for God is equal to a person's revelation of their own spiritual power in the poet's understanding. One will become a true and real humanist by loving God. Although God is the Creator, the Beneficent, He is the soul that serves humankind. God and human beings are meaningless and insignificant without each other. When God is true, human beings will never die. That is why it is appropriate for the poet to say, "Those who are ignorant call the separation of 'self' and 'mine' death. If God is eternal, then the truth about people is eternal too, that is, even though a man is not eternal, his soul, which is passed from generation to generation, is eternal. Both God and the truth about man are eternal."

Since Zoroastrianism is a very ancient religion, it could not reach Abai's times in a "pure" state. Thus, it is difficult to find the full principles of Zoroastrianism in Abai's work. One issue that is not openly discussed today, however, is that the religious philosophies of Zoroastrianism, Christianity, and Islam all have the same "theoretical" basis. Russian culture, especially, has plenty of signs of Zoroastrianism. That is probably why, after analysis of Abai's poem "Winter," Auezov concluded that the metaphor of winter as an old man was borrowed from Russian poetry, namely, from Nikolay Nekrasov. Perhaps he is correct, but referring to months as people is a well-established tradition in Zoroastrianism, in which months and days are often named after divinities. In the ancient Iranian calendar, each month, each day, and even each season had its own spiritual master. This is an effect of Zoroastrianism. This naming convention is also often found in the Avesta, the sacred book of Zoroastrianism.

In short, giving winter the image of a human being was Abai's novelty. And he did not limit this practice to winter. In the same poem, Abai described summer as a wedding couple: "The sun is the groom, the land is the bride, and their desire for each other is so strong." Was it Nekrasov's influence that caused him to define the sun as the groom and the ground as the bride? Probably not. The formation of such images was not typical in earlier folklore, so it was most likely the poet's own novelty.

Mukhtar Auezov studied Abai intensely and wrote a special article on him in the 1920s. He said, "Abai is not a philosopher. To be a philosopher, one must have a philosophical system. Abai does not have one. Abai has a philosophical opinion typical for wise poets."

I disagree. Abai was a philosopher, and though he may not have had a philosophical system, he did have a system for his worldview. Abai was a philosopher who had his own vision of the world and his own philosophical assumptions. His thirty-eighth Word is proof of this. The scholar Auelbek Qongyratbayev wrote about Abai's thirty-eighth Word in his article "Farabi and Abai":

> "There has not yet been a person who could analyze it properly. It is not enough just to know Arabic in order to understand this; one must also know Islamic philosophy. Here, Abai wants to reform the religion as Feuerbach did; he wants to adapt it to the new. There is the controversy. It is similar to Feuerbach's work *The Essence of Christianity*. However, in Abai's thirty-eighth and forty-third Words, God is not in the central place but in the qualities that are not found in man. Abai explains religion from an anthropological perspective. For God created a man similar to Himself and therefore the main inventor is a man, he must liken himself to God." [17]

Unfortunately, Abai's deep thoughts garnered no attention from other philosophers. The main reason for this is that Kazakh philosophers of the Soviet era did not study the Islamic philosophy Abai studied. It is very difficult to analyze Abai's views without considering his Islamic philosophy.

Abai was a poet who recognized the objective order of societal development and who obeyed those laws. His understanding went beyond fatal dogma, such as "the will of God" and "people will experience what is fated for them." By stating, "God will not change His commandment just because you are in a hurry," Abai was describing the order of the universe. For Abai, "the commandment of God" was not just a religious concept; it was an inescapable reality, the truth that would occur anyway. However, in Abai's time, there was nothing wrong with calling the law of development "God's commandment"; this was a comprehensible concept for people. As a realist poet, Abai provided his own worldview using understandable notions and not straying too far from his nation's consciousness. To reveal his own thoughts and beliefs, his own essence, in an understandable way, he did not rely on other languages but expressed the phenomena of the world in a clear language for his people.

The loan of philosophical concepts and terms in our lexical fund gave him this opportunity. Along with that, Abai also developed new concepts or added new ideas to the previous content of concepts and raised them to a philosophical level. For example, the word *pisiq* (excessively sociable) existed in Kazakh from ancient times. However, Abai transformed this word into a new concept that could reflect the social phenomenon of the new times. In his poem "Impatient, shameless, lazy," he described the word *pisiq* in detail. Unfortunately, during the harsh times, the *pisiqs* Abai mentioned turned into active performers of the government's tasks. The poet had prophetically predicted how these "activists," who would destroy the nation, would be formed.

We need to be able to see the contradictions in the dialectical perception of Abai's world. To accept, recognize, and describe the contradictions of his essence in a figurative way is one issue, and to suggest a solution to these conflicts by avoiding making them too tense is another. Abai felt with his heart and sensed with his mind the contradictions of life, but when it comes to the question of solving these conflicts, we refer to him as we do enlightener-democrats based on his "call" to art, education, and humanism.

However, it is a well-known fact that during the Soviet era, the words "enlightener" and "enlightening" were frequently mentioned. Kazakhs did not use the concept "enlightener" as having a concrete meaning. This is a calque translation of the Russian word *prosvetitel*; in short, it is an emulated word. For example, if you look at Abai's creative work, you will not find that word. Kazakh names for thinkers are *ghulama* (philosopher), *dana* (wise one), *danishpan* (wise one), and so on. There is no such word as "enlightener."

Bolshevist ideologists introduced the idea of "enlightenment." They claimed they were enlighteners who were bringing art and education to illiterate Kazakhs. They also began searching for enlighteners among Kazakhs. This was a necessary argument for the idea that "Bolshevism is a political thought that takes care of people." Thus, the concept of enlightenment was quickly developed and the Kazakh sons who were thinking about justice turned out to be enlighteners. It was a political-ideological maneuver to admit that the nation needed the concept of "enlighteners."

In fact, enlightening is a cultural movement that is perceived as a law that defines the essence of a society, and its driving force is a national idea. The concept of enlightening was borrowed from Europe, and when one analyzes the enlightenment of the French, English, and Germans, one has no choice but to acknowledge that the ultimate goal for each was a national idea.

However, when it comes to Russian enlightenment, the national idea was the decisive force there too, although, it had distinct characteristics. Because Russia's level of culture was much lower than that of Western European countries, the Russian intelligentsia formed two types (models) of enlightenment. One was an enlightenment that aspired to serve the interests of the Russian people, and the other was an enlightenment that tried to imitate the West.

Unfortunately, enlightenment reached Kazakhstan in the form of the missionary. A serious look at enlightenment in Kazakhstan finds that there were also two types of enlightenment there. One was the phenomenon itself, which attempted to make progressive reforms in accordance to the requirements of that epoch and, through these, to stimulate the consciousness of the people. These were necessary measures applied to the cultural system. They were implemented through promoting art and education and through appealing to the masses to get rid of social sicknesses and negative behaviors and to aspire to civilization. Enlightenment in such a direction is done for good purposes. In short, true enlightenment is a reflection of good intentions in action.

This type of enlightenment that leads to humanism was the Kazakh tradition, one that had been realized since ancient times. The content and creativity of the *zhyraus*, whose national preaching brought them close to the people, were mainly enlightening in manner.

However, when the Kazakh people were deprived of their native land, their heads bowed down and their knees bent to the ground, the second type of enlightenment, the missionary type, was introduced.

Before the October Revolution, missionary service that worked to spread Christianity was not hidden. The proof for that is in the work of Russian missionaries such as Nikolay Ilminsky and Kazakh teachers such as Ibirai Altynsarin who aimed to enlighten people.

After the October Revolution, missionary work was no longer allowed and it was accused of subversion, but its main characteristic was preserved. Now, in order to deceive people from an ideological perspective, Bolsheviks presented such work as an internationalist ideology. Thus, due to the establishment of the Soviet government, the two types of enlightenment were unified and joined together in Kazakhstan. The title "missionary" was removed, but its content was not changed, only its title, appearance, and form. From now on, the good intentions and aspirations of enlighteners who wished to enlighten the masses were under the influence of politicians.

New principles of enlightenment were developed, and enlightenment itself gained political-ideological importance. The enlightenment, which had had nothing to do with the revolution, had now become an ideological tool of revolution. Shoqan Ualihanov, Ibirai Altynsarin, and Abai were widely promoted by the Soviet government not for their achievements in science, teaching, or poetry but for their propagation and preaching of kindness to the masses.

According to the Soviet government, people such as Abai were the enlighteners who prepared the Kazakh people to shift to socialism. The policy of inventing the truth yielded results. The majority of the Kazakh people believed in the Soviet power and the Communist Party and were lost. As Abai had predicted, they did not distinguish between good and evil.

Abai was often referred to as an "enlightener," but he never said to the Kazakh people, "Do not practice the Kazakh style of life, turn to another nation and destroy your religion and language." He did, however, say, "Get rid of your negative behavior, look at other nations and correct your faults." If such preaching is considered as enlightenment, then it does not fit the Bolshevik description. The Bolsheviks denied the Kazakh lifestyle and destroyed the concepts of Islam, religion, and language. In short, they humiliated the spirit of the nation. They tried to create all possible obstacles to prevent Kazakh people from living as a nation.

Policies that destruct national interests cannot be considered as enlightenment. Hence, this was not an enlightenment but a tricky maneuver, a missionary consciousness hidden by politics.

Since enlightenment became a purely ideological concept, it became a political necessity to study such outstanding persons as Abai. In most research on Abai written between the 1950s and the 1980s, Abai was described as an enlightener, as a testimony to Bolshevik doctrine. Therefore, the enlightenment in Kazakhstan did not serve to lead people to independence—quite the contrary. It was an abusive policy that taught people obedience and a slave-like mindset.

Unless we know the essence of enlightenment, we must be forgiving of Kazakh intellectuals who were lost on the path to the truth. To be different from your times and to start a new path, to find unique wisdom, is not something everyone can do. However, there were many Kazakh sons devoted to the destiny of their people who were trying to do so. The next generation's duty is to be forgiving toward them and to know them. Everyone has their own destination.

Time is a tough critic; it reveals many things. Time is wise; it forgives many things. However, the question is in our contemporary times. If we do not understand today that we were lost and we keep being deceived by illusion, then how can we state that we are leading the way forward? As Abai said:

Then a poet will start his work
He will look around his environment
He will clean himself from the dirt of the world
And he will suggest wise words.

It seems it is time for the Kazakh intelligentsia to "clean itself from the dirt of the world."

Instead of relying on the statements told about us, it is our duty to "analyze critically what we have learned" and to form a science of Kazakh studies. Many of our social, political, and cultural ideas and concerns have been based on the imitation and worshiping of other teachings. And our tendencies regarding Kazakh enlightenment continue this problem.

For Kazakhs, there was a small gain from enlightenment—mainly, that it was destructible. We were led into a deadlock of development, to socialism. Now we are stepping back from that. But we have not yet reached the crossroads. We should have learned from past lessons to not follow others and to not imitate others, but in fact, we are now experiencing another type of enlightenment. A group of Kazakh intellectuals are imitating the West, rejecting the core of national development, and again pushing the people to the wrong path.

In Kazakhstan, enlightenment based on a national culture is a newly developing idea. Enlightenment is a cultural-political phenomenon that serves to awaken national consciousness. Today, we are witnessing the results of the missionary-enlightenment policy. The current Kazakh intelligentsia was brought up to be against the national idea. Its interest is Western culture.

Western civilization is valuable for its region, but the West is a different Christian world that does not suit the Muslim spirit. There is no doubt that it is useful to know Western culture. However, this is another factor limiting national development. Though Western and Kazakh cultures should not be rivals, we are a nation that has dispersed its own national genetic fund. We need time to get to know ourselves and develop ourselves. It is necessary to consolidate and accumulate our people. One of the main tasks of a sovereign country is to find out what it has and what it does not have. Before, Arabs and Persians introduced Turkic culture, but since those times, Russians have been moving to the east, and as a result, Christian culture has been dominating in Kazakhstan. It is reasonable to suspect a repetition of the same process in the future.

In short, Kazakh intellectuals are again encountering the spiritual problem of choosing a new path. Abai said, "The future path of a lost man is direct, and his past path is a trail." I would like us to find our own way after experiencing different paths and to make the future generation follow us, leaving them our own unique path.

Undoubtedly, there were other scholars, thinkers, and cultural figures from Anacharsis to Abai along with those I focused on. This is a very extensive theme. Thus, in this chapter, I have not been able to explore Abai in line with his own environment during the Soviet era. If one were to study Abai further, one would encounter histories of different worlds. This is called Pan-Turkism. Bolshevism invented Pan-Turkism and then struggled against it. In fact, it was not actually Pan-Turkism but just an attempt by those who wanted to explore the common culture and history of Turkic people. Today we all have the opportunity to study Turkic culture and its genesis, so I decided to discuss Abai from the early genesis. Doing so was not just a question of my desire. I had two other reasons for exploring this line.

My first reason is the Turkic language that has reached us in 2500 years (i.e., from Anacharsis to Abai). Certainly, it would not be correct to claim that the Turkic language has not changed, that it has remained the same. At the same time, no one can claim that the Turkic language has disappeared. It is one of the eternal languages. Once, Turks had their own alphabet, but with time, it was forgotten, and the reasons for that were explained above. Today, that alphabet is being revived in this new age.

Rabguzi, Baqirghani, Ahmad Yugnaky, Haidar Dulati, Jalairi, Turkestani, Al-Turki, Jamal Qarshi, Kashgari, Signaki, Barshylyghi, and others, all wrote their works in Turkic. They were talented people who lived before the Kazakh Khanate or the Kazakh Horde.

I do not argue with language specialists, but one thing is clear. It is a fact that the language we call Turkic language reached us from Scythian times. It is therefore very important to study Anacharsis's language. I hypothesized that Anacharsis spoke a Turkic language. What is needed now are concrete arguments. Turkology holds plenty of wrong conceptions about the Scythian language in my opinion. The main misconception is that the Scythian language is related to the Iranian language group. Speakers of Turkic language are listed differently in history: Scythians, Hunnas, Kipchaks, and so on.

My second reason for choosing this line of discussion is the ethnic consciousness that has not been interrupted for twenty-five centuries and that continues today. The theory, which has been proven by history, requires a unity in language among the people of an ethnos, since there is no ethnos without language, which means that the formation of a historical-social association of people without a common ethnic language is impossible. That is why ethnos and language are joined into one historical unity. The names of those ethnos that spoke in Turkic are the Scythians, the Kipchaks (Turks), and then the contemporary Turkic-speaking nations. Hence, the Turkic-speaking ethnicities did not disappear from history but only changed their historical names. The Kazakh ethnos is one branch of that Turkic world. In addition, the scholars I discussed here are those who lived in the "transitional periods" of those ethnic groups. All of them are renaissance figures. For example, if Anacharsis introduced to Scythians the culture, art, and political control system of Athens, the most civilized city of that time, then Yollug Tigin lived in the most prominent time of the Turkic world and inscribed that transitional epoch in stone. He is the creator of the liberation movement. Hence, he is a propagandist of ethnic consciousness. His essence is tightly connected to the Turkic Khaganate. The poem "Kul Tigin" delivers the notes written in Abai's poem, which sadly says, "Oh, my whole nation." That is why I did not include others in my discussion of thinkers from Anacharsis to Abai. Maybe I am right, maybe I am wrong. Other scholars might find out. It is a complex subject that requires special study.

My goal is to systematize the cultural-historical concept from Anacharsis to Abai and introduce it into school textbooks and thus create favorable conditions for younger generations to master the spiritual, historical, and cultural space of twenty-five centuries.

Despite the centuries-long gap between them, there are similarities between Anacharsis and Abai. The main similarity is their closeness to skeptical philosophy. I mentioned previously that Anacharsis is considered to be from the skeptic philosophers. As for Abai, he never "boasted" by stating useless opinions about science, the essence of life, or human beings. Indeed, he has more questions than answer in his words. He criticized the mind. He knew the limits of the mind. What, he suggested, if the mind is limited and it is impossible to recognize the universe? This is a philosophy of skepticism in Europe. However, this is not just mere skepticism, not just the rejection of something; it is an assumption that relied on reasoning. Only a mindful person can perceive the limits of the mind. Both Anacharsis, a Scythian thinker, and Abai are such people.

It is evident that in society, there is no absolute certainty about the truth, its existence is impossible. People often perceive a hypothesis as an axiomatic theory until time proves that it is wrong. Often, the theory is regarded as a hypothesis, and the hypothesis as a theory; they are equally interchangeable. Hence, what I am claiming is a hypothesis for sure, but who can guarantee its theoretical function? It is the theory that denies the theory. If there is no such theory, then the claim turns to into a hypothesis. In short, regardless of how it is viewed, as hypothesis or theory, this cultural-historical concept will be useful. If my arguments are proven wrong, then they served to reach the truth. They offer an initial path to those who might think this is the right direction, one that needs further consideration.

****

Before moving on, I will take a moment to say a few words about the next chapter of this book.

It is clear and reasonable that each intellectual should state their own opinion about Abai. Although the poet is common to all Kazakhs, each of us can have their own Abai. It is not surprising that each person and each generation perceives Abai differently. The content of consciousness is determined by the understanding of a subject. In this regard, I also focused on studying Abai's creativity.

It is impossible to speak about Kazakh culture and philosophy without mentioning Abai. Therefore, the understanding of Abai is closely related to the problem of Kazakh identity. However, what are the methods of understanding the poet? There are plenty of general statements circulating about Abai.

I used a different approach to understand Abai. This method is called 'hermeneutics' in European terms. It is a method of understanding concepts expressed in literary form. The explanations I offer in the following two sections are based on concepts in one of his poem-songs (Section Two) or Words (Section Three), or even sometimes in just one verse or line of a poem. I do not intend to compare my ideas about Abai's statements with the opinions of other scholars. My goal is simply to provide a clear explanation, according to my own study and understanding, of Abai's ideas and perspectives.

Endnotes:

[1] Plato, *Works*, Vol. 3, 1st chapter, (Moscow, 1971), pp. 427 and 642.

[2] Herodotus, *Histories,* (Moscow: Nauka, 1972), p. 198.

[3] Lucian, *Collection of Works,* (Moscow, 1935), pp. 95–101.

[4] Lucian, p. 96.

[5] Aristotle, *Collection of Works*, Vol. 4, p. 284.

[6] Aristotle, *Collection of Works*, Vol. 4, p. 280.

[7] Sextus Empiricus, *Collection of Works in Two Volumes*, Vol. 2, p. 69.

[8] Lucian, *Collection of Works,* (Moscow, 1935), pp. 95–101.

[9] Plutarch, *Essays*, (Moscow, 1983), p. 369.

[10] Michel de Montaigne, *Essays*, (Moscow, 1981), p. 24.

[11] Diogenes Laërtius, pp. 95–96.

[12] S. Kisilev, *Drevniania istoria iuzhnoi Sibiri* [Ancient history of southern Siberia], (Moscow, 1951).

[13] *Ezhelgi dauyr adebyety* [Ancient literature], (Almaty: Anatili, 1991), p. 110.

[14] *Ezhelgi dauyr adebyety,* p. 108.

[15] M. Auezov, *Zhyirma tomdiq shygarmalar zhinagy* [Collection of works in twenty volumes], (Almaty: Zhazushi, 1958), p. 15.

[16] Y. Bertels, *Sufism and Sufi literature*, (1965), p. 54.

[17] Qongyratbayev, *Qazaq eposi zhane turkologia* [*The Kazakh epoch and Turkology*], (Almaty, 1987), p. 329.

Section Two

'Concepts about Concepts' in the Songs & Poems of Abai

"Have you unraveled the simple secrets
That are carefully safeguarded by me,
My contemporary, my unknown brother?"
—— Al-Ma'ari

"Both God and His Word Exist"

Abai speaks of the knowledge of God in this poem. There was no thinker in the Kazakh land who had studied this as an issue of critical reflection before Abai's time. Even the saints who dedicated their lives to serving God did not go beyond the essential Muslim confession: "God is uniquely one and Mohammed is His Prophet." So there was no difference between faith and perception.

In Abai's opinion, faith and perception are different things. Faith is a religious term while perception is an epistemological notion. If we can call the first one a religious ideology, the latter is the category within the philosophy of religion. Both of these notions – belief in God and knowledge of Him – are the attributes of religious consciousness. Therefore, we call people who deal with this problem religious philosophers. Then Abai is a religious philosopher as well. This is neither praising nor blaming him, but an unbiased assessment of his work.

Abai is not a preacher he is a researcher of God's teaching. He is a thinker who strives to comprehend God. "Both God and His word exist. And their substance cannot be false," says Abai, considering the problem from the theological point of view and paying special attention to faith in God's veracity.

But what meaning does Abai assign to the word "is"? It is a measurement, which defines the content and quality of a thing or phenomenon. What was true at one time, however, may, ultimately in the course of time, change in terms of its significance, value or meaning. This is one distinction of the "substance."

The second distinction is the problem of knowing that substance. This is a philosophical problem. If we do not come to know the truth, we should be content only with blind faith in God. Speaking of the real existence of God Abai does not say it is an absolute truth, but considers it an opportunity to discover truth, as one of the kernels of existence.

In the first two lines of this poem Abai uses the word "exist" three times. It is not by pure accident. The reader is invited to think freely about this. "Think, ponder, try to get to the truth yourself," advises Abai. He approaches the problem of the essence of God from a perspective of His historic importance. The idea that "God exists" was true in the past, remains so now and will be in future. "Existing" in this case is the measurement of eternity. "God exists" is the eternal truth.

"Existence" can continue for eternity, but our life has transient elements as well. And the fact that these transient elements exist is true as well. So, in speaking of the eternality of existence we should recognize at the same time its changeability as times goes by. Does it mean that what exists today will vanish tomorrow? No, not necessarily. Instead there are times when people say that something is true and real when, in fact, it may only be their misperception.

What exists in the Universe is an objective reality. Objective reality can be misperceived, but this does not make it a false reality. From Abai's point of view, God is the truth. Thus, if the truth exists, God exists as well. If we say that our life is true, then God and His word are true as well. In recognizing our lives humanly, we recognize God too. This is Abai's view as a humanist.

Reality always remains real. That is why God exists and He is Eternal. Abai warns his contemporaries as well as us today from being light-minded in our attitude toward God, from making superficial judgments of Him. According to Abai, God is the one truth which cannot be comprehended with human reason. He came to the conclusion that love, more than reason, is the main link between God and humans. Abai, therefore, wanted to prove the existence of God via love. He says, "Life without love is meaningless." According to Abai, a true Moslem should be merciful and compassionate. Abai's words, "do not challenge existing realities," should be interpreted in the sense that the Word of God should not be challenged, otherwise those who follow God's path will lose their humanity and compassion.

Thus, in Abai's view, philosophically speaking, God is absolute, unchanging truth. But he is of a different opinion regarding those who preach God's word. He says: "As for times and people, their morals and occupations change; prophets replace each other in turn." By these words Abai wants to differentiate God's way and the way of His prophets. As the Kazakh poet Mukagali Makatayev said, "Powerful men change the face of the earth hoping that much better times will come." But if God is invariable and eternal, then why do the prophets replace one another? Is there any contradiction here? If so, it is only a seeming contradiction. God's word is invariable, but it is changed with the transformation of objective reality. The prophet who came to this world changed God's Word in accordance with the changes in the historical circumstance which had taken place between the last prophet and his own time.

If the words of the prophets were invariable and eternal, they would have become gods themselves. But because they are only God's chosen instruments who preach the word of God; the apparent contradiction is not in God' word, but in the prophets who preach it. The words of the prophets are limited by the scope of their knowledge. Only the word of God is infinite, all else has its limits.

God has no sin. We do not describe a prophet in the same way. Abai calls him truthful because he communicates the word of God to us. But the prophet came to the world by the will of God and when the time came he would leave this world, leaving his place under the moon to the others yet to come.

As Plato said: "Socrates is my friend, but the truth is more important." In the same way, Abai as a Moslem expresses bold antireligious thoughts. He expresses his point of view about God and the prophet. He understands how great his responsibility for each word of God is, but nevertheless he tries to open the way for a new system of thinking. One of the main conditions in Islam for those who want to be true Moslems is to recognize His Prophet and that God is one and unique. Abai does not violate this condition, but in his opinion the place and role of God and the Prophet are different. When Abai speaks of eternity, he uses general the categories and concepts of God and humans. Prophets are humans, that is, people like all the rest. Abai's philosophy does not follow the traditional scheme: God – Prophet – People. Abai speaks of both God and people. This is democracy in theology because he allows people to know their own selves. God is infinite. If you want to know Him, develop your own self infinitely, then you will be not only a great person but a true Moslem.

Abai says that God endowed His people with reason, aspiration and good deeds deliberately. God not only gives these qualities to people, He also lets people increase the capability of their various giftings. How does a person use this opportunity? Whom should they follow while believing in God and His infallibility? There are three kinds of people who can lead the multitude: prophets, saints and sages. If the prophets and saints served God with all their heart, disregarding all earthly concerns and pleasures, the world would have fallen into desolation and decay. Who would have then grazed the livestock, who would have sown the wheat and extracted the riches from the bowels of the earth? That's why true Muslims need sages. Although they are not religious workers, as the Prophet Mohammed said, "A good person is one who does good deeds on behalf of their fellows."

Abai's thoughts go beyond orthodox Islam. In the knowledge of God, he sees the solution of humanistic problems common to all humankind. Love of God according to Abai is self-perfection and he considers humanistic compassion one of its main principles. To achieve that, it is necessary to be cleansed from one's sins. You cannot love God and continue a life of sin because love for God requires a cleansing of ways. Then you will take the path of truth; your will, reason and feelings will be strengthened and your perception will be clear. Abai's call to become someone who pleases God does not sound fatalistic. He sees it as an opportunity to gain true freedom. Personal freedom to Abai is the perfection of one's human qualities.

Abai pays a special attention to the notion "will." When saying, "The will of God is invariable," the poet means the inevitability and objective character of the laws of earthly existence. People learn them from the sages. Abai values them for that even though they are not counted spiritual workers.

There are many paths to God says Abai. Ultimately, humankind should achieve harmony in spite of their different religions. The word of the sage should help them in pursuing the path of unity. Having known the power of God, people will find peace and be prosperous only when sages guide the people.

"There Were Many Messages from the Creator, Especially Four of Them…"

A Prophet is a mediator between God and humans. There are many prophets mentioned in the Qur'an, but only four of them left Scriptures: Moses, David, Jesus and Mohammed. The first book of Scriptures is the Talmud (or Torah). Surah 17, verse 2 of the Qur'an says: "And we gave Moses the Scripture and made him the leader of the sons of Israel: Do not take protectors except me…" The second book is called The Psalms (Zabur). The Qur'an says: "We granted advantage to David from us: Oh mountains, birds, worship together with him! We soften an iron for him…" The third book is The Gospel (Injil). Concerning how this book was created God said the following: "We sent our messengers with clear intentions and brought down with them the Scriptures and scales so that people could stand in justice and brought down the iron; it has bad and good to people, so that God knew in secret who helped Him and His messengers. Truly, God is powerful and great! Then we sent on Isa, a son of Mariam and gave him the Gospel and put it in the hearts of those who followed him in meekness and mercy, and they devised monasticism: "We did not instruct them to do that it if it is not for getting benevolence from God. But they did not do that properly." Book four is the Qur'an. There were forcible arguments for its appearance. "Women" surah says: "Oh possessors of the Scripture! Do not go to excess in your religion and say nothing against God except the truth because Isa, a son of Mariam is the Messiah, and His Spirit. Believe in God and His messengers and do not say three. Keep it – that is best for you. Truly, there is no god but God."[1] In the Qur'an, God is unique and He is God and Mohammed is his messenger. These verses are the main manifestations of God.

There are many books sent down from God, so it is natural to ask whether new revelations will appear in the future. In the Qur'an Mohammed is the last Prophet, but in Abai's opinion the sending of prophets could not be stopped. The idea that the prophetic stream would come to an end came from

---

[1] All quotes in paragraph above taken from *The Qur'an*, tr. I. Krachkovsky (Moscow: Nauka, 1990), pp.232; 351; 447-448; and 100 respectively.

the dream of "pure religion." As far as the truth was concerned, Abai never saw it from the point of view of only one faith and one religion. He had the same opinion regarding Holy Scripture, which indicates the way of truth. When choosing one's way, it is natural to be mistaken. In such cases, God sends to the earth a Prophet with new revelations. Usually God's revelations come from on high, first to the Prophet, then to the people through him.

In the twentieth century there are people in the world who still expect prophets; at least, there is such an idea. People in the world also still hold ideas about the coming of the Messiah. This tradition comes from old times. Some traditions may exist for a long time; others gradually lose their significance and are forgotten. Time will show what will happen to the tradition of the coming of the Messiah. We, on our part, should know that the coming of prophets usually coincides with a critical time in history, which has its distinctive signs and special marks.

Our time can be called such time. But there is no demand or need for a prophet now. We say that based on two things relating to faith in a messiah. Blind faith restricts people's freedom. It is better if a person does not have such a faith. We do not know of cases when the people have suddenly become happy having made for themselves idols and gods. A prophet is also a human being but he is a mediator between God and the people, speaking on behalf of God. Let's ponder whether we really need a mediator? What would happen if each person independently found their way to God? Abai was such a thinker who tried to find the way himself. But not everyone can be like Abai, that is why we need someone (a prophet) who will preach the word of God. Educated thinkers do not need the help of prophets. It is the multitude that needs messiahs.

The prophet is a thinker who reforms the public consciousness. It is impossible to do without them. The multitude needs not only the rulers, but thinkers and leaders as well. That is why the thinkers, just as they are, will not be accepted by those who are in power. First, the reason is that the prophets see the drawbacks and speak openly of them, criticizing the work of the rulers. Such a criticism negatively affects their political power. Second, when we consider the issue of whether the thinkers and prophets are needed to help manage the people, I would say this is a double-edged sword. The management system has its own logics, principles and established rules, which often do not correspond to scientific logics. Management of people is politics. It often needs little deep theoretical thinking.

Politics is the ability to keep pace with time, adapt to life and use all available means to practical ends. The prophets are bound up with eternal problems. They cannot wage war and stir up discords.

At present, we do not need prophets in their traditional sense, but rather savants and thinkers. As Abai said, we need sages. They worship no one with blind faith. In fact, sages do not demand anyone to worship them. They only aid in the promotion of free thought. Everyone is free to choose what he likes from word of the sages.

This is the meaning of Abai's thoughts about the content of Holy Scriptures. The name of God is eternal to Abai and the life of the prophets is limited in time. His words that messiahs come and leave in turn, one after another, is the understanding that their coming is associated with the changing times in the lives of the people.

No matter how great a prophet is, they cannot outdo those who will come after them. The fact that they exist a certain period of time is not a drawback at all, on the contrary, that makes them closer to the people and shows the level of the development of the society. Each time has its own prophets. These are the lines along which Abai expresses his thoughts about prophets and their role in history.

"Do People Know Iskander?"

The theme of Iskander was not new in Abai's times. There were many works in West European and Eastern literature about Alexander the Macedonian, that is, Alexander the Great. Why does Abai take up this theme? He was not a man who repeats things already known. What incited him to create the poem "Iskander"?

Certainly this poem is a result of Abai's long meditation. The first line of the poem ends with the question "Do people know Iskander?" It is not accidental. In asking this question, Abai wants to claim that he knows the truth about him. He is not satisfied with the existing stories. Thinking logically, let's ask the question in a different way: "Is the truth about Iskander known to the world?" It means there were many legends and stories about Iskander which pretended to be true. But Abai does not need a story known only to the Kazakhs. He asks his people not the whole world. The problem has two sides.

First, what is known to the Kazakh people about Iskander and, second, why does this truth not satisfy the poet. The fact that the poem starts with the question may serve as evidence that Abai's dissatisfaction made him take up this theme.

People knew about Iskander from two sources. One source is Islam; the other is the Eastern poetry. In the Qur'an, Iskander is known as one of the prophets. In religious books, Iskander is known as a mythic character called "The Two-horned." How might he have appeared in the Holy book as a prophet is a different story. Here is a legend explaining why he was called "Two-horned."

When Iskander started fighting with other peoples, the enslaved peoples took him as a liberator. The rulers of Egypt who had been suffering the oppression of Iranian conquerors for many years met Iskander as a hero-liberator. According to Egyptian laws, to be a ruler, Alexander should have been a relative to the Pharaoh. Some time later the rumors about his kinship were spread everywhere.

It appeared that Iskander was not Philip's son. In the absence of Philip, the pharaoh of Egypt, Nektaneba II, appeared as god of the sun, Ra, and met with his wife Olympiad. After this meeting Alexander was born. His birth from the gods was substantiated and he was given the name Zulkarnaiyn. They say that the god Amon Ra had horns. According to the tradition, a son of the Pharaoh was considered to be a son of the god Ra. All legends and stories spread among people were based on this plot.

Iskander from the point of view of the religious servants was a winning character. He is a prophet, he is just and he is a ruler. He fit the (messianic) image people had in previous times.

A historical paradox is that in spite of the fact that Iskander had conquered the Persians and taken their religion in the legends, he is a son of Darius III Codomannus. Thus, Iskander is presented rather as a mythic character in religious books, especially in the Qur'an, rather than as a historic person. The idea of Iskander considering himself a son of god was known before the appearance of Christianity, let alone Islam. Though the name of Iskander as a god and prophet was known before Islam, we know him as Zulkarnaiyn from the Qur'an.

Abai does not agree with that. The poet does not recognize him as a prophet, but portrays him from a negative angle. Abai's Iskander is a scoundrel who betrayed his father. He is envious and likes praise. Of course, such qualities are not conducive to calling him a prophet. This interpretation confirms again the greatness of Abai because in the nineteenth century it was a great sin and heresy to refute what was written in the Holy Book. By doing so, Abai tried to change people's views about Iskander.

The Kazakhs know Iskander from fiction. There were very few Eastern poets who did not write at least some lines about him. Their works were known to the Kazakhs from long back. Firdousi, the author of a favorite Kazakh poem, "The Shahname," wrote that Iskander was a son of the Persian ruler Darius who went to Mecca and became a Moslem.

The classics of the East which speak about Iskander repeated one another because there were enough legends and stories about him circulating. The Great conqueror had conquered many countries. There were lots of discussions among famous scholars and each of these legends and stories became the basis for another story. Nizami told the world about Iskander's meetings with Indian thinkers. He ranked them on the same level as Iskander. He also talked about the difficulties of Iskander's campaign. Of course, each poet gave his own interpretation of Iskander, but for us, it is important what made both them and Abai return again and again to the subject of him.

I suggest that one reason for the turning of Iskander into a mythic character and the great interest in him which it generated among famous poets is his early death. Iskander – Alexander was born in 356 BCE and died in 323. He lived only 33 years. The Greeks consider age forty an acme. The Kazkhs say reason comes at this age. Iskander died not reaching this age. The poets used Iskander to show the contradictions in human culture because Iskander as a historic character is very complex. Iskander, who replaced his father on the throne, was known for his cruelty, perfidy and despotism. But the humane education he received in childhood sometimes manifested itself in him and that helped the historians to create a positive character.

The Eastern poets were not interested in true facts of Iskander's life. In most cases they used the plots of the legends and stories in their works. And that is why it was not Firdousi, Nizami, Jame and Akhmedi who made Iskander popular, but vice versa, the character of the great conqueror aided them. It is appropriate to note that at the beginning of twentieth century many Russian poets wrote about Jesus. Alexander Block (1880-1921), in his poem "The twelve," describes Jesus Christ leading the twelve Red Guard soldiers. At the same, time the Kazakh poet Sultanmakhmut Toraigurov wrote a verse "Who is Jesus?' Later the character of Christ would appear in Mikhail Bulgakov's novel "The Master and Margaret." He is, likewise, the main character in Chingis Aitmatov's novel "Block" and Yury Dombrovsky's novel "Faculty of Unneeded Things."

In transitional times, people always ask the question, "Who is Jesus?" The Eastern poets, looking for the answer to this same kind of question, chose Iskander as the most suitable image to express their ideas. Human consciousness consists of contradictions. The theologians once made Jesus Christ both God and prophet. Islam ranked the tyrant Iskander among the prophets and the poets described him as a just and merciful ruler. Abai was against such interpretations of Iskander because for him the main thing in describing historic figures was truth. Here Abai displayed his quality as a historical-critical thinker. The poet admiring his teachers such as Navoi and Firdousi changed the character of Iskander created by them, that is, he disputes with them. Blind worship of authorities is alien to Abai. In his time, Abai could write freely on any topic, find shortcomings in the Holy Scripture and Eastern poetry. Abai's Iskander fully complies with historical truth. Abai is familiar with historic materials about Iskander and that is why the truth about him is already in the first strophe. As a ruler, he was envious and boastful. The reader then knows what follows thereafter.

"The Times, They are a' Changin'"

Abai accepted the thought that the world was in flux because he understood that it could not be constant, it was changing. Yet, it is not time itself that changes morals and occupation. How should we understand that? Let's first analyze the notion of "movement." At the lectures on philosophy the students more often are taught the notion "movement." Abai does not employ such a word. "Movement" of course comes from the word "move." Then the notion of "movement" is a simplified word compared to the term "change."

People and poets are changed, times change; every living being changes. That does not happen according to anybody's will and wish. These changes occur all by themselves. Abai does not explain the reasons of this process. If he were deep in a subject, then he would probably write a philosophic treatise, not a poem. But he is a poet and fulfills his mission by creating poetic images of the changeable world.

Each one has his own understanding of the changes in the world. Change fosters love for life as given to us by nature. In Abai's opinion, the reason for the changing nature of all existing things in the world is nature itself. The changes are not managed with reason; this is an inevitable phenomenon, which is impossible to avoid or avert. To understand the changes this way means to recognize its philosophical substance.

The poet raises a mysterious problem in this poem. Everything changes in the world but there is something that is not subject to changes. Let's read the following lines: "God is invariable, but people always change…" The principles of Shariah law change, but God is invariable. Every living being changes, but God is eternal." Abai clearly says that God is eternal and invariable. But can we really have equal approach to God and a man? There are no natural laws which apply equally to God and man, but Abai for some reasons does not say that. And so we come to the problem of absolute and relative truths.

Abai comes back again and again to the subject of change because he thinks that transformative time needs leaders. He writes: "The world is changeable; morals and occupation change with time, and the prophets succeed each other in turn."

Change brings not only the joy of renewal but sadness, suffering, mistakes and danger of the unknown as well. That is why to help people find the right way the prophets come to earth. Prophets are those who have new ways of thinking and change public consciousness. Only God knows the real number of prophets who have come down to earth. The following names of the prophets are mentioned in the Qur'an: Adam, Idris, Noah, Hud, Salih, Abraham, Lot, Ismail, Isaac, Joseph, Moses, Aaron, David, Solomon, Job, Elijah, Elisha, Isaiah, Johah, Ezekiel, Zechariah, John the Baptist, Jesus and Mohammed.

Abai gives the evidence that God's word changes. The prophets change each other's revelations and each one introduces something of his own into God's word. Such a statement could be considered a heresy. If God is invariable how can His word be changed? Is there any inconsistency? Of course there is. But the contradiction is the change itself. On the one hand, it is eternal truth of God, on the other hand it is the objective reality that always changes (time, occupation, morals of the people). The problem is how relation of these two facts – the invariable God and objective reality which continuously changes – should be understood.

God is invariable but His word addressed to the changing world cannot but be changed in accordance with the changes that take place, otherwise the bond between God and a man will be broken. The prophets come to the earth to keep that bond. The prophets have their own outlook but they speak the same message: God exists and is one. This is exactly what Abai means saying that God is invariable and eternal. God is the truth and we should come to know Him. There are many ways of knowing this truth and each prophet brings his own new truth to people. Ultimately all ways lead to the belief that 'there is no god but God.' Abai speaks of God in a broader sense than he is spoken of in Islam. It can be considered a reform in theology. Abai was seeking something valuable in God's word that could serve humankind, and if he did not find necessary thoughts and characters in the Scripture, he filled the gap with his own understanding and ideas.

"He Created Humankind in Love"

In strophe five of the verse "There is no god but God and His word is true," Abai is thinking of the purpose of life and says: "The Creator created humankind in love, that is why we love Him more than ourselves." Abai calls us to love God because He put love in people's hearts and created humankind in love. If it is so, then love has existed before humankind and the subject of that love was God.

It is His power and His Spirit, but this power is a mystery for Him as well, a certain truth, of which the Creator has a broad idea himself. When knowing God and His power in the creation of the world, including humankind, we should understand love as the very manifestation of God, His will and His power. Our duty is to worship and love God.

Love plays a special role in the outlook of Abai with respect to knowing God. How did he come to adopt that perspective? Before answering this question, let's see how the problem of love is considered in theological philosophy. You shouldn't be surprised that in religious teachings the notion of love is encountered regularly because love is a measurement of human qualities. Abai said: "Life without love is meaningless."

The thoughts of love are always the thoughts of the purpose of life. There are many works dedicated to the problem of love in Islam, the youngest religion in the world. The founder of the theory of knowing God through love was Rabia (or Rabia) al-Adawiyya (713 - 801 CE).

Rabia lived all her life as an ascetic. Her name became a legend. As an orphan, she was enslaved very early in life. Her master saw her fanatic love for God and her devotion to asceticism and gave her her freedom. Having received her freedom, Rabia preached love for God till her death. Al-Bistami, al-Khaladzh and ibn-Arabi – who were her followers and disciples – raised the philosophy of love to its highest level. In the 10th -11th centuries, the philosophy of love was extended to the arts, particularly literature. Firdousi, Nizami, Rumi and other poets wrote about love. The tales, "A Thousand and One Nights," also are dedicated to the topic of love. The story of Leili and Medzhnun was a form of the religious philosophy of love in the poetry. I say that because E. Bertels, one of the well-known orientalists, once noticed that an author described Medzhnun's love as his love to Leili. For Medzhnun, everything that surrounded him – mountains, stones, walls, houses and other things – meant Leili. That means that Medzhnun loves life. Life made Medzhnun fall in love. His love for Leili is an allegoric image and you can feel the influence of Rabia's philosophy.

The appearance of Rabia's philosophy and its popularity can be explained by several reasons. By Rabia's time Islam had existed for more than a century. At that time the preachers of Islam, keeping their distance from the common people, started transforming religion into politics. Rabia's philosophical teaching became a form of people's protest. The preachers of Islam persuaded people that hard work on the earth would provide a paradise in the heavens. Rabia was against such a theory. She said that love for God must be unselfish. According to Rabia's teaching, God and people are united. A person must love God with all their heart, asking nothing in return.

Asceticism prevails in Rabia's teaching. A person can do nothing but show the proof of their love to God. Her teaching is a step along the path to knowing God for Abai. Abai, however, supported a pragmatic philosophy, which stood for life interests. He did not accept asceticism.

In the course of time, Rabia's teaching became a leading philosophical school within Islam. Rabia's "philosophy of love" is the basis of Sufism. The "philosophy of love" greatly influenced the Arabian and Persian culture and poetry of Central Asia and Kazakhstan because the subject of love in art and literature allowed us to think democratically and freely. Maybe because of that, no literature of the Middle Ages could be compared to the Arabian and Persian love poetry. No matter how paradoxical it sounds, the teaching of love flourished within Islam. The "philosophy of love" was a healing remedy for Islam, which was infected with politicization; it breathed fresh energy into the religion.

Abai, too, understood that Islam needed renewal and proposed his view on how to know God. Abai believed that love could clean the soul from filth. The "philosophy of love" became love poetry in the Kazakh steppe. A person's love for God could be transformed into the love between a man and a woman, but the meaning remained the same: love must be unselfish, it should not be the subject of bargaining. Devotion and faithfulness is God's way.

Love stories and legends came to Central Asia from the Islamic world of the East. The poets wrote verses and people learnt them by heart. Thus, the "philosophy of love" came to people through poetry, but the form of expression was a bit different than in the "philosophy of love." While Rabia spoke of love sitting alone for years, in the love poetry two people, a young woman and a man spoke of love. Love became a human feeling. But the asceticism and sacrifice in love remained. There are few stories which have a happy ending in love poetry. Much more often the lovers die, as for example, Bayan-Sulu and Kozy-Korpesh, Kyz-zhibek and Tolegen.

The outlook and public consciousness are historic notions. Abai's words, "The Creator created humankind in love," were accepted and understood by all of his contemporaries because everyone heard the parables that came from Sufi literature.

The love of God is infinite, that is a holy truth. That means that the knowledge of this love is infinite as well. Love is an eternal subject. The purpose of life is love. In the course of time love for God was expressed through both carnal and spiritual love. This is what Abai meant when he wrote: "love and passion are two different things because passion is satisfaction of flesh."

"Love for Three Things is Like Fragrant Flowers in Your Heart"

Abai is a thinker. He has deeply analyzed such notions as "being a Muslim" and "holiness." Let's consider these notions and the expression "Love for three things."

First, a person should love God: "Love God with all your heart." Second, "Love all humankind as your brothers," that is, you should love all people irrespective of their faith, language or race. Third, bearing in heart and mind God's love for humankind, you should be fair and love justice.

Abai called love for these three things sacred feelings which are like fragrant flowers. He says, "Think and try to scatter the seeds of these flowers everywhere. Spare neither riches nor life for that. If you arrange your life in this way, you can consider yourself a true Muslim. But if you simply keep the fast, pray with beads and observe other traditional rituals, they will not make a true Muslim. The same thought is in the following lines: "Prayers, alms, fasts and pilgrimage are necessary things. But if you do not love God, your neighbors and justice, all your good deeds will be in vain."

Abai said nothing bad about other people or religions. As a humanist, he dreamt of mutual understanding among the people – peaceful coexistence – and approached the interpretation of Islam and religion from humanistic point of view. A 'Muslim' according to Abai is a person who does everything for the good of other people. Acts which result in detriment to people are evil deeds.

"God is Perfect and the Prophet Brings the Light of Truth"

God is pure and perfect and people are not. God endowed humans not only with reason, but human frailty as well. Who then is responsible for human failings? Abai answers this question. He says that God is perfect and people should recognize this and worship Him. The Creator sets this goal for people only because he endowed them with reason and freedom of perception. The rest of the creation does not have such qualities.

The prophets whom God sends to the earth help people with their choices. Mohammed is the last Prophet. Abai speaks about him. If God is perfect, then His messenger is virtuous as well. God cannot make mistakes, only people make mistakes, but it is the prophet who should correct them and show them the right path. That is why he must be truthful. People do not need all the truth, because when he has doubt, a person needs only sufficient truth, which is told him through His prophet who we should recognize as a benefactor.

God gave people freedom, that is why they cannot be without sin. People are sinful. There are no sinless people. A person who refuses the pleasures of the world becomes holy. They do that to rid themselves of sin. The notion "holiness" is ambiguous because complete refusal of earthly things and fanatic worship of God cannot be the way to truth. First, a person should live a worthy life as given them by God: sow wheat, marry, beget and rear children. It is natural that a person makes mistakes, gets tired and rejoices. Some people do good deeds and others do evil things. The belief in God's perfection gives a person strength and motivation for life, it brightens their perception.

We call a mystery or mystique something we cannot comprehend with our reason, which beyond our reason. If there were nothing inscrutable, neither would there be anything comprehensible to us, otherwise how would we determine the border between comprehensible and incomprehensible?

Then, what do we call a mystery? The simplest explanation is the following: A person perceives unknown phenomena and tries to develop an idea about them. We call it a notion. A notion, depending on who perceives, can be subjective or objective. But such division is relative because subjective or objective do not exist in a pure form. In most cases the problem is in understanding unknown phenomena. Discrepancy occurs when people take a narrow point of view of things and develop their own understanding of them in an uninformed way. The superficiality and discrepancy of some things are explained by the relative peculiarities of the mysteries of the Universe, which will never be revealed by a human being. Perception of the mysteries of the Universe is in the mystery itself.

It is useless to ask questions about such mysteries. The question is asked by each according to their own abilities to comprehend. A person asks questions and seeks answers. They study the mysteries of the objective reality and try to understand them. Love for life inheres in us. Those who ask many questions we call passionate people. They are keen to understand the mysteries of the

Universe. They admire the mysteries and are ready to dedicate their lives to disclosing them. To admire the mysteries of the Universe is to recognize infinity. The mystery of Universe cannot be comprehended with reason.

Many prophets and savants tried to explain its laws in their own way, but all their efforts were vain. People feel their weakness when they face mysteries. The strength of a person is in recognition of the mystery of the Universe and their weakness in useless efforts to solve it. Nevertheless, mysteries awaken love for life in us. The Universe is God's mystery, and God is perfect.

"Old Age Approaches, No Hope Remains"

The word "old age" includes three things: aging, regret and dreams. Old age is inevitable and its coming will surprise nobody because it is like birth and death, which do not depend on our own wish and will. A person can only feel and understand and adapt to them. In different periods of time, people's perception of the world changes. With age their feelings cool down and they become a more sober-minded person. We can consider "the golden age" the time when the reason and soul are in harmony. In Kazakh poetry, they call the age around 25 "the golden age." An old person feels sadness and melancholy. They are discontented because of their love for life. In Eastern poetry, as well as Kazakh poetry, love is not suffering and anguish, but sadness.

Thus, discontent causes suffering and suffering causes disappointment. This is the first distinction between sadness and suffering. Second, sadness is spectral and shows uncertainty. When a person is sad and suffers, their thinking is sharp. But cold rationality cannot lead to the truth because suffering restricts it. It cannot go beyond the suffering and that is why it has to "beg the Creator or some infinite great reason." Sometimes sadness and grief, being essentially different as they are, supplement each other and merge into a single whole.

In this poem Abai spoke of grief, not sadness. Abai was always strict in his choice of words. In my opinion, he used these words not in a biological sense, but in a philosophic one. People go through old age differently. They may live long, yet have a useless life. Abai thinks that old people have great life experience, which they should pass on to their descendants and others in the coming generation. And it is natural that a person who lived an interesting life may lapse into sadness in their old age. Of course, sometimes some people lapse into sadness when they are young.

Sultanmakhmut Toraigyrov, a Kazakh writer and reformer of the early 20th century, became sad when he was thirty years old. The English poet Lord Byron and the Russian poet Mikhail Lermontov did as well. Some people, having lived till a ripe old age, may not experience this feeling. Dreams of the "golden times" come back. These cannot be called regret of the past or grief. It is ignorance, because grief is addressed to the future, not the past. When Abai says: "We grew old, our hearts are touched with sadness," he means such sadness that does not kill one's dreams.

Grief is a philosophic notion, which plays an important role in the perception of the world by people. In ancient times, the Sufi Abu Nazid said: "When sadness comes to your heart, consider it good fortune, since it is because of sadness people achieve something." When a person grieves, it means they try to solve the mysteries of the Universe and discover the truth about life. We are accustomed to thinking that only young people dream. Abai's life proves that a person who has lived a long life may still have a dream even in older age, which becomes the purpose of their life.

"The Past Errors of Those Who Stray Lead Them Down the Right Path"

At first glance these words of Abai may seem fallacious and cause confusion because in our understanding the word "error" has a negative meaning. Humans have erred from the earliest times. There was no genius or prophet in history who has never been mistaken. All attempts to find the right way and free humankind have failed. Doesn't that mean that error is justified?

To err is human. It is in human nature. A reasonable person may err because usually such people are possessed with some ideas. They have thirst for knowledge, wish to know the mysteries of the Universe and it is natural that a person errs in their way of understanding the truth.

Once a wise man asked the Sheikh: "Who is understanding? Understanding can be compared to a bird that left its nest in search of food and found neither food nor the way back to its nest. It is perturbed, wants to go back home, but can't."[2] A person who takes the path of knowledge is like that bird, which once has left the nest and cannot get back to its nest. A person errs, but it should be taken into account that realizing one's mistakes is a part of knowledge as well. Those who do not realize that have no true knowledge. A knowledgeable person should become aware of their mistakes.

According to the Qur'an, the first people on the earth who tried to know the unknown were Adam and Eve. Eve wishing to know the unknown ate a

---

[2] E. Bertels, *Sufism and Sufi literature*. Moscow, 1965, p. 257.

forbidden fruit. They were banished from Eden to the earth to earn their living by hard work.

Humankind, like a baby making his first steps stumbling and falling, will eventually find its way. On their way, people will make mistakes and then try to steer down other paths. A person who becomes aware of their mistakes is able to steer down that right path.

But those who do not are in the majority. There are few people who can influence this majority. An error in its essence is associated with faith. Faith and cognition should be considered separately. According to Abai, recognizing the changeable nature of the world means transcending the bounds of faith. If we look at history, we see that not only Adam erred, but the prophets did as well.

Frederic Nietzsche, in his work *Zarathustra Said So*, expresses the following opinion about faith: "You say you believe in Zarathustra? But what do you do with Zarathustra? You believe in me, but what's the use in all the believers? You have not sought yourself yet, though you sought and found me. That happens to all believers and that is why any faith is of little significance. I ask you now to lose me and find yourself and only when all of you disown me I will come back to you."

Attributing these thoughts to Zarathustra Nietzsche used the authority of a Persian philosopher. Actually these are the thoughts of Nietzsche. To trust anybody in blind faith, even God, is not always a good thing. Abai speaks much of God but does not demand to believe in Him blindly. In his verse – "Don't fall for the flatterer's praise" – Abai says, "Trust yourself! Know that your reason and honest and industrious labor are your support and happiness."

Abai and Nietzsche have similar views on faith. Both of them think that faith is to be born in the heart. If you have such faith in your heart then there will be a place for both Zarathustra and God.

We read in Abai's verse: "Look into your heart and, finding the pearls there, keep them, do not throw them away." The majority needs faith, along with an ideology and a leader. The multitude blindly believes in its leader and will follow them wherever they take them. We know examples of national psychosis in Hitler's times and the idolization of Stalin by the Soviet people.

Is it not a mistake to divide the world into a Christian world and others; divide people into Christians and Moslems? Until recently the world was divided into capitalist and socialist camps. We also had a notion of the "third world." Isn't that a mistake? Thus, the multitude can make mistakes and only few progressively thinking people who are ahead of the epoch are not mistaken.

Abai speaks of the changes from the philosophical point of view but he has never mentioned such a notion as "development." Much was said about it, but what we understand as "development" in reality is our misperception. Is 'development' good or bad? In my opinion, 'development' is a sign of civilization. Development is an objective process. But can the human perception understand the logic of development? Kant doubted that. Abai speaks of the limits of human reason as well and, because of those limitations, we cannot precisely determine whether 'development' is good or bad, but we must try anyway.

The essence of the historic teaching of Marx was rooted in laws of history. He led people to the building of a communist society and by delivering them from their mistakes, "opened their eyes and wakened them." That in itself was a mistake and the convictions built on that mistake penetrated our minds. Irresponsibility was one of the consequences. It took shape from the conviction that the future is clear and mistakes are impossible. His teaching restricted (the) people's freedom. People were promised a paradise on earth. But people should look to the future without any pre-determined assumptions about it. It is the element of the unknown which makes people responsible for their acts and wakens their minds.

Abai is right when stating that errors are justified. We are more anxious about those who make no mistakes and do not go astray. The leaders should be very careful to avoid mistakes. They should be responsible for their actions. It is about such people Abai said, "the past errors of those who stray lead them down the right path."

If I were asked who could be called great thinkers, I would answer that there were two groups: those who clearly showed and detailed the way to the future (Marx, et al) and those for whom the future looked vague (Kant, Abai). I prefer the latter because they give people a choice to independently choose the course of life.

True thinkers are those who understand that people can make mistakes. They are guided by a thirst for knowledge. They are eager to know the unknown phenomena. People are not interested in familiar things. Science is associated with unknown phenomena. Investigation of familiar things will not result in any discoveries. That is why Abai says that mistakes at the beginning are natural and understanding that point is knowledge as well.

The advisor to Ablai Khan, Bukhar Jirau (c. 1693-1787), speaking about the future, surmises that there will be times when the world will turn upside-down. His words warn us to be more responsible about the future. Unfortunately we did not follow such warnings in order to avoid many mistakes. People seeking for the truth make mistakes. The small path is hidden. It is not a wide road showing the way to the future. People will make new mistakes until they find the right way.

"Lyrical Song is the King of Words, Their Highest Heights"

Using this line from Abai's poem – sometimes appropriately, sometimes not – we often do not even think of its true meaning. But careful reading causes various thoughts. The first line reads, "lyrical song is the king of words." It should be noted that the Kazakhs understand the abstract nature of a word. They have such expressions as "the word left to us by the ancestors," "The ancients said that." The people appeal to folklore, including much lyrical verse. "*Soz sarasy*" is the "acme of the word," its culmination. The Kazakh language has notions "*sara bagyt*" and "*sara zhol*," which mean the right direction and the way of justice.

Did Abai use the right meaning? Studying the literary heritage of Abai we come to the conclusion that all of his words have particular meanings. These word combinations supplementing each other generate new ideas, thoughts and notions. The verse, word, king and height are used in one line. On the one hand each word represents an independent notion but used together they generate a new notion. They are the bricks of the general idea. These four words in Abai's verse include the idea of the purpose of the word. The poet considers the problem in two aspects: verse – king and height – perfection.

Abai thinks it is impossible to show the nature of the word using only the first part of the definition. Words carry various meanings and it is necessary to differentiate the proper use of a word from rubbish. Abai thus says, "do not insult the ear with rubbish." Rubbish is the words and phrases which have neither thought nor sense. They cannot be referred to "*sara soz*." To find the best possible word out of a thousand is long and laborious work. The word found in this way is a real word, it becomes true poetry.

Thus, the word is the highest manifestation of human spirit, its perfection, and because of that Abai calls a poet, who has such a word, a genius of humankind (*er danasy*). Abai, unlike us who often use the word "culture," has never used this notion. But he speaks of the destiny of humankind, his necessary qualities and brings us to the idea that an educated person is a person who can differentiate meaningful words from rubbish.

"Nature is Temporal, Humans Eternal"

Since Abai's times there are many legends and stories about humankind. To know the mystery of human nature the prophets and their assistants contrived many religions. Knowing a person through religion bore its fruit. There were lots of religious trends which asserted that God had created humans and He has the key to the mystery of human nature. Thus, the mystery of humankind became an external abstraction and people started investigating it using well-known truths. Here they faced such notions as "eternal life" and "mortality." So what is mortal and temporal and what is eternal?

Life is short; it is only a moment in the universe. So this moment is vague and delusive. And what about eternity? The statement "a person is a child of nature" was known before Abai's time. The poet thinks that people are a part of nature, therefore they are mortal. Similarly as winter comes after summer, a person is born and dies in their time. There are sayings "a time to be born and a time to die," and "everyone is mortal." They confirm that people from ancient times understood and accepted that rule.

Abai knew these sayings as well, but he spoke of the rule in a different way. According to Abai, it is the body that dies, not the person themselves. The natural body of a person dies so they are not among the living any longer. Other people come after them. This is a law of the Universe and nobody can explain it. Human perception and reason cannot understand the mystery. It is by ignorance that some people have called death the means of transmigration to another world. Death of the body does not mean death of the spirit. Not everyone can get to know the secrets of existence and the nature of a human life. Only few can do that. Abai writes:

> "When "I" and "mine" are finally separated,
> It is called "death" by those who are ignorant."

What, then, is "I" in Abai's view? It seems to be a person's body, but there is one philosophical problem. The notion "I" is related only to a human being. Other living beings do not have "I." According to the laws of nature, "I" is not only the natural body, but also indicates a measure of perception. Each "I" is a step toward knowing the subject. That is, the "I" of the people who try to know God or nature.

Abai's "I," therefore, has three meanings: body, soul and spirit. The body is mortal. That is a biological law. Islam paid great attention to the cleanliness of the body, which it associates with the purity of the soul. A healthy body has a healthy spirit. People are responsible for themselves and their responsibility is expressed in their "I." "I" is a philosophical category, which describes human nature, so it is connected not only with the body and soul, but spirit as well. When the body is dead, the soul and spirit are transformed into other forms. "I" separates from its nature. After the death of the body, the soul and spirit leave it and start seeking other forms of existence. Having lost a material embodiment, they do not lose their objective essence. On the contrary, becoming eternal they are united with eternal truth.

The Kazakh people surmise that the soul after death becomes one of the spirits of the ancestors. Each people and religion has their own myths and legends about it, but these are at the level of supposition.

A person cannot know a spirit, that is why Pluto proposed to recognize the spirit as a certain idea. To seek the reason which causes an idea is useless because the reason is inside the idea. According to Abai, God is an idea, that is why there is no need to look for God's origin. But a person can get to know God through his word. A person's perception cannot go beyond the notion of God. In Western Europe this is called mysticism.

The cognition of human nature has been the basis for the creation of many religions and world philosophies. People realized the separation of a body and soul, but nobody has managed to get to the root of the matter. Abai recognized the separation as well. What Abai said was not new, but he analyzed the ideas existing in the people's minds and expressed his views on the subject.

The Kazakhs knew of the separation of the body and soul before Islam. The notion "the spirits of the ancestors" was a dominant one in the outlook of the Turkic people. In the song about Kultegin (685-731 CE), ruler of the second Turkic khaganate, it is said that "the soul flew away," not "the man is dead," i.e., he took a different form and went to heaven. The word "Tengri" refers to an inseparable, wholistic world. It does not exist outside a person; it is the measure of the person's world.

According to Abai, the one who says that a man is dead is ignorant. Indeed, forgetting a person after their death and erasing their memory from among the living causes contradictory ideas about public principles. It is an act of disrespect. We honor and respect a person when they are alive; the same attitude should remain when their soul flies off to the heaven after separation from the body. Abai speaks of it as follows:

> Nature is mortal, a person is eternal
> But where are they? Where is their life? Where is their time?
> When "I" and "mine" are finally separated,
> It is called 'death' by those who are ignorant.

"Earthly Life Is Like a River of Water"

Pondering the problems of life and human nature, philosophical thinkers have very often used the image of water. The ancient philosopher Thales said that water was the basis of life. Chinese and Indian philosophers distinguished four elements: fire, air, soil and water.

Water more often was used as the synonym of the variability of phenomena. The Greek philosopher Heraclitus said: "It is impossible to enter one and the same river twice," meaning that nothing could be repeated in nature. Such variability made him think of the essence of life. The idea that "earthly life is like a river" has existed in Kazakh philosophy for a long time. Did Abai, then, add anything new?

The poet's use of this phrase shows first of all that he was familiar with the teachings which existed before him. Having thoroughly studied them, Abai tried to bring to people their deep meaning, speaking frankly about the tragic meaning of life. Those who obtained deeper insight into the meaning of earthly life always refused to interpret it optimistically. Thus, Buddha, meditating on the meaning of life, spent all his life wandering. Diogenes, hiding from vanity, whiled away his time in a barrel. That is why Abai says:

> "Earthly life like a wave
> It runs fleetingly,
> Whether good or bad,
> It is full of poison."

If we think of the origin of these statements within Abai's worldview, we will find similar thoughts in the outlook of the Sufis. It is possible that the Sufi expression "Life is a delusion" has originated from such definitions. Sticking to the relativistic principles in interpretation of the universe, people came to the idea of eternal life, which is common to many religions. Thoughts about the ephemeral nature of earthly existence in contrast to eternal life are innate within people.

Human life is short and as irretrievable as flowing water. Similarly though, as water, it does not disappear – the human spirit is eternal. Water may disappear, but it will reveal its properties in a different form, for example, flora and fauna are the result of the effect of water. Likewise, the human spirit does not disappear when someone dies. The Kazakhs call it "the spirit of the forefathers." I do not agree with the interpretation of this idea in a religious sense alone. The philosophy of the spirit of the forefathers appeared long before the religious teachings which came later to the Kazakhs. In the later religious teachings this idea became associated with eternity. If there were no idea about the spirit of the forefathers, our ideas about life and existence would be impoverished. Eternal life and vain delusive habitation in this life are different things and the distance between them is as between the earth and sky.

We call people who have taken upon themselves the burden of responsibility for humanity sages and thinkers. A person who has dedicated all their life to learning the mysteries of life and the universe cannot expect that they will find the one and only true conclusion. There is no one who can fully open the meaning of life. The mystery of life, to use Kant's words, is a "thing in itself" and the meaning of life as explained by the great thinkers is only a guide. Thus all their thoughts contain sad thoughts about the vanity of human existence. The meaning of life is a mystery and the clue is beyond human consciousness. If one sage opened the great law of life, what would the others do? The word of the sages should not be taken as absolute truth, but only a guiding path which leads in that direction. The role and significance of great thinkers is precisely that. A sharp person tries to find their place in life and only they can decide what suits them best. To find their path, they need freedom.

"When the Number One is Gone, What Will Become of the Old Number Zero?"

We are the generation that was brought up believing that history is not created by individuals (great personalities, kings, rulers, commanders, and such) but by people. Indeed, there is no doubt that people are the authors of history. A Kazakh thinker who lived long before Marx described this truth in the following way:

> *How does an onager survive without tail and mane?*
> *How does a snake survive without legs and arms?*
> *How do people survive when they are oppressed by kings and rulers?*
> *Then people would be furious, their anger would give them power*
> *And the people's revenge would become strong.*[3]

The word *halyk* ('a/the people') is a meaningful and significant word. Hence, the existence of the proverb "The *Halyk* (People) do not say anything without a reason" is not a mere coincidence. However, most people do not fully understand the concept of *halyk*. Today, the word is usually used to refer to manufacturers, to people who produce material items. This is a Marxist-Leninist

---

[3] *Ertedegi adebyiet nusqalari* [Ancient literature options], (Almaty, 1967), p. 105.

conception. But the word actually has a much wider conception, one that includes everyone from rulers and khans to mere shepherds.

To divide people into two groups, the oppressors and the oppressed, is not correct. As a concept, *halyk* means unity, so when the word *halyk* is used to refer to different groups, it loses its meaning. It is worth mentioning here that each *halyk* (nation) has rulers and citizens in accordance to its own nature. Sometimes we criticize other countries' politics or their government leaders, but this is not a right thing to do, since each country has a ruler who fits its principles, traditions, and understandings. Abai discussed this issue in his thirty-seventh Word: "A man becomes adult thanks to the characteristics of his epoch. If someone is bad, then all his contemporaries are responsible for that."

In the Soviet times, concepts such as khan, rich man, *bi*, *batyr* (hero), and *haziret* (honorific title similar to "Your Honor" or "Your Holiness") were removed from the content of the word *halyk*. But is it possible to exist as a *halyk* without these people? Undoubtedly, no. Thus, in Abai's time, it was typical to understand the word *halyk* from only one angle or perspective. Abai was born in 1845, after the 1822 Charter of the Siberian Kirgiz through which the Kazakh people lost their right to be a *halyk* (a united nation). It is difficult to say a nation is a *halyk* if they do not rule themselves, because the will of a nation is reflected through its self-regulation. The Kazakh nation, without its khan and *bi*, started to deteriorate. Being thoroughly aware of this situation, Abai did not use the word *halyk*; instead, he used the word "majority," and he equated "majority" to zero. What happens to zero if there is no unit, no "one"? If you add zeros to zero, its value will not change. The "one" is a person who gives it value. Hence, Abai concluded, "What would a noisy majority achieve if there were no one leader among them?"

Transferring Abai's "majority" to a more comprehensive term, it is closer to the concepts *Lumpenproletariat* and "the masses." It is interesting to note that the Russian word *tolpa* ("the mob") has an equivalent in Kazakh: *tobyr*. However, the poet did not use *tobyr* but *kop* (majority). It seems that there is a reason for this. It is likely that "the majority" has a different meaning from "the mob." Indeed, Abai used the word "the majority" in ways that had different meanings, whereas, "the mob" only has one meaning. Therefore, the poet did not define "the majority" as "the mob" but instead described the word from different angles. He stated, "Do not call all majorities the majority, majorities can be diverse."

The first way that Abai used "the majority" was to refer to "the mob," as shown in these examples: "What would a noisy majority achieve, if there was no one leader among them" and "Ignorance relies on the majority and the masses." In two of his poems, Abai described how the *halyk* (nation, people) cannot be turned into the majority, but the majority can be turned into a mob. The first example is in his poem "Masghut." Even though most Kazakh people are familiar with its content, let me remind you about its plot. When Masghut was a vizier to the khalif, he had a prophetic dream sent from Khidr (prophet, angel):

> *Oh, my son, there will be rain in one day*
> *That rain will make people sick.*
> *The one who drinks it will lose his mind for a week*
> *He will recover after seven days.*

Masghut delivered the message to the khalif, and they prepared clean water. When the day came, it rained, filling rivers and wells, and people lost their minds. Those crazy people forgot about resting and made noise and wandered purposelessly. When the khalif came to calm them down, they said, "The khalif and his vizier have lost their minds, we must kill them!" Realizing that things were going to become serious, Khalif asked for advice from his vizier:

> *There is no way to escape from those masses*
> *The only way to escape is to drink that water too.*
> *Otherwise, these crazy men will hunt us*
> *And kill us thinking that we went mad.*
>
> *Then both of them drank the water*
> *They went crazy and appeared among the masses*
> *The crazy men said they were sorry for their deeds*
> *They worshipped them and prayed to them.*

Here, Abai used "masses" to mean "mob," for it would not have been correct to name the misguided masses as "the majority." The masses, or mob, had to lose their minds in order to make false assumptions. Undoubtedly, the masses in the poem, with khalifs and viziers, are the *halyk* (the state). Whatever the state does is done with awareness and reason. When the masses lose their minds, people's consciences are lost as well, and they get sick with the illness of the masses. It is unacceptable to rely on the masses just because they are the majority. Abai described the situation in this way:

> *All majorities are like that if you look at the examples,*
> *If you are deceived by their massiveness and trust their promises.*
> *You will be misguided and lose most things*
> *If you follow the majority by mistake.*

The mob characteristic of the masses was also described in Abai's thirty-seventh Word: "Who is to blame for poisoning Socrates, for burning Joan of Arc alive, for crucifying Jesus Christ, for burying the Prophet Muhammad under a camel's carcass? It is the masses; therefore, the masses have no wisdom. One just needs to know how to manage them and lead them to the right path."

In the society in which Kazakh's lived, which was called socialism, everything was considered the responsibility of the masses, and this was called the *kollektiv*. Therefore, justice was turned into a political game. Those masses were the mob who went crazy after drinking from the Bolsheviks crazy water, as in Abai's story. Kazakhs claimed that it was what the people wanted, but in fact, the people were already in that situation before they even realized what was happening. People went crazy for seven days in the poem, but it lasted for 70 years in real life. In the poem, the khalif and vizier survived by drinking from the same water, but among the Kazakhs, those who were sane were destroyed by Bolshevism, and those who were scared had to accept being "insane" with the others, that is, being "in control" with the majority.

The word "revolution" is itself the activity of the masses, their political government and the dictatorship of the proletariat. It is clear that Abai, who knew about the poisoning of Socrates, definitely knew about the French Revolution. He knew about the French Revolution, but he thought about it as the action of the masses. He stated, "There are many fools, but few wise men." "Many fools" are not the *halyk* but the mob in this saying. He wanted to warn us about a similar mob's action, but unfortunately, history did not go the way Abai wanted it to. In 1917, the mob achieved its goal.

Even though Abai wanted to save his *halyk* from the masses' calamity, even though he tried to warn people, the Kazakh *halyk* could not escape its fate and therefore experienced its fate's sorrow. As the poet said, "Sagebrush grew in the place where wheat was planted."

In his second meaning of "the majority," Abai used the word not only to mean "the mob" but also to mean the masses, the people, and even the *halyk* (the state).

> *Do not call all majorities the majority, majorities can be diverse.*
> *The majorities can beat the mischief-maker and make his life hard*
> *Cursing and praising people are the things people are always doing*
> *Wherever you look, that is what they are always doing.*

Abai gave two opinions about the majority. Though the majority can do good things, the masses can also be misguided; taking care of them and serving them are different issues. Praising and justice are the things the masses need.

Justice is the power that supports the masses and wakes their consciousness. Hence, to serve the majority honestly and to work for their interests is a person's duty because "Tangri (God) has been taking care of the majority, so your Creator will love you, since you love those whom He loves." If you are taking care of the majority, for whom Tangri also cares, then you are on the path of Tangri. To go against the masses is to be against Tangri. If you can, then "act, so that you can be helpful to people," as Abai said. The proverb "Do not disgrace all people" (*Kopke topyraq shashpa*) has a similar meaning.

In his third meaning of "the majority," Abai described how the majority can be misguided and make mistakes. They cannot identify what is gold and what is copper. What should be done in this case? Abai answered this question in his fourteenth Word. First, he analyzed the person who is called brave heart and concluded that Kazakhs do not call people brave hearts, only heroes, but it must be an individual who can direct misguided masses to the right way and who is smart enough to do that. Such people are "the ones," the individuals. "The ones without zero can still be dominants": by these words, Abai called prominent individuals "the ones."

Kazakhs called such people *kosem* (leader). *Kosems* were those people who could direct misguided masses to the straight path, and they could be khans, sultans, or *bis*. Kazakhs knew the value of speech: "Orators come out from hundreds, and *kosems* (leaders) come out from thousands" (*Zhuzden sheshen, mingnan kosem shigadi*). This means that orators come out of the masses more often than do leaders. Few "ones" and leaders can lead misguided masses to the right path. Hence, such people must be respected.

"Poor Satan, the Spirit Banished by God"

Let's start with concept of a demon. Does it exist in nature or is it a product of our imagination? If we set aside for the moment the question of demons in other religions, in Islam a demon is a reality. Even the Islamic prayer which is read five times a day says that it is necessary to have protection from a demon. The Qur'an says the same in surahs 113, 114. Based on that it is not easy to define this word. One of the terms for demon is a devil ('iblis'). In most cases he is called a leader, a main demon. Abai speaks of the main demon, the devil. What did Abai say about him?

It is impossible to comprehend the human spirit without understanding what a demon-tempter, a devil, is because these notions are applicable only to a human being. It means that we cannot speak of the spiritual development of humankind without the idea of a devil. Such a conclusion obliges us to consider the notion "devil" in greater detail.

According to Abai a human being is neither a devil nor an angel. "If people are spoiled, that benefits the devil," says the poet. Spoiled morals give the devil a happy chance to possess people's freedom and then their acts cannot be called other than the devil's intrigues. Abai saw how the morals of the people who had lost their independence to the Russians and thus had to obey strange customs, with rules gradually changing for the worse. In this state of dependence, the people tried to resist and live according to their customary rules and laws.

In Abai's time there was a struggle between these two trends. Ordinary people were at a loss, not knowing whom to follow. Powerful people were in doubts themselves. If they accept Christianity and learn the Russian language, was it worth then to be called Kazakhs? It was still impossible to live. Where is the way out? The smartest fellow quickly accepted the new rules. The sense of duty to the people and serving to their interests were quickly replaced with the thoughts of one's own benefit, wealth and easy money. They were ready to sell even their fathers for easy gain. That was a logical consequence to all the peoples, who became the colonies and experienced hardships of colonial oppression. Their spoiled morals can be explained by the fact that the people lost their freedom and became dependent. But people arose who felt comfortable being slaves. Such people started prospering in Abai's time.

If we consider carefully Abai's words, "if the people are spoiled that benefits the devil," we notice two forces helping the devil to tempt people. "An ignorant person likes the crowds and entertainments," says Abai. Ignorance is an action directed against the human spirit and human nature. Ignorance occurs not only because of the lack of knowledge, but it may be a deliberate action, which is called a misdeed. Fear is another of the devil's weapons. Fear binds a person's will. The colonizers drove fear into the people using weapons and prisons for this purpose. A person could be punished being guilty of nothing. The old customs providing fairness and justice were forgotten as the new rules of the colonizers appeared.

Educated people, understanding that resistance was useless, started thinking and acting like the Russians. Thus, a missionary policy concealed behind the mask of the so-called enlightenment was introduced. Some educated Kazakhs supported this policy. Some did that not understanding the issues involved, others intentionally implemented the policy of russification. Filled with fear, they were frightened by cruel tsarist policy expecting people would not be able to anticipate future events. In the time of the Bolsheviks, this fear increased still more. The Kazakh intelligentsia accepted the Bolshevik's ideology. Fear turned into their drama and tragedy. Bolshevism was the time of flourishing for the devil's power because if in Abai's time there were thinking people capable of leading the people, the Bolsheviks eliminated everyone who resisted them.

The descendants of the poet experienced that hard time. The ideology is delusion of the consciousness. It has fear as its basis, which is a weapon of the devil. A person is free if they do not have fear. Faith generated by fear misleads. If we think of the meaning "poor Satan," we feel pity for him because sadness, which is at the root of the word here, is a moral category. "An anguished soul" is a person absorbed in deep thought. Sadness leads to grief. Grief generates sorrow. Very often people do not grieve long. Only few people can endure it. Therefore sorrow is a moral and philosophic notion associated with views and outlook of a person.

Abai's words about "poor Satan" are actually his thoughts of the devil's outlook because a person cannot understand God if they have no idea of the devil. The devil is an attribute of habit or custom which determines human nature and one's level of consciousness.

"Poor Satan, the spirit banished by God" is, in fact, a line from Mikhail Lermontov's poem "Demon." Abai did not plan to make a full translation of the poem; his task was to talk about humankind. In Abai's understanding, a demon is one of the forms which reveals the mystery of human nature. It is a link between humans and God. The devil wronged God, not humankind, but he wronged God because of humankind. Humans can only protect themselves from the devil by the will of God.

God could have destroyed the devil, but he did not, because the devil's presence was a vital necessity. The devil wants to bind a person's will, make them vicious. An angel protects and preserves a person's will. Their task is to induce humans to do good deeds. Thus, humans need angels as well.

Such thoughts come when you read Abai's translation of Lermontov's "Demon." We can understand the notions "angel" and "demon" not only through human consciousness. This problem is important *a priori*. I have concerns about people who do not tolerate objections and declare their primitive thoughts about these two forces. I think these forces are the demonstration of human power and mystery.

"Tangri, Who Decorated the Earth, is the Master"

Master is the name of God. The one who created the universe, its owner, is God himself. Everything in life is done by the will of God. If we speak in a mythical sense of "the universe of a thousand planets," the one who made them all exist and who made them co-exist and be dependent on each other and who gave power and energy to all creations is God.

The word "universe" itself consists of presence, not of absence. To create something from nothing is meaningless; the truth of life is in its presence, in the nature of things. The word "world" itself means to be present. Absence has only one meaning—non-existence—whereas existing has diverse meanings, since truth has endless qualities and is immeasurable.

You cannot just accept the existence of an existing thing; humankind is unable to list all the characteristics of existing things. That is why it is said that only God knows the secret of all things, which is the secret of the universe. If God is the name of all existence, then the secret of existence is in Him. Thus, there is no person who should not bow their head before the master skills of the Creator—who made one thing different from another thing, who gave special characteristics to things and phenomena in the world, and who made each of them unique.

Humans themselves are the secret of the universe; they themselves are spirits and things that were made by the Master. If the true Master is God, then each human is a sacred individual who can reflect the quality of the Master's skills. Hence, God's mastery is identified through His creation of humans with their intentions and attempts to own the universe, with their blessed intellects, warm hearts, and strong efforts. Humans and God, one is a flawless masterpiece; the other is a creator, that is, the owner of infinite mastering skills. The word "master" should be reserved for God. When people are amazed by someone's impressive skill, they usually say that the person's skill comes from nature, God, or God. This idea exists in all religions. Christians also say that talent comes from God. It is then up to the person to learn and to practice. Talents, or gifts, are from God. I think that the words "talented," "gifted," and "wise one" can be described together as master skill. When Abai wrote, "Tangri, who decorated the Earth, is the Master," he did not mean a master who sews or who works with iron. He meant the Master, the one who lit the space between heaven and earth with the light. This means that "master" is a measure that can be expressed as the power of God, beyond the will of a person; it is the composition of consciousness and of the thing, the rationale and the feelings, soul, and body, the chance and the truth, all in one unity.

To say a master's skill is infinite is a superficial notion. Being a master is the space of freedom for a person's perfection. Being a master is limited for an individual and infinite for God. Infinity is God's mystery, and its meaning is mysterious both to humans and to humankind. It is typical for humans to be surprised, to suddenly recognize and enjoy a piece of the mystery.

People are often ready to describe a master's skills with positive emotional traits such as pleasure. Indeed, to master a skill includes passion. In religious legends, God himself created people with passion. The universe was established as a result of love. In the verse "Zhazghituri" (Before Summer), which I mentioned earlier, Abai wrote about passion:

> The sun is the groom, the earth is the bride,
> They missed each other so much.
> Their passion is so strong

As a result of this passion, the ground blossoms and becomes as silk; youth hang out with friends; old men and women become more industrious in their housework, as if they just stood up from their graves; songbirds sing in the air; and geese and swans start honking. The earth missed her husband all winter long; after being filled with the light of the sun, the earth flourishes and turns into a colorful parrot.

All this is the mastery of God. Abai said:

> If you look in amazement at the work of Tangri
> You melt away and your energy dissolves.

I mentioned earlier that a person's skills are limited and God's skills are unlimited. Let me explain this principle by way of passion. For example, no matter how skillful and passionate someone is in raising their offspring, they are unable to create a person by relying only on their own mind and intellect. God gives the child to a human being. A person is unable to create another person without nature. If humans were to reach the level where they were able to make human beings, then the world would lose its humane characteristic. That is probably what is called the Apocalypse. A person has no right to reveal the secrets of God and compete with Him. Therefore, if this were to happen, there would be no question of recognizing humankind and God.

Indeed, it is advisable to keep distance between humans and God. This distance is a person's space of perfection, the human space. The more this space is expanded, the longer the distance becomes between humans and God. The more people believe in the mastery of God, the better they feel His infinity.

Abai did not just depict spring in his poem "Before Summer." He would not be Abai if he only depicted the spring season. He added God's mastery to the poem. The lyrical heroes here are the sun (the groom) and the earth (the bride). The arrogant star and the moon, the Heavenly Father, and so on, are all eternal

79

concepts. Abai said that "Tangri is the Master" because He could "decorate the universe" systematically.

"Anxiety is a Person's Safeguard, A Sign of Their Thoughtfulness"

Anxiety and sorrow are similar ideas, but worries do not always lead to sorrows. Indeed, a person with worries most likely does not have sorrows. However, sometimes anxiety and sorrow can be united into one. Then what is anxiety?

According to Abai, "Anxiety is a man's defense, a sign of his thoughtfulness." Hence, worries are a sign of thoughtfulness. One who can feel anxiety is one who knows the value of life. All thinkers had anxiety. This is the impulse of consciousness; it is a characteristic of people that leads them to reasoning. It is likely that this characteristic is not typical for animals.

There is a legend and a *kui* (Kazakh traditional music played with the dombra, a traditional musical instrument) about a mother camel who is searching for her baby. However, this situation is described through people's feelings. The *kui* "Bozingen" (Mother camel) is not so much about the camel as it is about people's skills of perception.

For Kazakhs, the word "anxiety" has two meanings: responsibility and regret. One meaning is reflected in this proverb: "The end of anxiety is the abyss, you will just sink in it; the end of challenge is a sailboat, you will sit in it and cross the river easily." In this sense, anxiety is a person's inability, and that person cannot achieve anything due to anxiety, but at the same time, it implies that anxiety is a deep thought. Anxiety is related to thoughts. However, anxiety is not just a matter of thinking: only one who is responsible for oneself and one's country is able to be anxious. That is why Abai stated, "Man's defense is anxiety." The anxiety of an ignorant person is a pity. It makes them depressed.

An intelligent person does not regret the past, does not feel sorry but takes lessons for the future. The core of a thoughtful person's anxiety rests in responsibility. It is not about regretting one's past, but it is reflected in one's understanding of the analysis and making conclusions. Sometimes people may say that they are anxious about something; in this case, one should find out if they are anxious or regretful. It might be that they are not able to distinguish between anxiety and regret. Although anxiety occurs in an individual, its content involves more than an individual's interests. In this sense, anxiety means one's responsibility towards their country, the unity between the individual and the country, and intelligence. A person without anxiety is a person who has no feeling of responsibility. Such a person could not protect the nation; such a person is not wise. This is the meaning that Abai gave anxiety.

"Livestock – the Beauty of Humanity"?

Abai used each Kazakh word here in its original meaning. As proof of that, let us consider the word "livestock." In Abai's poems, "livestock" was used not only as a word but also as a concept. For example, in his poem "Would a hungry stomach be satisfied without fatty food," the poet wrote about livestock as follows:

Work for money; go to foreign lands, if needed, to find livestock;
If you have livestock, everyone will respect you.

In this verse, Abai did not mean horses, cows, and so on, by the word "livestock"; he meant possessions in general. Whether it is gold, silver, or money, livestock is the sign of wealth and richness in general. He also used "livestock" to mean wealth in the following verse:

It is impossible to find livestock without taking risks or working
A lazy man who does not work will never become a true man.
It is ok to wash a donkey's a..., if for livestock
Its dirt will not stay on your hand, and no one will humiliate you.

In the above-quoted poem, Abai repeated "livestock" seven times. And in each case, the word was used as a concept. It was used to mean not only cows, horses, lambs, and camels but also 'capital' and 'wealth.' In short, Abai described livestock as an economic concept in the language of poetry.

Thus, the notion of livestock is understood by such terms as "wealth" and "capital." Journalists are still debating on how to translate "capital" into Kazakh, but Abai, who lived at a time when capitalism was just beginning to be introduced into the Kazakh steppes, described it quite clearly. There is a basis for Abai's using "livestock" in an economic sense. "Livestock" (*mal*) in Arabic means "property" and "capital." Let us consider how *mal* is defined in the *Universal Dictionary of Islam.*

Mal (pl. - amval) - possession, property (among sedentary Arabs—money, property; among Bedouins—camels, cattle). According to the explanations of medieval authors, *mal* is divided into four categories: dumb (precious materials and money), speaking (slaves and cattle), goods, and real estate. In a narrower sense, *mal* is finance, cash (many treatises on finance and taxes were called *Kitab al-Amal*), hence the notions of *bait al-mal* and *mal al-muslimin* (funds belonging to the entire Muslim community); in some cases, *mal* means taxes in money, in contrast to natural products. In one form or another, all the languages of the Muslim peoples borrowed the word *mal*.

The funds invested in production or trade were called *ra's al-mal* (fixed assets, capital) as opposed to profits (*galla*, *ribh*); the cost of the product in contrast to the sales price, which is included in the profit, was also called with the same word. Today, *ra's al-mal* is identical to the concept of "capital."[4]

Obviously, if I were to say that the word "livestock" was not used before Abai, I would be wrong. When the Kazakhs greeted each other, they would say, "Are your livestock and people okay?" In this case, they were also using "livestock" to mean a person's treasure or their possessions. Asking about the health of one's camels, cows, and horses is a very simple concept. But to ask "if your livestock is safe" is a much more philosophical issue, an example of being ethical. Thus, when it comes to today's market economy, it would still be up-to-date to follow the traditional ritual and ask about one's livestock.

Abai considers finding livestock not only as a labor but also as a way that leads to humanity and freedom:

One cannot collect livestock by being sly and thieving
If your lust is eager for this, then it will be hard to overcome it.
You will not be left without punishment
You will lose your livestock and peace, and your conscience will not be with you.

And the following verse shows his high regard for honest labor:

Your authority does not give you the chance to become full in your own home
You search for food in the other village.
The one who gives you one bone and one cup of qimiz
Will soon send you to one of his tasks.

According to the poet, if you do not have livestock, you will not have freedom; anyone can send you to perform any task, and you will stop respecting yourself; you will be satisfied with what you have eaten and drunk, and will turn into a mumbler. If you want to be free, then do not feel ashamed about working and earning honest money. This economic pragmatism Abai mentions is indeed needed for our people. It is typical for Kazakhs to choose certain jobs and to feel

---

[4] *Islam. Entsiklopedicheski slovar'* [Islam. Encyclopedic dictionary], (Moscow: Nauka, 1991), p. 158.

ashamed to perform some types of work. In foreign countries (in developed countries), any type of labor is respected, but it must have its price in the market. We Kazakhs are still not ready to earn for our livelihoods, as Abai instructed; we are still not free from our unproductive "show off" characteristics. But a life built on showing off can disappear quickly like melting snow. Abai's call to establish economic pragmatism in the country's consciousness is still a necessity today.

"The One Who is Friends with Livestock Will Think Only about Livestock"

Abai is a poet who supported economic pragmatism (necessity). In the late nineteenth and early twentieth centuries, trade capitalism began to be introduced freely in Kazakhstan. Tatar traders initially took part in this social activity, and then, gradually, the Kazakh youth began to be involved in it. Abai approved of this:

The next generation will be all in benefits and livestock
They will not find their income leaving their house but through the trade of livestock.

He expressed his appreciation of getting involved in trade by these lines. Undoubtedly, Kazakhs involvement in trade was a worthy thing, but Abai also spoke about the other side of it, about its wealth, about its shadow. He criticized some people with the following verse:

Some would curse and sell their souls,
Would lie and deceive others for the sake of livestock

The poet's dream was to make youth earn livestock in an honest way. He wanted youths to not go astray, to work honestly and to have a positive authority among people.

However, the number of people who were ready to go against their consciences was growing. The poet criticizes them in the following way:

Gathering livestock by theft
They are happy if someone says them that they are sly.

Abai's views are in accordance with current Kazakhs, who are living under the rules of the market economy. It is not surprising if those who are eager to become rich by any means cannot distinguish humaneness from dishonesty. If the goal is only to be enriched, it will not be productive. Abai described such people with criticism:

> *What can a boastful, greedy man understand*
> *Only one in a thousand can be selected among them.*

The poet believed that the skill of earning one's livelihood was the result of intelligence. Hence, he assumed that the people who had found their livelihood were the people who had found their minds. Similarly, people who found their reasoning were able to earn for their livelihoods. This is the way of humaneness and honesty. The intelligent and conscious people should live in such way. God curses the other ways. Those who are on that way:

> *They aim to earn their livelihoods by theft*
> *If someone is against them, they will attack that person's village as a warning*
> *Such people are cursed by God.*

Are there any issues that Abai did not discuss? The poet's legacy is so true for our modern epoch. When you visit suburban regions, you can hear about rises in thefts and feel regret about that. But those who achieve heights by theft are those who are going to be torn down. There is no theft in the cultural states. It is a sign of immorality.

When Abai said, "The one who is friends with livestock will think only about livestock," he was referring to philistinism. To be friends with livestock is to lose one's humanity, to be entrapped with the ties of wealth, to become its slave. This is a dangerous situation for people. Feelings like generosity or purity are not typical for a "friend of livestock," or for a philistine. Such people are usually ready for betrayal, blackmail, or any act of wrongdoing.

There have been narrow-minded people who have served in the fascist and even more aggressive policies of the past. Thus, Abai's line about being friends with livestock is his warning for people who decide to go their own way for their livelihoods. According to the poet, one who thinks only about livestock is an ignorant person. Ignorant people can create only ignorance. They are slaves to their appetites, friends to livestock, and enemies to other people.

Grief is a feeling of muddled consciousness and concern about one's fate; it is an immersion into deep thoughts about how to escape from deadlock and find a way forward. Feeling grief for one's livestock is a fool's action. Livestock is possessions and wealth, and Abai wrote a lot about it. For example, he stated, "If you turn to science, it will be both possession and livestock for you." By this, he valued science higher than wealth.

Wealth is like a drive. It is endless actions, but it leaves no trace. There is no phrase like "there was one rich man in our history." Some rich people taught children, built mosques, went on *hadj*, and created the necessary conditions for scholars and poets to leave their names in the people's memory. Due to such deeds, their names were remembered. Such people were not worried only about their livestock. They used their livestock for the people. If you are rich and choose this way, your humanity will not be forgotten. However, if you make livestock your friend, you will forget about others, you will have no mercy for others. Such people are usually unbalanced, aggressive, and greedy, and they often make shortsighted decisions. They measure everything in a very limited way and live with only one idea: to be friends with livestock and to care for nothing else.

"Being Nimble is in Fashion"

At the beginning of the twentieth century, many "weeds" (bureaucrats) began to appear among the flourishing new-literate groups of colonized Kazakhs. Abai called them "nimble ones." Nimble ones did not appear accidentally; there was a demand for them. The royal government needed minor bureaucrats from the local population to carry out its colonial policy effectively.

Abai identified two types of nimble ones. The first he described as follows:

Which Kazakhs have a conscience?
They are ready to place blame for any reason at all
A sign of being a nimble is to lodge complaints
For no reason

The poet reveals the social image of such nimble people:

If you ask who is nimble
It is the person who goes to the city center frequently
The one who lodges false complaints
And does not feel guilty about it.
Now the number of ill-intended nimble ones has increased
They are yapping like puppies
They are not conscious of their flaws
What they are involved in is their business.
God curses him
Would he care about anyone except himself?
Would he feel sorry for anyone?
No truth is in his word
No blessing is in him.
He will paint the truth with false boasts.

No lies are in my words
No words are left to say,
Be careful, be aware
That is how the situation among people is.

Such nimble ones want people to become broken down and impoverished. For them, people's tragedy is a source of income. Were there not similar nimble ones in the 1930s among those who led people to total starvation? Is it not true that similar nimble ones appeared after the Jeltoqsan event (December 1986 protests in Kazakhstan)? Is it not true that some nimble journalists, scholars, party representatives, and office workers added fuel to the fire? Have they not succeeded in destroying their own native language, their knowledge, their history, their growing youth and students?

The second type of nimble ones are "the screws" of the state bureaucratic machine. In Abai's time, these were *bolisis* (district leaders), translators, and the like.

Bolis is so pleased that
Authorities praise him.
Is pleased that Russians dress him in
Expensive clothing.

Hence, to work for status and expensive clothing, to exchange the people's interests for personal reward is also a sign of being a nimble. One thing to keep in mind is that a nimble is a social type. They can be found in all nations. However, the consequences of nimble ones' actions in Kazakh history were severe. "Nimbleness" became too frequent on Kazakh soil because it was established in tribal consciousness and developed into tribalism. Thus, it grew stronger and became a nationwide disease. There was always a need for the nimble ones, who turned their people into orphans. It was no surprise that the bureaucratic administrations that were subordinate to one center were made up of nimble ones. Abai described such *bolisis* as follows:

If a Russian yells,
The polis yells too,
Like a dog barking while staying inside the house

A dog barking from the house will never be like a real dog.

In Abai's time, people were under colonial rule with no self-ruling government. The united Kazakh land was torn into pieces and divided into provinces. At the top of this government were governor-generals, and then there were royal officials in the administration. The Kazakhs were divided into *volosts* (administrative divisions consisting of several *auls,* or villages). The senior sultan system, which existed in historian Shoqan Walikhanov's (1835–1865) time, was also destroyed later. The interests of the different ethnic groups were not a concern of the state, and thus, tribalism developed. The agenda was not the country's interest but the tribe's interests. Tribes fought for land. The colonizer took almost all the good lands. The rest of the lands were left for the tribes to fight over. *Zhesir daui* (the issue of widows) and *zher daui* (the issue of land) became intense. For colonizers, the tribal disputes and issues of concern did not cause difficulties; on the contrary, they were beneficial for them for two reasons. First, a self-destructive country was no longer able to oppose the king, and secondly, the seekers of justice would come to the Russian officials and pay bribes to further their cases. Therefore, the nimble ones Abai described—egoistic *bolisis* and judges—began to appear. Such nimble ones, whose number rose rapidly in the colonial times, were later called *sholaq belsendilers* (self-proclaimed active people) during Stalin's dictatorship. There were many similarities between nimble ones and *sholaq belsendiler.* Particularly, philistinism and ignorance were so common among them. Both were with the people only when the people's interests were beneficial for them. They felt no blame for betraying their own nation and destroying the country's treasures for their own interests.

The deeds and actions of nimble ones and *sholaq belsendilers* were directed against humanity.

"It is Easy to Say 'God'"

In a four-couplet poem, Abai raised a number of issues. First, he called for people to avoid using the word "God" in non-serious ways. God is not just the truth that is pronounced but the truth that comes from the heart. To speak about God requires having the light in one's heart. In the next couplet, Abai interpreted the concept of love in terms of Sufism: "The heart is the holder of water for the mind if one loves for the sake of Tangri." The owner of love is God. To understand Him, the heart must be nourished. Abai described this with the phrase "The heart is the holder of water for the mind."

Finally, he paid attention to the fact that God is the truth that is unrecognizable by reason. Many Western European scholars had previously mentioned that it is impossible to recognize everything through intellect. Abai, however, was not imitating Western thinkers on this issue. No matter what topic he was discussing, Abai never went beyond the Islamic world perception. In Islamic philosophy, it is repeatedly stated that it is impossible to know God through intellect. Abai depicted this situation as follows: "He is God, and he is beyond our understanding, Oh, it is so hard to describe it!"

Noting the limits of language to describe God is a metaphoric way of depicting the limits of the mind. However, God's existence is undeniable, because we feel him with our hearts: "Mind and quality are not cognized in the heart, but are felt." This demonstrates the significance of sensory knowledge in how Abai perceives the world. To those who intended to debate this question, Abai said, "Do not bother and do not waste your time." Abai read, met, and debated with many "thinkers" who rejected the existence of the obvious and who made up problems from nothing and pretended to be smart. He did not waste his time on useless debates regarding the existence of God. In the poet's understanding, God is the obvious truth, the name of everything in the universe.

"My Heart Bleeds Like an Open Wound"

Abai left a lot of thoughts about his time, himself and his contemporaries. He says that people are really happy only when they are young because youth is thoughtless and careless. But as soon as one grows they face problems. Suffering is the lot of great people. A reasonable person cannot lead a careless life. Abai, as a thinker and philosopher, could not be a romantic, seeing people's suffering and hardship and anticipating a gloomy future. In this poem, Abai does not speak of the society at large, he speaks of himself.

These thoughts are Abai's philosophical views of life. In spite of everything, he expresses his innermost thoughts without any fear. He finishes the poem with the following words: "Here I will stop telling my secrets." If it concerned personally the poet his grief would not be so deep. The poet grieves that people do not want to listen to what he has to say. He did not have a chance to fully express his thoughts to them.

What is this force which resides in his thoughts and will? In my opinion it is the sense he had of his fate. A person can master themselves, but they cannot escape their fate. We are mistaken thinking that fate is a certain external energy. Yes, fate is the expression of fatalistic power, but this is only one of its components. There are other components of which it consists. Abai wanted to explain it, but could not, therefore he grieved and was sad. Of course, if Abai more precisely defined his fate, it would be easier for us.

Abai always had a thirst for knowledge. He restrained his aspirations for he understood that some time his heart would stop, his speech would become meager and it would be impossible to escape his fate. The poet tries to find his place in this life. It may seem that he is not disappointed with life, but speaking of the caducity of life, he writes: "Poison and hell are inside me, though I look different outwardly. I will end my life having done so little." These thoughts are similar to the thoughts of Western European existentialists. Is it good or bad? Should we blame or praise the poet? I think we should do neither, because the essence of our reasoning is Abai's outlook. These thoughts are valuable because to know and understand Abai we should look at the world through the eyes of Abai.

It is difficult to understand Abai's poems and much more difficult to explain and interpret them. Because what we say may not always be Abai's conception. We have read different books and are familiar with the history of philosophy. It is natural when analyzing the poet's works that we use ideas expressed in later generations. Some thoughts help us to better understand Abai, others on the contrary confuse. No need to use modern philosophy while interpreting Abai's "My heart bleeds like an open wound." This expression is common throughout history. Abai says that he is lonely in his grief. Loneliness is the destiny of wise people and great thinkers. To feel lonely among the multitude means that he has no equal among his contemporaries, he is beyond the multitude.

"There was a Time When
I Did not Acknowledge Ignorant People"

Abai wrote a lot about ignorance and ignorant people. It is therefore important to ask, What is ignorance and who is an ignorant person? To answer these questions, I refer to Abai's concepts. Since his ideas on ignorance are sprinkled throughout his poems, I decided to group his thoughts on this issue.

First, Abai believed that there are many ignorant people. If life is full of Ignorant People, is it not true that life is hell? What is the reason for there being a majority of Ignorant People? Perhaps he thought there were so many Ignorant People because of his disappointed mood? He wrote in his poem "We passed so many years":

My soul intends to say
However, I am alone, and there are so many Ignorant People
How can you explain it
To immoral people?

In looking deeply into the content of these verses, it seems that in the phrase "I am alone, and there are so many Ignorant People," the many Ignorant People were a "mob." How else can there be many Ignorant People if not in a mob? Since ancient times, a mob has been the symbol of ignorance. The psychology of a mob is limited; it is a destructive power that is ready to easily reject the existence of existing, to state good as bad, to name white as black, to follow someone without critical analysis.

Abai understood the Ignorant People as a mob in the poem "Eight legs":

I am disappointed with the many Ignorant People
Who do not hear you
And who do not heed you.

As noted above, the mob is a destructive power that is ready to follow anyone. But what else might Abai mean by "many Ignorant People who do not heed you." The complexity of the problem is that many Ignorant People (a mob) do not hear the word of an intelligent person. An intelligent person does not destroy the world but makes it flourish. However, a mob (many Ignorant People) does not hear such words, nor do they heed them. When Ignorant People group together, it is the start of an atrocity. We find proof for that from his poem "I am disappointed by a friend and enemy."

Even smart people are not happy with their deeds
And Ignorant People are not feeling grief for people's lechery.

Ignorant People will not be sad about people's lechery, but they will be happy with it. Peaceful life is dangerous for Ignorant People because, in peaceful times, they become as noticeable as crows in the white snow.

Ignorance increases in times of hardship, and it becomes hard to understand who is who. This is a comfortable condition for many Ignorant People, for their deeds and actions.

Many Ignorant People (a mob) is a destructive power. Abai wrote in his poem "I used to not acknowledge Ignorant People":

I was useless
In the fight against many Ignorant People

Alternatively, in his poem "Useless yelling," he concluded:

All along the way, I just met Ignorant People and cursed ones
They do not understand, even if you tell them many times, are they really
human?

Here, it is worth considering one thing. If you notice, Abai is using many Ignorant People, who are a mob, in relation to himself. Then, what was it that Abai could not explain to them? What made him desperate? It seems Abai was being mischievous here by calling the masses Ignorant People, since it was not easy for his contemporaries to understand his words. This is probably the case.

Is it possible for anyone to perceive and understand life as Abai did? Is it necessary for everyone to be like Abai? It is appropriate that there is always a significant distance between thinkers and ordinary people. This should also be taken into account. Not all lack of knowledge is ignorance. Even the scarcity of the space for intelligence is a forgivable thing, but there is no excuse for a man to live like an animal. Therefore, the subjective assessment of ignorance cannot be overlooked.

Abai was displeased by the fact that when ignorant people gather into a group, they are easily manipulated. He was sad that the mob's actions lead to the mob's consciousness. They do not heed you, and they commit cursed actions. It is a great challenge to one's humanity and a threat to the country; it is a barrier to the future and to the mind's prudence; it is an obstacle to courage.

A second aspect of Abai's view on ignorance involved thoughtless people, whom he criticized:

The worries and thoughts of an ignorant man
Are limited to his eyes only.

A thoughtless person is one who will not do conscious actions, does not understand the meaning of a word, or cannot determine the state of affairs. Such people are blinded in their hearts and see only what they can see with their eyes. That is why the poet identified them as Ignorant People.

A thoughtless person does not have sorrows and grief. Such a person should be considered simply a two-legged animal. One of the most important traits of human beings is their ability to think. A thinking person knows what sadness is and what joy is. Those feelings make a person think; they make a person think about the meaning of life.

There are two types of thoughtlessness. One is thoughtlessness in its literal meaning, a defect in development. The second is ordinary thoughtlessness, which is caused by laziness or irrationality. Some people say that depression can be considered as thoughtlessness, but to some extent, even depression can be a product of thought. However, if one is depressed because they do not understand that the truth is life itself and because of a lack of skills, then such a person can be considered an ignorant person. Life is the power of God given to people; to escape from it is certainly ignorance. That is why Abai said:

The soul of an ignorant person is covered
By the veil of darkness.

Why is a person's soul veiled with darkness? What is the way to overcome it? Abai has a ready answer for these questions: only when one does well will the light shine and the darkness disappear from their soul. Doing well is the foundation of humanity. Abai never thought otherwise. Recognizing, obeying, and edifying God is a sign of consciousness. It requires acumen, intelligence, reasonableness, and diverse knowledge, that is, it requires reasoning. The soul of a sensible, clever, educated, and intelligent person will never be under the dark veil.

Though Abai concluded that a thoughtless person is ignorant and a thoughtful person is not, one should not understand his words literally. A careful reader of the poet's poems will ascertain that he does not give an absolute final conclusion. Even though Abai depicted all issues clearly and thoroughly, his thoughts had deeper meaning. For example, Abai's purpose in exposing the ignorant person is not only to talk about ignorance but also to suggest ways to overcome the state of ignorance. When he said that an ignorant person is a thoughtless person, Abai also described the solution to the problem of ignorance. The solution is in one's intention to acquire knowledge and art. To do this, undoubtedly, one needs thought and awareness and a wealth of feeling.

In his third view on ignorance, Abai said that ignorance is a sign of illiteracy. This statement calls on us to answer the question of what illiteracy is. The word "illiteracy" itself is not a clear concept. Usually when we refer to illiterate people, we mean people who did not study with a master. We often speak of uneducated people as people who were not educated by a teacher. Undoubtedly, this is true for some cases, but we sometimes also encounter ignorance among highly educated people. This was also common in Abai's time. Abai therefore spoke about two kinds of illiteracy: illiteracy among those who studied and illiteracy among those who studied but did not learn anything. Abai took the characteristic of humanity as a measure of literacy. When literate people demonstrated ignorance, Abai considered them Ignorant People. The poet said:

> *Both sayer and listener are Ignorant People in a majority*
> *Most people are not able to understand*

and

> *Poets are thoughtless and ignorant*
> *And they make up a poem from nothing.*

One should understand these verses cautiously. Recently, Kazakhs have made it a habit to criticize Abai by saying that he did not express his thoughts about people and poets in the right way. However, we must remember that not all of us have the art of words for some issues like Abai had. For example, Abai said, "Most people are not able to understand." The poet said whom people do not heed, but he no doubt meant his own words. And Abai had good reason to make this statement because he knew the weight of his own words. He fully understood who he was for Kazakhs. Hence, he said, "Both sayer and listener are Ignorant People in a majority." Likewise, Abai said poets were thoughtless and ignorant. Here, too, he had the right to say that because not only did he know what it means to be a poet but he proposed a reason for his claim. These statements are worthy of Abai, and to identify degrees of ignorance is acceptable for people like Abai.

In general, to be arrogant toward an ignorant person is also ignorance. Ignorant People are also human, so it is fair to pay attention to them. This worldview is a characteristic of piety. Abai goes in this direction even though he was not pious. He felt that malice toward others would create hatred and freeze hearts. So he wrote:

My goal is to improve my language skills and to spread art
To awaken the ignorant person and reveal his soul.

By saying "I used to not acknowledge Ignorant People," he is criticizing himself. His criticism suggests that none of us is guaranteed not to be ignorant. Is there anyone who was bypassed by ignorance during their life? Is it correct for even someone like Abai to look arrogantly toward Ignorant People? Each person should answer these questions for themselves.

Abai said that God created illness, but God does not make you ill. Similarly, God created ignorance, but He does not make a person ignorant. If this is correct, then what is the cause of ignorance? According to Ahmed Yasawi, God gave free will to humans. However, this will is an enemy. Why is free will given to humans? It is given to them so they will be able to recognize and love God. These are Abai's words. If free will were not given to people, they would turn into animals.

A person with free will is responsible for their deeds. The issue is whether someone with free will can take the right path. Free will is an opportunity that has not been realized yet. Turning opportunity to reality is up to each person. The question is in how a person will be able to represent themselves. Presumably, one who feels the existence of ignorance will not be an ignorant person. Indeed, the way to avoid being called an ignorant person is to have the ability to feel and recognize ignorance.

In his poem "Segiz ayiaq" (Eight legs), Abai described how ignorance is caused by a lack of knowledge.

He has no brain in his head
No personal opinion
Arrogant and jolly are all Ignorant People;
Easily manipulated
Agrees with the majority
This is what is typical for Ignorant People.

A person without a personal opinion has no self-respect. That person is easily manipulated. That person has no free will. A person without free will is unlikely to be able to overcome ignorance. Abai saw such thoughtless and arrogant people and said, "The ignorant relies on the majority and the masses."

"The Living Live with Hope"

Where there is no life there is no hope. Life is a power, which requires the activity and efforts to overcome earthly problems; it gives no rest to the living. Hope is an idea about the future. People say only Satan lives without hope. Humans cannot live without hope. Even on their deathbed in illness they hope for a miracle that they will recover. Life ends when hope disappears.

In Abai's opinion a person is both petty and great. The one who understands their greatness has a certain dignity and honesty. Such people live with hope for the future. Their hopes are often related to the perennial problems of the world. Abai's says: "How can we say they are dead if they have left us immortal words?" So great people of the world live hoping to leave a word after their death.

At the same time there is hope related to everyday life and concerns. But life does not consist of lofty feelings alone and not all the people were born great. There are daily concerns in life as well. That's the truth and you won't be able to avoid it. There are no great battles and heroic deeds in the life of ordinary people because every day cannot be a holiday. Most of the days are just humdrum life with ordinary worldly hustle-bustle. Day to day affairs and hopes constitute the core of life.

Unwittingly you recall these ideas when you read the first lines of Aba's verse "young men celebrate with feasting." The core meaning is a person's hope for the future. The poet tells a love story of two people but the dream of their happiness has not come true. The girl's beloved dies defending his honor. The girl also dies and her white wedding dress becomes her burial cloth. She dies hoping to meet him in heaven. It means that her hope leads her to death. So hope is not only love of life but also a power, which can make one defy death. Is there anything that is dearer than life? Or is it a delusion? Why does a person decide to commit suicide for the sake of another? What is the problem? We say that a living person has hope. What hope can a dead person have? Is there any hope when one commits suicide? The answers are in the last strophe of Abai's poem. Having left this world with hope her beloved she will not be upset. When he meets her in the other world, he will no longer recognize her.

There is nothing new in the first two lines because there are many legends about lovers who choose death for the sake of love. The last two strophes, however, sound unusual to us. The young people die hoping to meet each other in the next world, but Abai says that they will not meet. In other words, Abai ponders whether such sacrifice is necessary.

First, the lovers, once they have made a decision to die, have a long discussion about it. The purpose of their life is in their being together and if one of them dies life seems meaningless. Life for these lovers is their dream of happiness. They recognize only their feelings and dreams. There is no other reality which they can conceive. During their lives they dream of being together, but when one dies the other commits suicide. For them it is not coercion or torment, but a dream. To fulfill a dream even at the cost of one's life is the law of life. The lovers understand the world in this way, even though it senseless to others.

Second, Abai opens a truth which the lovers do not know. Love is an earthly pleasure, it does not exist in the next world because the soul leaves the body and takes other forms while love is grounded in our earthly experience. There may be other pleasures and torments in the next world, but we do not know about them here. But we know for sure that there is a young girl and young boy. Most likely they do not exist together in the next world. I think Abai's two last lines – "But when he meets her in the next world he will not recognize her" – are precisely about that. It would be irreverent to try to disclose the poet's secret beyond that. We know well that as long as a person remains alive they will never stop hoping. As the saying goes: "Hope dies last."

"God Will Not Change His Commandment Just Because You Are in a Hurry"

The concept of commandment has been an issue of debate since the ninth century. This concept is related to free will. Does a person have free will or is everything done by God's commandment?

If one's deeds and actions are performed only by God's commandment, then what is one's free will? Thinkers have recognized the ontological significance of commandment: namely, a commandment is synonymous with a regulation. A commandment is an inescapable truth, and it is accepted as "the commandment of God." But what would happen if the reality were beyond an absolute scope, beyond God? The question is therefore whether God's commandment corresponds to one's free will. According to Abai, no matter how quickly one tries to go, God will not change His commandment. Since a commandment is a reality that is the truth, it is an inescapable law, a necessity of life.

Therefore, it is only right that people should admit there is "a commandment of God" and recognize it. I am convinced that Abai was talking about the desire for knowledge when he concluded that "God will not change his commandment just because you are in a hurry." If people recognize God's commandments, they will not hurry; they will accept the necessities and act accordingly.

Therefore, the matter is in the recognition of God's commandments. This is the path where one has free will.

Abai explained one's free will and God's commandment in that way.

"Love and Passion are Two Different Things"

There are diverse strong expressions to reflect the human emotions. They are love, affection, passion, and lust. Although all these are related to human beings, there are striking differences between them. We often use them as synonymous terms. Although it is acceptable to interchange them in colloquial speech, we have to be specific about each one of them when we want to reveal human nature. For the nature of human nature is exhaustive. And people's natures are identified by how and why they act throughout their lives. For example, it is humans who aim to destroy human beings, and it is humans who fight to protect the universe. Everything is related to humans. There is no enemy of people, other than other people. Marx wanted to solve this dilemma through class struggle.

The nature of a tribe is based on the psychology of the masses. Human beings do not live in a mob, since each person's nature is in their own individuality. Each person is like a unique universe, with their own life and understanding. Likewise, each individual has feelings, which they feel only in relation to themselves. The strongest feeling among them is the passion for wealth.

Passion is the power that protects humanity because it is determined by the need for human beings. Such power is natural; biological laws determine its basis. If there were no human passion, humans would have long ago vanished from the surface of the earth. Although passion is typical for both humans and animals, their qualifications are different.

We call the passion of humans "sexual desire." That is why the poet said, "Passion comes only for 'sexual desire.'" The problem of sexual desire is a very difficult question; let me explain it through the philosophical category of "opportunity."

Sexuality is the capacity of a person's opportunity. It is, on the one hand, a hinged appearance of human nature. Sexual desire can be both realized and not realized. Control over it is in one's will. On the other hand, sexuality is one's destiny. For example, those who deny their sexual desires and reject them are called saints, pious people, monks, arhats, and so on. They are those who control their sexual desires and accept their fate, and every moment of their lives, they struggle with their desires.

Resisting passion is the most difficult thing in human existence. Numerous cataclysms in history were related to the size of controlling that desire. Being called sinful is also related to this desire. The location of sexual desire is not in the mind, nor is it in the senses; sexual desire is located in the lowest level of humans' natural and historical nature. Sexual desire is comparable to the foundation of a solid house. Psychoanalysts such as Sigmund Freud, Erich Fromm, and others, wrote much about that. Though Kazakh scholars have not conducted profound research on sexual desire, Mukhtar Auezov wrote a story called "Qaraly sulu" (Widow Beauty), which is devoted to this issue. There is no talk of love in "Qaraly Sulu" but only the problem of sexual desire. In the story, a young widow, whose husband was killed during a *barimta* (theft of cattle), promises that she will never get married. However, being unable to keep her promise, she had sex with an old man named Bolat.

Abai said that love is different from passion. Love is born from control over sexual desire. True lovers will not deceive or betray each other. Love is an infinite evaluation of human beings, which is between a man and a woman. On the one hand, love is the freedom of feeling, that is, the will of each person to choose their partner. On the other hand, love is the limiting of every human being's will. For the person in love, their lover is the symbol of the whole universe. That is why lovers are so inclined to sacrifice for their partner. Not every human is capable of love, since it requires a beauty of the soul and the flesh. According to Abai:

> When affection comes, it comes over you
> It will make you sick, like malaria
> It will get cold and cool down if it loses hope

It will burn like a fire if it has a hope.

Affection requires spiritual purity. Only a pure person can fall in love because to be in love is to take a risk, to reject the world, to be challenged. The path of love is very difficult. There is a deep meaning in Abai's statement that passion and love are different things.

Love is the measure of humanity. Love is a feeling that cannot be considered conscious. However, love has two forms in a person's life: one is the love of God (this is the mystical outlook), and the other is the passion between two people (this is a feeling).

Those who are in love with God, or God, are called Sufis and saints in Islam. The closest true Sufi and saint to us (Kazakhs) is Khoja Ahmad Yasawi. The Sufis regarded love as *iman* (a state of being pure). Yasawi announced, "Oh, people, those who are not in love have no iman." One who is in love with God is one who overcame sexual desire and was cleaned from the dirt of life. Abai used the concept of "dirt of life" to mean "sexual desire."

Love is a mystical outlook in Sufism. Saints are people who are in love with God. For saints, love for God is not just a worldview but also a fate. Saints are not people who are in love with God because they want to be in heaven in the other world; they are ascetics who made meeting God and seeing His face their life's goal. Saints do not think that if they do righteous things in this world, they will go to paradise. The good deed done to enter paradise is a sin for saints. Their love for God has no pragmatism. It is an unconscious idea; therefore, such an outlook seems incomprehensible to most. It is called mysticism in Europe. The truth is that there are two channels of mysticism in nature. One is the worldview that gives priority to paradise over this life and that is constructed on faith; the other, which values both worlds equally, is the worldview that accepts the mystery of both worlds. Sufism's outlook follows the latter channel. This is the first direction of love.

The second direction of love is the feeling between a man and a woman. A man falls in love with a woman, or a woman with a man. Other than that, there is no love between a father and a child or between a relative and a relative. There are other concepts that represent such feelings. This is what Abai meant by "The lover's language is a deaf language."

One who carefully reads Abai's poems does not doubt that he knew the specifics of love and affection. When the poet talked about love, he paid special attention to it. Love is a feeling that is independent of a person's sexual nature. There is no consciousness in love. Abai used "love" mainly in gnoseological, or cognitive, terms.

In his book *Sufi Orders in Islam*, the scholar John Trimingham described seven stages of difference between love and affection according to Sufism. The fourth stage of this scheme depicts the seven stages of the soul: (1) to get rid of your common thoughts and deeds in order to be purified from sexual desire (*shaqawat*), (2) to replace it with love, (3) and then to burn in the flames of love more intensely (4) and to be one and united (*wusla*) with the Truth (5) so as to be transformed into another state (*fana*) (6) through the grace and patience of God (7) in order to enter the eternal world after going through hardships. These seven stages have their own colors. The color of love is yellow, and the color of affection is red. Hence, the separation of love and affection was known before Abai, especially in Sufism.

Love is not a worldview; it is a way of recognizing reality, and affection is the worldview. Love is first. Affection, which is second, is not directed toward the Creator, but it is between two people. However, Abai used "affection" to refer to both the light of the Creator transformed into human emotions and the affection between a man and a woman. In this sense, Abai used "love" and "affection" as synonyms.

"Initially the Bright Mind is Cold Ice"

Abai compared the mind to cold ice. The mind is acumen. However, why is it cold? Wisdom is astute, but why is it cold? Wisdom is typical only for people. There is no dispute about it. Intelligence is the level and dimension of knowledge, and Abai respected it highly. There is no science without intelligence. If God gives intelligence as an opportunity, then each soul is its lone realizer. A wise person is a well-educated, intelligent person. There were, are, and will be many wise people in the world. It is a legitimate fact that the number of intelligent people will increase with time; it is a demand of civilization.

If Abai were limited to talking about these issues, then there would be no discussion of his wisdom. All these are known things. But Abai came to this issue from a different angle, for he stated that the mind is cold ice, and in the second line of the poem he wrote, "A hot heart is what warms up a man's flesh." The question then arises: If a mind were to remain cold, what would happen? Why do we need a hot heart? When the mind is cold, it does not differ between good or evil, and such distinctions do not matter to it. They are only a matter of knowledge that the world knows and realizes. The mind's only goal will be to know, to identify, and to turn knowledge into education. It will aim to know, identify, and reveal reason. In addition, the mind will not care about who or what this knowledge will serve. The revealed knowledge may serve both vicious intentions and justice, and the cold mind does not care about that.

The mind only knows its own business. When deeds have such content, the intellect threatens a person; it threatens a person's essence. That is why Abai raised the issue of a "hot heart" as a companion of the mind. It melts cold ice, illuminates the mind, and makes the mind feel sympathy for people and their good deeds.

Abai did not limit himself only to combining mind and heart:

Self-control, patience
Comes from courage

Now courage is added to mind and heart. It gives the mind self-control and patience. Only then does one have a "full mind." That which I call "full mind" can also be called wisdom. Hence, Abai concluded:

Keep your mind, courage, and heart in balance
Only then will you be unique.

Keeping these three in balance must be the goal of any person. However, in real life it is not always like this; one can be smart but impatient or patient but heartless. By "hot heart," Abai meant humanity; therefore, struggle without kindness is meaningless.

There are many diverse types of people. You might meet a kind, humble, pure person, but because they lack courage, they become as dry as water under the hot sun. Abai spoke of the consciousness that is formed when mind, heart, and courage are joined together. But how they come together is a difficult question: What does a cold mind give to the hot heart? What does courage give to those both? What do we get when all three are combined in one person? That is the issue.

I mentioned above that there are many smart people in the world, but are there many people who keep their mind, heart, and courage in balance? It is not necessary to determine the number of such people, because the world is about thinkers. There were never too many thinkers in the world. To long for them is to long for "full people," for *hakims* (philosophers) and Muslims, in Abai's lexicon.

"The Blacks of My Eyes"

The blacks of my eyes,
the state of my mind,
never ending is
the inner wound of love.

These often-cited verses not only impress me but also lead me to unusual thoughts. First, I want to say that Abai never tired of searching for rhymes in poems; his rhymes were always in accordance with the content of his thoughts.

For example, Abai wrote about an eye's pupil in the first line and mentions the soul's consciousness in the second. What is the relation between these two things? If we look from that angle, are the words "pupil" (*qarasy*, lit. 'black'), "consciousness" (*sanasy*, cf. 'state of mind'), and "wound" (*zharasy*) used only for the sake of rhyme or do they also have a conceptual function? Let us try to find the answers to these questions. What does the expression "pupil of my eye" mean? Presumably, Abai was not speaking about the eye's pupil. The poet wrote a poem about feelings, so the point is in the glance, which in Russian is *vzgliad*. The love is born from the glance of an eye. As Abai said, the feeling would not have appeared if there were no glance. Does the feeling also not appear because of a glance? Perhaps, I would understand the phrase "pupil of my eye" in its physical meaning if the second line of the verse did not have the phrase "consciousness of my soul."

The two lines are identifying, supplementing, and complementing each other. The poet's pupil is his soul's consciousness; therefore, consciousness is born from a glance. It is the consciousness of love. This consciousness is not revealed or identified; it has not found its own unique way. Though it is an opportunity of consciousness, it is still in darkness. Since consciousness has not been transformed into light, it has turned to sickness. Therefore, the poet said, "Wounds of love in my heart do not heal."

The word "wound" in the fourth line is a spiritual term. It is also consciousness, but it is the consciousness of a person who is in love. The soul is something that is beyond the flesh. Not everyone's soul can be wounded and feel the pain of love. Love needs a deep consciousness of the soul. Consciousness is born from one's worldview. In addition, love is not just a matter of human existence; it is also unrealized dreams and impossible chances; it is the consciousness that is made up of a longing for the creator and a natural need for unity and harmony. By this, I mean that love is the worldview. Love is an inestimable passion, and it becomes meaningful when it turns into a sickness and a wounding of the soul. Love is the truth, which is beyond lifestyle and flesh.

If you find love in a lifestyle or in the passions of the flesh, then it becomes self-destructive. Just as a soul flies away from the flesh, love will leave passion. This is the power of poems, stories, epos, and songs about love. This is how they impress, make your soul tremble, and strengthen your passion for life.

Abai's poetry focused not on topics of everyday life but on major themes of human life. Moreover, it is a well-known fact that the language of poetry need not be comprehensible, or clear and easy to understand. Poetry is a mysterious consciousness. Its secret is in its inner side. That is why it is poetry and why it is unique. Abai used this power of poetry without falsity.

The love born from the eye's pupil is the consciousness of a soul. What, then, is the consciousness of a soul? Is not this soul a person's consciousness? Does it mean, then, that consciousness has its own consciousness? This is a philosophical question. The famous poet Qays ibn al-Mulawwah expressed his deepest opinion on this subject:

> You asked: "Who is she? Does she live far away?"
> I answered: "She is dawn, whose dwelling is in the heavens."
> People asked: "Can't you understand that to fall in love with dawn is meaningless?"
> I answered: "This is my fate, and so it is hard for me."[5]

Usually one's consciousness would be reasonable. But the "consciousness of a soul" (love) is beyond consciousness. Only the sole creator knows its secret. However, the existence of that secret is a necessity for people. Just like people were created in the world with a need, it is obligatory for them to long for that need and to be passionate for it. The eagerness of this need gives birth to love. Being in love with the dawn of the poet leads to this truth.

Thus, love in human beings is when one puts one's needs higher than life's interests. However, this natural affair, this passion, has two facets: a passion of the soul and a passion of the flesh. Love is a passion for life. Therefore, the wounds of love can never be healed. If a wound is healed, then it was usually a wound of the flesh's passion, not of love. Love is a dream, and dreams will never become reality. A dream that comes true is not a dream. The meaning of Abai's phrase "Wounds of love in my heart do not heal" should be understood in that way.

---

[5] *Arabskaya poezia srednih vekov* [Arabic poetry of the Middle Ages], (Moscow, 1975), p. 143.

"The Pleasure of the Eyes is for Parents"

The content of this six-versed poem, which ends with a concise conclusion after each couplet, does not overlap with simple concepts. The poet is considering the issue of a child and a parent. It is well known that all people are born with sorrow or pleasure for themselves and for others. Abai turned to this question. People usually say that a child is the image of their parents, but Abai used the word "eye-pleasure." The poet immediately described what this concept is:

> *For parents, eye-pleasure is*
> *Their baby in their hands.*

Hence, to coddle a baby is parents' eye-pleasure. Here we come to one thought. Is it not theatre to coddle a baby? Is it right or wrong for a parent to coddle a baby just because the baby is their eye-joy? I guess two issues are going to be revealed here. First, who needs the eye-pleasure, parents or children? In the poem, the owner of the "pleasure" is the parents. Then, what benefit does the child get? If the child's cuteness is not for a child but for the parents, then coddling is the parents' joy. What is the logic of using a child as an object of joy? One should think about this.

Second, is it a natural need for a child to be naughty? It is difficult to provide a specific answer because naughtiness is a reflection of a child's free will and actions. There is no doubt that a child's behavior should have some limits. This is a general rule. Moreover, what kind of adult will a child who has no limits grow up to be? Abai did not respond but asked questions:

> *Cuteness has gone,*
> *Now he is grown up,*
> *What was achieved?*

When Abai mentioned that a cute baby is eye-pleasure for a parent, he also mentioned the goal of coddling. Parents coddle their children with some hopes. However, hope is not a matter of timely realization in science. So Abai said:

> *If the soul of the parent is not pleased*
> *If there are no achievements in art*
> *If no one knows him, except his relatives*
> *If he is not even aware of his own deeds*
> *Where is the hope?*
> *Think about that.*

Be cautious!

The poet clearly explained the vindication of hope's space. It is a difference between traveling within and between countries and knowing only one's home.

Traveling is the criterion of individuality and citizenship. In addition, what if a child never leaves home? What is going to happen to this child? If the parents' souls are not pleased and the eye-pleasure becomes a house-bound child, it means the collapse of hope.

Yes, as the poet said, it is not easy to turn comfort in the heart into happiness. Although children can be born with better qualities than their parents have, it is rare in life. And though children can be born with better qualities, it is also possible for them to be born with lesser qualities. This is because we look at children from the angle of the parents and the elder generation. We do not always understand childishness in children's behavior. A children's deeds are incomprehensible to their parents. That is why a child's cuteness is like eye-pleasure for adults. Abai described this issue very accurately. For a parent, a child's life is similar to a horizon. The closer the parents get to the child, the further the horizon will be from the parents. When it comes to this situation:

You will complain and feel anxious
Thinking what will happen to me now.
You will feel uncomfortable in front of your friends
But just obey the commandment of Tangri.
Have you ever seen
A person with no sorrows?

There is no one in this life without grief. So, what does it mean to escape grief? This is meaningless. Tragedy is the consciousness of life. Why do we, then, want to be without sorrow? I assume that parents turn their child into eye-pleasure and coddle them because they want to be without sorrow. However, life does what it wants. People who are deprived of grief can be mentally diseased. If mentally healthy people coddle their children and turn them into their eye-pleasure as a way to escape from grief, what is wrong with that? The last lines of the verse includes these thoughts:

If Tangri wants a man to be sad
Then what can be solved just by crying?

The problem is in two directions. The first is that being happy depends on the person themselves, and the second is that it depends on Tangri.

If it is Tangri who made you sad, not another person, then what can you do? There is no reason to cry in such a situation. This is destiny. You have no choice except to obey. People often accept despair as legitimate. If one does not have enough courage and intelligence, one will not achieve many things. The poet wrote about this situation:

Did you say deep inside yourself
"I myself am this kind of person"?

These are words of despair but ones with meaning. If people feel their wrong deeds, then they also know the way out of them. Such people are not Ignorant People but people with light in their souls. Though Abai was such a person, he said these words because he was desperate about his child, his eye-pleasure. Everyone wants their children to grow up and leave the family's surroundings, to reach the level of being able to travel within and between countries alone, and with this aim, they coddle their children, make them their eye-pleasure and the consolation of their souls.

"Heavenly Mist Portends the Future"

Only a true thinker can understand a wise person. The proof for this opinion is Ahmet Baitursynuly's 1913 article entitled "The Greatest Poet of the Kazakhs" in which he praised Abai's wisdom. Take for following excerpt for example:

In 1903, I came across a notebook with Abai's words. His words are not similar to other poets' works. Their difference is so vivid that when you read them for first time, you feel amazed. He uses few words, but with deep meaning. For a person who is not familiar with his texts, it is hard to grasp all his ideas from the first reading. If one is not skilled, then it is hard to understand some of his words, even if one rereads them repeatedly. *Only if someone explains can one understand the meaning of his words.* Hence, it is true that for a general reader, his words are hard to understand. However, this is due not to Abai's failure to express his thoughts but to the reader's ability to understand. In this case, the accused is not the writer but the reader. Whatever Abai writes, he writes about its roots, basis, inner details, and attributes. Since he always takes into account the topic's details and attributes, his words are like a test of the reader's knowledge.[6]

Ahmet develops his thoughts further and gives as an example Abai's eight versed poem "The future is blue mist" to prove its difficulty. I would also like to give my opinion on some lines in that poem.

1. *Heavenly Mist Portends the Future*

It is useless to talk about the future with those who have not yet understood the current society. Each epoch has its own troubles; each person has their own fate given to them by Tangri. All of this is the burden of the false world. Though God, as a forthright being, created humans, people need strong courage as they struggle to remain human. Is it easy to think of your future when you are burdened by the troubles of daily life? Of course not. Abai was aware of this situation and wanted to discover the essence of the present day through the approaching day. For Abai, the future was important not for the sake of the future but for the conversation about the present. He wanted to understand his own place in the present life. What is the essence and meaning of the present if there are no prospects? Hakim Abai reasoned on this subject and described the coming epoch as "blue mist." One can agree or disagree with Abai on this issue, but the problem is not in this. The topic of the conversation is the essence of life. How can one master it, understand it, and explain it to others? According to Abai, the future is mist, that is, an unclear image; its origin is uncertain and dark. The only light that can enter into its essence is hope. The future can be sensed only through hope. That hope is human. Only the devil is hopeless. A person with hope is a real person. Such a soul should have a sense of the future. That is why Abai said:

> The future is blue mist
> So eyes are staring at hope to make it light

There has been no thinker who has not referred to such futurologist thoughts. There is no person who does not care to think about the future. But it is mist. The events to be realized, to be born, and the stories to happen in the

---

[6] Abai, Vol. 3, 1992, p. 23.

future are not yet clear. That is what makes the future interesting. If the future were clear and obvious, how would our lives be interesting? The interesting side of our lives is in fact that we can never know for sure what is going to happen even tomorrow, to say nothing about the far future. What is going to happen tomorrow is a question about the future. Though the future's reason is in the present, its reflection is in the future. Does this mean that people have no chance to know their own futures? Undoubtedly, they have no chance. But many people have wanted to change this order, and various utopian and other theories have been created for that purpose. Revolutions have been organized to realize such theories. Nevertheless, the blue mist of the future was not revealed. Prophecy cannot remove the veil of the blue mist. Those who can understand the future and clear away the blue mist are the descendants of the next generation, the philosophers of that time. People of the present can only rely on their hopes. Hope is not one's deceitful consciousness; it is the power that leads one to the next epoch. The power of the hopeful is abundant. Hence, the desire for the future is unique. Abai himself is among such hopeful people, for his "approaching epoch" is not just an abstract concept but one's life that has not yet been experienced. It is one's still unfulfilled job, one's unspoken speech.

The coming epoch is one's future life. The nature of that life is blue mist, that is, uncertainty. One's actions turn uncertainty to certainty. Since the actions of the coming epoch are unknown, it is like a blue mist. Abai described the mist as follows: "Many years, many days have passed away, and there is no image, no picture, my eyes are tired."

This raises a question: If so many years and days have passed, who is their chaser? The chaser is time. It is time that moves years. What, then, is the symbol of time? What is the relationship between human life and years and days? Can they exist without each other? According to Abai, the passing of many years and days happens without people's involvement; it has an ontological attribute. In addition, its attribute in relation to people is reflected through the "image." Abai, however, said he could not find the image or picture of the coming epoch, and so his eyes were tired.

The key element of human thoughts about society and epochs is integrity—integrity of the present and the future. In order to fill this integrity with meaning and significance, the coming epoch must turn into the present epoch, which means that people must live. This is the path to the truth because the truth is human life.

2. One of Them is the Special Day of Apocalypse

Many years, many days come and go. What is left after them? This fast-passing life is full of grief. However, one day among them has special significance; it is a vital day. Abai called this day the "special apocalypse day." On that day, all the spent days of your life will become as tiny as if they could fit into the tiniest hole. Life turns into a momentary fragment. Your many years and many days will become a symbol, attribute, and image of that special apocalypse day. The attribute, image, meaning, and significance of life are all determined on that same day. That is the miracle of the special apocalypse day. However, one should come to this day prepared. It is a fateful day, but not everyone succeeds in transforming this day into the meaning and philosophy of life. One can even say, "Take it easy, do not worry, when the time comes, I will see," and not take any actions. Alternatively, maybe one can foresee that special apocalypse day and can act and direct their actions toward that day. This is also a personal matter. However, it is clear that every single person will have their own special apocalypse day.

The topic of there being a special apocalypse day was discussed before Abai and will continue to be discussed long after him. The special apocalypse day is also the main basis of religion. On that day, one must be cleansed of sin and worldly dirt. This can be found both in Christian traditions and in Islam. There is no innocent human soul. The day when one accepts one's sins is on that apocalypse day. In addition, one understands the meaning of this life on that day, and then what kind of concept can one understand? According to scholars, it is evident that on that day, one understands that the meaning of this life is in its meaninglessness.

There are many philosophical movements in the West concerning this consciousness. One of them is existentialism. This has two directions: atheistic and religious. Intellectuals know all of this. What they are talking about is the connection between the special apocalypse day and the meaning of life. The meaning of life is a mystery to people; they can reveal life's secrets only in this last moment. However, at the same time, the correct perception of death also requires lifelong consciousness. In short, it is desirable for one to come prepared for the moment of separation of flesh from soul. What Abai wants to say is that many days come and pass, but one of them is the last day; will you have enough intelligence to accept it? Because after that day, human consciousness stops its existence and starts living in another conscious mood, and its secret is known only to one: God.

The special apocalypse day is the border between life and death, the measure of life. The change from life into death, the transformation of one life form into another life form, is a phenomenon that is similar to existence and the change of day and night, and it happens beyond people's control. In Islam, it is called the commandment of God, and in the atheistic viewpoint, it is the law of nature. There is no mistake, however, because God's commandment and the nature of nature are the essence of ontological content, regardless of human nature. They are both truths with ontological content that happen beyond people's control. Each is a substance with its own mystery and secrets. The philosopher Immanuel Kant called these things "things-in-themselves." Meaning and phenomenon go through transformations, and eventually, it is hard to identify what is phenomenon and what is meaning, and they get used interchangeably. The most striking example of this is the socialist society.

It turns out that a social opportunity can only represent the phenomenon of a person, not the essence of a person. However, people believed that it was one's essence. People's division into classes or groups and people's cooperation are not their essence but external phenomena. One's essence is in one's personality, one's character, one's actions, and one's deeds. A person will never gain anything valuable from imitating others. The actions of others change, get worn out, and a personality crisis begins at that moment. A person must first believe in themselves, and as Abai said, they should listen to their heart and believe in their courage. Humans are very complex, deep, bottomless abysses, and their substance cannot be identified with a group classification of attributes and properties. This approach is only for politics. Politics is not a person's essence but a consciousness that regards human beings as a phenomenon.

Thus, the moment of the special apocalypse day will give individuals the opportunity to understand their essence. The consciousness that is born at that moment must be about the fullness of life, its evanescence, instability, limitedness, and relentless cruelty. The human life should consist of a person's responsibility and irresponsibility toward their Creator. I think that those who take responsibility for their actions have a high consciousness, and those who do not responsibility for their actions are Ignorant People. But even their fates come to life because of God's commandment: on the special apocalypse day, both wise thinkers and thoughtless poor will be equal, both will suffer equally, both will regret that it is impossible to return to a past life, and both will not want to leave life and will be eager to stay there.

Fate is a mystery that cannot be weighed, measured, or reasoned. That is the destiny that Abai described as the special apocalypse day.

3. *The Destiny of the "Self" is not Death*

Death and (eternal) life are the most vital problems that the world cannot resolve. So many religions, philosophical systems, and theories have been created around this problem. Scientists and thinkers have expressed so many great ideas about life and death. All of them have searched for the cause, but none have been able to give a full answer. Abai did not give an answer to this question either; he did not even attempt to. What he talked about is the separation of "self" and "mine." I do not know of any Kazakh thinker other than Abai who regarded the concept of self not in its mere meaning but as a philosophical and worldly fertile concept.

Abai, in the third verse of "The future is blue mist," defined the two terms "self" and "mine." First, let us discuss Abai's idea of "self." He said, "The mind and the soul are me myself." Thus, "self" is the synthesis of reason and soul. This is true but requires clear understanding. Would you ask why? Well, what are the mind and soul? I have discussed a lot about the mind in this book. It is the dimension of human intelligence and imagination. Usually, those who make the right choices and who can foresee things are called "wise ones." The soul, however, is mysterious, and there is no complete understanding of it. There are expressions such as "let your soul fly," "my soul is wounded," "I love with my whole soul," and so on. These are phrases that are used in simple terms, but they do not have worldviews or philosophical attributes.

The most fertile concept of the soul is that it relates to a living person, that is, when someone dies, their soul is extinguished. A live person has a soul. Even for the person who passed away, the term "soul" is used for identification. In addition, Abai identified the mind and the soul with the notion of self and said, "The destiny of the 'self' is not death." He used self as a dimension of eternity. What does this mean then? Does this mean that both mind and soul are permanent? Indeed, let us say that mind and soul are eternal; then what are their shapes in life? Can the mind be soulless, and can the soul be mindless? Abai did not say anything on this point.

Next, let us consider Abai's idea of "mine." If self is a unity, a relationship, between mind and soul, then the notion of "mine" has a relationship to it as well. Abai considered this problem and said, "The mind and the soul are me myself, and the flesh is mine." He separated the flesh from the soul and named it "mine." When a person is alive, the body and the soul are together. They are separated only at the end of life. Abai described that situation.

To make this idea clear, let us look at the verse:

The mind and the soul are me myself, and the flesh is mine
The meanings of "self" and "mine" are different.
The destiny of the "self" is not death
But mine can die and just accept it.

The meaning of "self" and "mine" changes when the special apocalypse day comes. The flesh dies, that is, "mine" dies, and the soul and the mind turn into the "self," which continues to exist. Destiny has no power to change this. Abai's "self"' is probably a person's soul. The spirit is eternal.

When Abai talked about "self," he referred not to a lyrical hero but to a real person, himself. The "self" of people like Abai will never die. This is the rule for human beings. Their nature, their body dies, but their "self" does not die. Generations need this power. Without such a rule, there would be no change in human nature.

4. *Do Not Call All Majorities Majority, Majorities Can Be Diverse*

"Majority" is a social philosophy concept. Abai used the word "majority" as a concept. There are many alternative words for majority in science, such as society, class, social group, collective, caste, mobs, masses, people, and so on. Scientists have created these concepts for their own needs, depending on their political objective. Abai expressed his opinion in one word: majority. According to Abai, the one who defines the direction of a majority is an individual. The individual is the one who gives meaning to the actions of a majority. But in most cases, a majority acts without an individual (without the one). Do not expect anything good in such a situation, because the minds of a majority have the attributes of a mob. A mob is a destructive force that has no other goal than to destroy everything in its path. The destruction creates special concepts, which lead to revolution. This is a catastrophe philosophy. However, the catastrophe also has the power to attract people. When a person is involved in destruction, they change their nature and accept another person's consciousness, replacing their own consciousness. They start living in the space of two consciousnesses. Sometimes a person's own consciousness leads them, and sometimes the other person's consciousness dominates, thus one person lives in two spaces. For this person, the hatred of others becomes a habit, and those who criticize this person are regarded as enemies. The name of such consciousness is fanaticism. The consciousness of a mob is the consciousness of a majority. Though, initially, a mob may have good intentions, it can take actions that are against humanity to achieve its goals. How can a mob know that good deeds are needed to achieve goodness?

Those who seek to drink and cause the flood are also a mob. What is a mob? The shortest explanation is that a mob is a group. They used to sometimes be called a collective. Why do people gather into groups? First, people are often intentionally gathered into groups because a group is easy to manage. Second, people who are panicked and anxious are easily grouped. Increasing the number of people in a group is not a sign of braveness but a sign of fear. Third, there are groups headed by "the one"; this is a different issue. Obviously, if the power of a mob is in the will of the intelligent, good-willed person, there will be humane ways of achieving their goal. The notion of the wise ruler is born of this idea. Abai said:

> Cursing and praising people are the things people are always doing
> Wherever you look, that is what they are always doing.

Justice is required for the majority. A country's ruler is supposed to first be fair to the majority. Otherwise, people will go astray; they will turn into a mob and regress. Hence, the leaders of the country should know that the power of the people is within them. Abai said on the second line of his verse:

> The majority dogs will torment others daily

That is, a mob will use its numbers and make those who are alone suffer. What, then, is the benefit of a majority? There is no hope for a mob that is lost. The problem is that the majority must be kept on a humane path from the very beginning. Otherwise, it is obvious that "the majority dogs will torment others daily," as Abai said. One can find many examples of that from history; my readers know them well.

"Who Would Give Their Soul for This Life?"

The story of the two worlds (life and afterlife) has been a topic of discussion since ancient times, but the terms of this and that world have not yet been clarified in religious philosophy. The main reason for this problem is the fact that when this world is described, it is usually described as being separate from that world. The central issue in religious philosophy is that discussions of materialism and atheism have ignored that world, and only the ideas of this world have been discussed. All these perspectives are one sided. In fact, there are not two worlds; there is only one world. The worlds called this and that world are actually two facets of the one world, and it is a very special reality.

Therefore, partial recognition of the world does not lead to the goal; the issue is in considering both worlds in unity. Only then will people think about what this world is and what that world is.

It is impossible for thinkers to find an answer to this question. All their assumptions are just a hypothetical and descriptive design. This is understandable. The truth about the universe is the universe itself. The secret of the universe is its essence, and people cannot comprehend it fully.

Humankind's recognition of the universe is endless. The world is infinite, and people have no choice other than to accept that its cognition is endless.

Abai also raised this complex problem, but he came to this issue from a different perspective. He said:

> *Who would give his soul to this life?*
> *Eternal life will see the flaws of evanescent life.*

Thus, that world will see the flaws of this world. What does this mean? Why would that world see the flaws of this world, when this world comes first in chronological order? What is the issue here? In my opinion, the problem lies in the nature of this world. Let us then discuss the concept of the flaw (of this world).

"Flaw" is a deep worldview concept. People often say "flawless beauty," "flawless soul," and so on, in colloquial speech. In this sense, it is not used as a concept. However, Abai used "flaw" as a philosophical outlook. When he said, "Who would give his soul to this life," he meant that this is the flaw of this world. To give one's soul to this life is to forget that there is another world, to be limited to this evanescent life, and to not think deeply about this world. This is humans' flaw. But what does the flaw of this world mean? In short, the phrase the flaw of this world means the flaw of this life. It reveals the existence of terms such as humankind's flaw and the flaw of this world. The relationship between these two is their common attributes of shortness and evanescence. The life of a human is measured: that is, this world is false and it is not a person's eternal residence. Not understanding this is humankind's flaw. Even if one does understand it, they cannot change it, because it is the flaw of this world. *The flaw of this world* is the *destiny* of humankind. Any attempt to change it is futile. Again, there is a question: If this world is imperfect, then why do humans need another world? The answer for this can be found in human's essence.

Abai wrote in the first verse of this poem, "Nature can die, but not a man." That is, the flesh of mortal humans is their nature, but their souls are eternal. A person passes from this false world, where their flesh remains, and their soul returns to eternal life. Probably, that is the reason why Kazakhs do not say "died" but "passed from life" or "returned." Thus, it reminds us of the idea that a soul has returned home.

However, if we stopped with idea that the flaw of this world is in its shortness, we would not thoroughly analyze Abai's thoughts. He said:

Who would give his soul to this life?
Eternal life will see the flaws of evanescent life.

and continued:

You cannot find its flaw
Unless you sink into deep thoughts.

Abai posed a problem for readers by asking what the flaw of this world is. Indeed, which of a person's actions are flawless and which are flawed? If the world itself is imperfect, can a person's deeds be flawless? To address this point, it is necessary to answer the question of what the flaw is.

First, consider the relationship between the terms "flawed" and "flawless." Perfection is inherent only to the Creator, so no one can be perfect. The issue here is just in knowing the difference between flawed and flawless. In life, people mostly cannot see the perfection in absolute imperfection. Undoubtedly, there are a number of reasons for that. Sometimes, even if the imperfection is vivid, it is forbidden to speak of it, or people ignore it or they do not want to see it. This is particularly commonplace in politics. In contrast, there is a tendency to show flawless things as useless. In short, there is a lot of talk concerning the difference between flawed and flawless. People themselves created it. When it comes to comparing humans and God, God is flawless, humans have flaws. This is the interconnection between the two terms. That is what people must understand and what Abai was trying to impart.

Second, when speaking about flaws, the main problem is in immersing oneself in the term's content. In other words, a person who does not understand the word "flaw" cannot master the essence of this world, because they will not see the difference between this world and that world. Flaws are the internal rationale of this world's essence. The world is self-approving through its own flaws. Abai said that this world's fault is identified by the eternal world. Therefore, imperfection is the secret of the general world. It is not related to humans; the problem is in the recognition of it. If a person has the ability to let God in, then they have comprehended the flaw of this world and they have understood the internal rationale of the world.

Third, according to Abai, finding the flaws of this world is a big deal.

You cannot find its flaw
Unless you sink into deep thoughts.

Though the poet said that you should immerse yourself into deep thought in order to find the flaws of this world, he did not say where you will find them. This is because it is impossible to find them, but it is necessary to immerse yourself in thoughts about it. Reasoning is a process that does not always produce results. If all thoughts could reach a final point and find their exact answers, thoughts would not be thoughts any more. The depth of thoughts is endless and unstable.

Fourth, Abai said clearly that the most obvious flaw of this false world is demonstrated through human nature. He wrote this in the first line of this verse:

Who would give his soul to this life?
Eternal life will see the flaws of evanescent life.

Consequently, it is not good to give your soul to this life, because there is an eternal life on the other side of life, on the other side of this world. Forgetting that and being unable to rise above everyday problems is a flaw of human nature.

Fifth, what is the reason for the imperfection of this world? Why is this world short and faulty? This matter concerns all religions. There is probably no precise answer to this question. I can say only this: according to Abai, who intended to explain humans through the terms "self" and "mine," human nature can be divided into two aspects, the nature of the flesh (me) and the nature of a soul (mine). When a person's nature and soul are intact, their life space is this world, and when the two are separated from each other, when a soul begins its own life, the life space is that world. There is no other way to say it, because the Creator created humans like that. Such creation has its own power. It is human freedom. On the one hand, it is the imperfection of this world; on the other hand, it is its advantage over the other world.

Humankind is free in this world. That is why both an angel and a devil are needed. If free will is a field of goodness and evil, it is a path with dangers and threats, and perhaps this is the fault of this life that Abai mentioned. But if this world had no flaws, humans would not be free; we would turn into a toy of fate. The meaning of this life is in the fact that one can fight against one's fate, that is, one has freedom of actions, freedom of thought, and freedom of faith in this world.

The flaws of this world are manifested by human freedom. They are seen in people's actions that go against human nature, which is His creation. This is why people are in need of religious consciousness. If this life were flawless, there would be no need for religions.

"To Use Trickery, Just Forget Your Nobleness"

This is taken from the second verse of the poem called "Where are you, oh, flame of youth?" Abai put two notions in these two lines of poetry—the concepts of trickery and nobleness. These two things cannot exist separately, but they are concepts with two different meanings. Let us discuss each of them.

The topic of trickery was discussed long before Abai. It is not something new. The proverb "A man's day with a man" means that someone is involved in the problems of using trickery. Kazakhs also describe this hardship as "the key to the belongings of others is in the sky." To use trickery means to catch someone in your cage, making them serve you, making them do the things you need to achieve your goals; but it also means you end up serving that person, becoming their slave, and living a bustling life; otherwise, you will not be successful in your endeavor. So what can a person do? One can just accept the challenge and begin using trickery. This way is not stable; it is slippery and dangerous. However, the necessities of life can bring one to diverse situations. You have no other choice than to obey your fate. You know exactly that your destiny is in the hands of a person, not God. One begins thinking not about God at that moment but of how to use trickery. In this case, there is a risk of losing nobleness.

Nobleness is a person's conscience and self-esteem. A person who lacks nobleness is a miserable person who has become a victim of fate. It is unlikely that someone who has lost their conscience can ever find themselves. Abai raised that question. It is important to not lose your nobleness by trying to use trickery. A person without nobleness is not a full person. A person with nobleness is a "full person"; they are a "true Muslim." This is connected to my earlier discussion of an advanced person, one who is *lichnost* in Russian.

The concept of *lichnost* can be well expressed with the Kazakh word *kisilik* (nobleness). Sometimes Kazakhs say "that person has no nobleness," or "that person is really noble." These colloquial phrases have truth. Nobleness is a concept that is especially needed in the political sciences. Therefore, it must have its own place in society's consciousness in the meaning suggested by Abai. However, one should not perceive Abai's phrase "to use trickery" in a negative way. Using trickery is also a significant question. It has a vital pragmatic significance. A thoughtful person will never forget about trickery. It is trickery that makes this world both paradise and hell. Branches of science study it. These include law, diplomacy, science of upbringing (pedagogy), science of the soul (psychology), science of the conscience (ethics), and so on. What Abai is saying is that a person should act, but they should not lose their nobleness.

Trickery is a bottomless act; the possibilities are endless. The Creator has given conscience and will to people, but He has not restricted them. A person of conscience can think and can do. It is impossible to list all of the possible actions. Only a person can notice trickery. To notice it is also trickery. Thus, figuring out which actions are right and which are wrong is also trickery. How can one get out of this kind of communication, or as Kazakhs say, how can one escape from the complex net? If the problem was not complicated, Abai would not have written about it. The problem has no solution; there is only one aim, and it is nobleness. If you are using trickery and thinking about nobleness, then you are headed on the right path, but if you forget about nobleness, then there is nothing to say.

In Abai's understanding, nobleness and humanity are not the same. In colloquial speech, they are sometimes used as similar notions, but in academic language, there is a qualitative difference. Moreover, today, Kazakh scholars use the term *adamgershilik* (humanness), which was coined in Soviet times as a substitute for both nobleness and humanity. However, analysis of these terms shows that the word "humanness" cannot express the meaning of the words "nobleness" and "humanity." I discussed the meaning of nobleness above, but what is humanity?

Humanity is the consciousness of human qualities. Its meaning will be determined in the following matters. First, humanity is the set of qualities that keeps a person away from "non-human" qualities. Humanity is a set of properties that separates a person from "unbelief." There are types of consciousness particular and not particular to humans. Human consciousness is humanity. In addition, there is a kind of consciousness that is not typical for humans. This is evil; it has diverse types of appearances and forms. A second aspect of humanity is recognition of the Creator. While this issue is different in different religions, the issue here is one's responsibility before God. If one lacks that responsibility, they will encounter a morality that is the opposite of humanity. These principles of humanity are directed against human beings, making them invalid instead of making them perfect. The most convincing proof of this is the principles of communist morality. According to communist morality, dividing people into classes—creating and killing class enemies—is humanity. There is no doubt that such a moral consciousness led to the adolescence of people in the communist system of upbringing, but it made their spirits and morals invalid.

All religions are against such moral perception. According to religion, a person is guilty of an offense committed against another person. Human life is not in the hands of people but in the hands of God, in the power of the Almighty, which people often call "fate," "script," or "line." Hence, humanity starts with a person's feeling of responsibility and duty before their Creator and with their acceptance of God.

A human being is a creation of the Divine Power, and therefore, recognizing one's own power without breaking the laws of the Creator is the basic principle of humanity. Then, the main treasure for people will be people, because humans are the most precious treasure of the Creator.

People often fail to grasp the word of God, and they often fail to connect God's words to people. If the word "humanity" is replaced by another, the term will become less significant and full. Religion has strictly adhered to this issue, so religious commentators' words are logical because all their words have a single root. Humanity is a purity of words, and if it is pure, the thought will be pure. Ideas should not be overloaded and overrun with possibilities, in which case thought will be exposed to dirt and sickness. Thinking has its possibilities and levels, but everything beyond those limits is in the power of God, in the mystery of existence, in the secret of the world. Everyone should understand this in their hearts.

"Oh, Young Men, the Game is Cheap, Laughter is Expensive"

Why is the game cheap and laughter expensive? Is not laughter an attribute of a game itself? Do we not talk about games and laughter together? Abai discussed them separately and identified their value. He said that laughter is closer to humanity; the meaning of a game is lower than that. The game is entertainment, and it is very fast. There are many games, and their purpose is so people cannot just live a life but live a cheerful life. It is well known that discouragement will cause discomfort. Therefore, people need a game. Abai did not deny the game, but he revealed its value compared to that of laughter. Everything is understood through comparison. Abai compared game with laughter and determined that laughter prevails over game. In other words, in the mind of the poet, game and laughter are not terms that go together; instead, the game is one consciousness, and the laughter is another consciousness. Thus, Abai treated them as separate concepts. Game and laughter are general terms, not clarified ideas, and there is nothing bad in pairing them in colloquial speech. Abai, however, clarified these concepts and determined that games are cheap and laughter is expensive. Here, he is speaking particularly to young men. Undoubtedly, if we speak about children, the meaning of their life is a game. In addition, it is appropriate for young men to see a game as cheap because, for them, the meaning of life is not in a game but in living a life. Gambling is an aimless condition that turns adults back into children. For those who have no definite aims, the game is interesting.

Life is not a game, it is a purpose; it is the path you did not follow, the actions you did not take, the fun you did not enjoy; it is your future opportunity. What is expensive is not the game but the actions taken to live a life. Young men have to understand that. The game is cheap, and now you have to analyze what is expensive.

When Abai said "laughter is expensive," he did not mean meaningless laughter or jokes. He meant the significance of laughter in the essence of a person. Each of us can laugh at meaningless things. This is a stupidity that is born from not feeling what laughter is. Oh, if we could experience something that could make us feel the real laughter! This is not a feeling given to everyone. In this case, laughter is expensive. Does this mean, then, that uncontrollable laughter because of a game is not real laughter? That is how Abai understood it. Therefore, the problem is in understanding the difference between what laughter is and is not. Laughter is a manifestation of the sadness of a person who is involved in the suffering and joy of life.

There are genres of tragedy and comedy in culture. In my opinion, a real tragedy transforms into comedy. To express grief with laughter is high comedy. Dante's *Divine Comedy* and Honore de Balzac's *The Human Comedy* are proof of that. In Abai's understanding, laughter requires high consciousness, so laughter is expensive. Similarly, Kazakh people have a saying: "A person's happiness and sadness are the same."

Laughter is one of the treasures of the Creator, and laughter is a dimension of humanity. Usually people say a person is known by their deeds and words: I would add laughter to this list. Laughter is a mirror of humanity. The nature of laughter has a symbol. A person's purpose can be understood through their laughter. The "language" of laughter is the parable and the mystery. One's behavior is lightened with laughter. The character of a person whose soul is rich will have meaningful laughter. Abai came to laughter from this perspective and thus explained to young men that a game is cheap and laughter is expensive.

The second line has the following statement:

Mystery and attractiveness are two different things

Abai's "mystery" and "attractiveness" made me think for a long time. What does he mean? What is the interrelation between these two, and if they have a relation, why does he say that they are two different things?

Indeed, to understand Abai, it is important to start by focusing on the jobs during his time. Therefore, it is necessary to find an answer to the question of what were the values of "mystery" and "attractiveness" during the poet's time.

People say, "*Syrly ayiaqtyng syry ketse de, syny ketpes*" (A mysterious dish's paint can be erased, but its value will not be lost). This is said about a woman who was beautiful and unique in her youth, but who is no longer young and beautiful. In this case, mystery is identified with beauty and attractiveness, an idea I will discuss later. But Abai did not mean that. He meant that the essence of mystery is different from attractiveness in its meaning.

The second meaning of mystery is related to secrets among people, that is, the question of keeping secrets. If Abai discussed this popular meaning of the word, would Abai be Abai? He seems to be discussing a secret or "mystery" that is unknown among the majority. To understand Abai, I must start the discussion from an earlier time than that.

Abai was deeply familiar with Sufism. There are plenty of reasons for that, one of which is the broad application of Yasawi's *Ḥikmet* among Kazakh life. Poetry was recited by memory during Yasawi's time. The philosophical treatise written in Turkic and as poetry is quite understandable for Kazakhs. In this Sufi philosophy, the notion of mystery is important. Along the Syrdarya River in Central Asia, the debates between Sufi scholars have never ceased. Though mystery is a vital philosophical term, it is interesting that it became almost an authentic part of the Kazakh vocabulary. Now, before discussing the etymology of the word, I must try to answer one question. Could the word "mystery" in the

Kazakh language preserve its philosophical content from early Sufism? I find an answer for this question in Abai's poem, where he separates mystery from attractiveness.

Yevgeni Bertels wrote about mystery in Sufism as follows: "The teaching on *sir* (mystery) is one of the darkest questions in Sufism, and the definitions given to it are extremely vague. Apparently, *sir* was initially understood in the literal sense, as a 'secret' that a Sufi keeps in his heart (that is, hiding his knowledge). Subsequently, *sir* began to acquire terminological significance, and it denoted the left side of the heart (*kalb*), which is like a cache into the depths of which even the owner of the heart cannot penetrate. *Sir* is what God hid and what the creature cannot attain."[7]

For those of us (Kazakhs) who were educated in Western-style education, of course, the above meaning of mystery is unclear. But Abai knew what mystery was like. Abai's concept of mystery was similar to the concept of humanity because humanity is connected to the mystery.

In his book *The Rebel*, Albert Camus wrote the following about Marx: "The aims and prophecies are generous and universal, but the doctrine is restrictive, and the reduction of every value to historical terms leads to direct consequences. Marx thought that the ends of history, at least, would prove to be moral and rational. This was his utopia."[8]

The issue I am focusing on in this text is the unity of morality and mind. I will try to find out if this is a problem by asking counter questions. Is morality just intelligence, and conversely, does the mind always have a moral quality? Of course not. Morality cannot be justified by intelligent measurements, nor can intelligence be measured by morals.

There is no place for the third. As Camus stated, "But nothing can discourage the appetite for divinity in the heart of man."[9]

According to Camus, the main failure of Marx's philosophy is that "Marx destroys all transcendence."[10] In Kazakh, transcendence is *tylsym* or *tylsymdylyq*.

Abai put the heart ahead of morals and talked about courage and wisdom. Instead of the concept of morals used in Western European philosophy, Abai

---

[7] Y. E. Bertels, *Sufizm i sufiiskayia literatura* [Sufism and Sufi literature], (Moscow, 1965), p. 260.

[8] A. Camus, *Buntuiushii chelovek* [The Rebel: An Essay on a Man in Revolt], (Moscow, 1990), p. 281.

[9] Camus, p. 232.

[10] Camus, p. 281.

used the concept of humanity. Kazakh's *adamgershilik* (humanness) is an alternative to Western European morality. Humanity is not considered separately from the individual in the Kazakh mentality. Morality is a phenomenon that lives beyond the will of the individual as a form of public consciousness. Consequently, morality is close to the ideological meaning of consciousness. In the Kazakh life, humanity is not beyond an individual. Humanity is manifested by an individual's actions, deeds, and behaviors, and its demonstration is called kindness, justice, courtesy, admiration, and intelligence. Opposite actions are called disobedience, immorality, stubbornness, blindness, and ignorance.

Being cultural is a concept that has come later to Kazakhs, but its meaning has been defined by the above terms. In addition, there is the concept of "a man from the correct mold." Such a person is rich with wisdom, able to keep the secret, and full of courage. The mystery is a person's secret. A person without mystery is a person who is easily blown by the wind. The person who keeps the secret is highly respected among Kazakhs, because the secret is not just a matter of one day; it is a channel of knowledge that stems from the situation, the essence of the case, the line of events. The mystery of humankind is indefinable, but it is revealed due to necessities. The term that we consider now as being cultural is directly related to the problem of secrecy. Mystery is born from sensing. We humans feel one thing, the unity of God and people, and what is beyond that is only hypothetical in the cage of consciousness. To enlighten one's consciousness is to sense the mystery. To deny that this feeling is superior to consciousness is the path to injustice.

Abai was no doubt aware of the meaning of mystery in Sufism, but he did not duplicate it. Instead, he shaped it with new meaning. It would be a compelling idea for a reader to speak about the two terms together—the unity of mystery and attractiveness. Their unity is one of good will, purpose, and aim. However, though they need each other, it is important to distinguish between these two words and to understand that they are indeed two different things.

"No Youth can be a Worthy Parent"

1. *No Way to Rebel*

"No way to rebel" is what Abai said when he was in a joyful mood. The thinker Abai used the word "way" as a Kazakh conception of going beyond the limits. Therefore, it is a statement that something is more than its size; it is about using something in too much abundance. When something crosses over its way, it ceases to be itself and transforms into a different state. For example, the water that overflows its banks (its way) will never become a lake again; it transforms into a puddle, and then it slowly disappears. That is the way things are. Thus, to go beyond the borders means to squander. Why, then, did Abai show his sadness by saying, "No way to rebel." How was he using the word "way"? Have you noticed that one needs energy to go over boundaries? That is what Abai means. The action of going over boundaries is one thing, and the thing that happens after that is another state. Abai was speaking about the first one, the action. Oh, if there were enough energy to go over boundaries! What a delight it is to long for that! It is not hopelessness; it is the knowledge of measuring an action and sensing the power required to go beyond the limits. In summary, it is a prediction of the size of the case: that is, it is about energy.

2. No Energy (Shama) To Live A Full Life

In saying "No energy (*shama*) to live a full life," Abai was describing the energy that makes you cross over boundaries. This is called *shama* (energy's possibility). This concept was probably borrowed from Sanskrit. *Shama* is a qualitative sign of size but not the quality itself. Quality is a property, its own attribute, and it is itself a volatile phenomenon. But it is also a character (an attribute), a fluctuating one. In Kazakh, the word *qubylghan* (fluctuating) describes such a phenomenon. It is close to the Russian word *hameleon* (chameleon). Is not the world's quality in its fluctuating character? There is no doubt that the world is volatile, and when we perceive it, we accept not it but its volatile state. Abai called the perception of this state *shama*. He described attributes of the changeable world in the following phrases: "Sleep and food lose their taste," and "beard and hair lose their color." Are not these signs of a volatile world, for those who understand? You know the world's volatility by your energy's size. If you do not estimate your energy, you will blame not yourself but others. Do you have enough energy to live a joyful life and to enjoy your life?

3. No Slandering the Youth

"No slandering the youth": Abai stated this thought in relation to energy's limits or to *shama*. But what about the concept of slander? This is a thought that has been discussed in all time periods. Youths are always to blame for everything. They are dangerous. Why is this opinion formed about young people? The basic reason is clear. In short, young people are ardent, they do not analyze their actions, and they are as sharp as the sword. But what is bad about that, and why should we fear it? There is a reason to worry.

Young people are opposed to things that are sorted out in practice and transformed into practice. This has two meanings. First, it is common for young people to be against things that have already been established. It is typical for young people to rebel before analyzing the matter at issue. In this case, the results are not going to be good. As time goes by, these young people can go against the stream of the epoch and endanger society. There is also a danger that the number of such young people can be multiplied. They should be criticized on this point but not slandered.

Second, young people have energy and strength, so they are active. This is a serious concern for adults, who are conservative. That is when, as Abai said, young people are slandered. "Slander" is a deliberate ignorance. You are young, so you are guilty. Undoubtedly, this is a negative intention toward young people that does not look at the essence of the case. This is not because of youth's failure; it is because of thoughtless people who are not confident in their own deeds. Such people rely only on their long lives. One can live a long life, but not everyone makes valuable conclusions from it, especially not those people who are ready to blame the youth for problems. Alternatively, some fanatics of strict discipline and strong faith are ready to punish and slander young people who do not follow their initiatives. Such people existed in Abai's time. He saw them and encountered them. He heard their words and said, "No slandering the youth."

Abai did not say his thoughts openly in the line "No slandering the youth," but it is clear that he was raising the question of the generation gap. Though this problem is well discussed in literature and academics, Abai's poem covers the issue in relation to specifics of Kazakh life such as respect for the elderly, respect for one's father and one's grandfather, respect for the elders of the village and the tribe. These are all correct and good. But now we are losing them. However, Abai spoke about this in terms of energy possibilities. If we value things in accordance to our energy, there will be no problems, but if we cannot estimate our strength and we analyze everything from the perspective of respecting elders, we will not be able to analyze things critically, and then we will start slandering youths, not taking into account our own weaknesses. Abai clearly described his point of view on this matter: if you are contrary person, then you will have no value; if you are concerned with the finances of others, then you have no consciousness. What would such people do if not slander youth? Abai discussed this situation.

4. No Respect for Contrary Views

Each thing has its own significance, and the term that identifies it is "value." There is an academic sphere in the West called axiology, which is the science of values. Sometimes we misuse the word "price" instead of "value." Price and value are not the same things. A thing can have both a value and a price. Abai discussed this issue. He did not discuss an individual's value but their price.

Does an individual or humanity have a price? Price is an economic and legal concept, whereas value is a philosophical concept. If one cannot understand the price of something, one can understand it through its value. If price is applied to a product, value is applied to a person. We ask about the price of things in the market. We talk about the value of a person in relation to their qualities. Abai used the word "value" in this way.

Abai mentions the word "no" in his poem "There is no place for the disappearing of birth and death." And in his three-versed poem called "No youth to be a worthy parent," he used the word nine times. One could regard that as a poetic approach, but Abai used the word "no" in a true philosophical sense. Let me try to prove my thought. For example, in the first lines, he used the phrase "no mother, no child." He did not use "no" to mean a lack, or in its absolute meaning; he used it as the measure and strength of possibilities. When he said, "no way, no strength," in the second verse, he was not totally denying strength but was speaking of its amount. In the last verse, when he said, "no price, no slander, no consciousness," he was referring to making full the price, slander, and consciousness.

****

The idea of this poem was related to the family. The family was in crisis. Abai was telling the truth. A family cannot exist outside of community, society, and country. The family has significance at the community, society, and country levels because children are the future of the present life. That is why Kazakh people say, "*ul erzhetti, qiz boizhetti*" (a baby boy and a baby girl are grown-up). Communities were interested in the early adulthood of boys. Thus, there is a saying, "*on ushte otau yiesi*" (the head of a family is thirteen years old). From today's perspective, early youth marriage might seem weird, but in reality, this situation was a natural-historical necessity. It had two reasons: first, the need for early adulthood in a youth's development, and second, the need for population growth, which was a demographic need. At those times, many human deaths were caused by accidents and wars; therefore, the number of men was important. Hence, the family had to compensate for the needs of the community. But Abai did not raise this issue; instead, he was concerned about the family's attitude to the country, and he expressed his depression. He made it clear that two things were lacking in the country. One of these was that "no youth can be a worthy parent"; the problem was with parents. Were parents ready to bring up children? What kind of training should they have? How should they prepare? This was the problem. What was parents' responsibility to the country? In order to be responsible for this, the country had to have integrity. There was no integrity among the people, because the Kazakh people had been left without self-government due to the colonial system. If the purpose of parenthood or family was to educate citizens, such a demand did not exist in the Kazakh society.

The colonial administration did not need citizens from Kazakh families, but they did need interpreters and lawyers who could perform its ideology. Frankly speaking, those who were educated among the Kazakh people were needed to keep people under the colonial regime. In this situation, both the parents and the family were in crisis.

The poet recognized the situation and raised the issue, but he did not suggest a solution, and he did not aim to, probably because he did not know a way out of the situation. The poet accurately diagnosed the disease, and that was a help to healers.

In order to get rid of a disease, it first has to be identified.

"If God's Wills It, One has No Choice"

This is the line from Abai's poem that starts with the words "My soul is suffering." Fate is an often-used word, but its essence is not defined. The discussions about fate began when contemporary religions were not yet formed. For Turkic-speaking people, including Kazakhs, the idea of fate existed before the arrival of Islam. The idea that fate is given by Tangri was present in Kul Tigin's inscription. At those times in the Turkic world, fate was supposed to be given by Tangri; then in Islam, it was thought to be given by God. This means that fate is related to the Creator: that is, it is a substance of ontological significance beyond human consciousness and will. What happens if this issue is addressed from such a perspective? Only a few philosophers did not discuss the topic of fate; a few did not make assumptions and give their opinions; most wrote many books and invented diverse conceptions, one of which is fatalism. The intelligentsia is aware of fate.

The matter of fate was common for every nation's consciousness and life. Fate is a well-established concept in the Kazakh language. If we look at that concept, the fate of the Kazakh people is largely related to grief, to a deadlock with no solution; in short, it is used in a negative sense. The word "happiness" is often used for good deeds and kindness. Abai also used this negative sense of fate in this poem:

My soul is suffering
Without you
I have no strength
It is the insidious fate.

According to the poet, evil is from destiny. The question is, why is destiny inclined to be evil? Why is fate not a source of good?

I think that we Kazakhs are not familiar with the positive side of fate, because we do not feel it and because we take good things for granted. For example, we are not surprised at the sunrise and sunset; we do not feel excited when we see them, because it is a natural sight, one we do not accept as fate. However, if the order were changed a little, we would be frightened and scared and say that this was fate. If so, then one can assume that fate is the Creator's warning to His servant. Does relentless consciousness need a fate, then? Is it not the power of destiny to make a person resentful? Everything in the world, including the phenomena that seem to cause each other, is the Creator's command. If this order is broken, fate appears and warns people. But though the Creator sends fate, it is the people who call for it and need it. Is it possible that fate is the Creator's punishment for humans' ignorance? Fate is a punishment; I think that is right.

Understanding destiny is a challenge for human consciousness. Some of us call as fate things that are not fate. The results of our actions are caused by our ignorance, and we call this fate. However, destiny is the Creator's reflection. It is not the direct action of humans but the way they are compacted. Fate comes in a form of pure consciousness and puts limits on a people's minds and wills. Abai said, "A man has no choice if it is God's will." If fate follows you, there is no escape from it. The question is why destiny would choose some people. Destiny also needs height. It is going to choose the noblest people with the highest minds because destiny is the power of revelation, the essence of the times. The times will follow destiny's lead, and the times' consciousness will be defined as fate. When we speak about life, we usually say the fate of history, but in fact, fate is identified as the reason first, and then it becomes a historical phenomenon.

"But Now I Am Calling You to Me, Oh Hero, Death"

When Abai translated the poem "Prisoner Knight" by Mikhail Lermontov into Kazakh, he translated it as "*Tutqindaghi batyr*" (A captured hero). Both the original and the translation contain five verses. The meaning of the poem in translation is delivered fully. Those who have read Abai's translations may be surprised to learn that he was fluent in Russian. For example, the line "By a porthole I sit in my prison" is translated excellently into Kazakh as follows: *Qaranghi ui terezesi - tutqyn orny* (The window of a dark house is a prisoner's place). There is no word-for-word literal translation; the translation is based on the essence of the idea. Abai's translation is no different from the original.

All the words and notions in Kazakh are understandable: For example, Lermontov said, "On my dry lips, I have not any prayers." And Abai said, "*Tauba zhoq, dugha da zhoq, tentek boida*" (No repentance, no prayer in a rebelling soul), which is a pure Kazakh concept.

In the fifth and last verse, Abai demonstrated himself perfectly. In my opinion, he went deeper and reasoned about the meaning of heroism. No warrior sorrows for his captivity; he is accustomed to his fate. As Abai said:

> *Zhuirik uaqyt sharshatpai qoimas aqyr*
> (Going fast will make you tired in the end)
> *Denemdi sauyit-saiman qysyp zhatyr.*
> (My armor is compressing my body.)
> *Buryn seni bireuge kop zhumsap edim*
> (Often have I sent you to others)
> *Endi ozime shaqyrdym azhal batyr.*
> (But now I am calling you to me, oh hero death.)

The phrase *Azhal batyr* (hero death) is a novelty of Abai's. There is no such phrase in Lermontov's version. But if Abai did not say it like that, then the poem in Kazakh would be unclear, and Abai expressed his thoughts as clearly as he could. *Batyr* is the one who kills dispassionately, and now it is his turn. If his bravery is true, then he must not show fear in the battle with "hero death." He must meet death bravely. This is heroic. This is not a hero who is afraid of death. One needs deaf courage to call for death. Abai used the notion of "hero death" to clearly express that idea.

"Is There a Sweet Whose Taste Never Spoils?"

Nothing in the world eternal. We all know that. Many other philosophers talked about that before Abai. Perhaps, the thought is so valuable not because it was discussed but because of why it was discussed. This is one aspect of the topic. Another aspect is that the thought has its own lifetime, its own birth, growth, and adulthood. An adult thought needs to be heard by one who is adult enough to understand it. What Abai said is a mature idea. It is hard to make a mature idea comprehensible to young people in their twenties because they have not yet tasted the spoiled sweet. If they have not yet tasted the sweets of life fully, how can they know the spoiled taste of such sweets. They do not know what a sweet is in life. Those who are mature and who have tackled their own assumptions, especially those who have a sense of repentance, can understand all of this. In the first line of this verse, Abai said, "The insidious world is plundering, do you have anything to do with it?" Only a person who is disturbed by the fact that the world is insidious, who has started to sense its essence, could say such words. How can a life be insidious for the one who regards life as celebrations and parties? Why, then, is this world insidious? Because it is unstable, floating, and it does not leave people anything.

The world robs people. It is a pirate. What does it rob from us? Abai said it would take your strength and color: "The strength will leave you, every single step will be so hard to take, and your cheerful face will lose its color as a tree without leaves." That is why Abai said the following about life: "Its future is hope, its past is regret and a life of mischief." People open the door of life with hope, but what is the benefit of life? When someone reaches an exit door, they realize the deceit of life, and their regretful conscience burns their heart. At this point, I would like to focus on Abai's definition of "regret."

Abai's "regret" is not the regret of a person who is sorry for their ignorance and says, "Oh, what a pity, I wish I had not done that." Abai regarded regret in its wider meaning. Regret, here, is given as a rule of law. It is a regret that no one can escape; not a single soul can skip it; all will experience it. Both the philosopher with deep thoughts and the average person will face it. The question is how this regret is reflected, how one values it, and how one understands it. Alternatively, how do people identify it? This is the only problem. There is no person who does not know that the world is a life of mischief and regret. Religion is based on this issue. In Islam, there is a tradition of *iman* (true faith), whereas in Christianity it comes as purification from sins. Religion is a way of overcoming the perverted consciousness, the methods used to eradicate it; otherwise, it would be painful to pass from life. The key to the Buddhist doctrine of "Samsara cycles" and the Pythagorean theory that life shifts from one to one are very similar to the law that the meaning of life, which destroys the consciousness of life, is in death. While reading Abai's poem, one gains the clear idea that the concept of death is destroyed and its meaning is only in life. Hence, the death of a person does not happen on one day; it seems that a person dies gradually. Abai clearly defined the criteria:

The insidious world is plundering, do you have anything to do with it?
Do you still have that power and color?

Yes, it is important to think about death while you are alive. There is no meaning in describing the final day as a death. Life and death are not two ends of one thing; they are one thing. They divided only with the purpose of making them easier to understand; otherwise, both of them have one meaning. The intrigues of this insidious life lie in the fact that it is a power that leads us to live as a deceitful Satan. We usually say that we need to live life to receive joy from it, but having read this poem, I think that the joy of life is something that leads us to death and that this is a mythical consciousness. Therefore, the meaning of life is in its mythical essence. Myth is defined by death.

Abai used the following epithets about life in this poem: insidious life, deceitful life, and violent life. Thus, how should one categorize Abai's poem? Should it be regarded as pessimism or optimism?

I would say, neither. Pessimism and optimism are a dualism of philosophical meaning, that is, one needs the other. They are not found as separate concepts in Abai's works; therefore, they cannot be applied to Abai's poems. Abai's "insidious life" is neither pessimism nor optimism but a secret of a mysterious life. Although the truth is about to be told, it encounters many barriers, and the most difficult among them is lust, the joy of life.

Do not utter a word if it is not from your heart
The tongue is accustomed to lust's insidious behavior
The tongue has no bones, the lips have no borders
They will hide the face of the truth like a veil

So the truth about life will never be revealed, to say nothing about the world. Mysterious world, mysterious life, and there is a person who has a passion to learn its secrets.

"The Vast Kazakh Steppe is the Cradle of its Children"

Mikhail Lermontov translated Friedrich von Schiller's "*Das kind in der Wiege.*" Then Abai translated Lermontov's version into Kazakh. People like Schiller, Lermontov, and Abai were involved in a branch of science called the philosophy of life. The essence of all things in the world is in human life. In order to survive, people are exposed to uncontrolled actions and deeds, and they even cause threats to life itself. However, this issue has not yet been revealed in the child's cradle. It begins with maturity. Schiller's poem is about this. Let us compare two lines:

A baby is happy!
(Schastliv rebenok!)
And his cradle is vast enough for him
(I v lyuilke prostorno emu)
But as soon as gets mature
(No dai vremyia sdelat'syia muzhem)
The world will seem too narrow for him
(I tesen pokazhetsyia mir)[11]

The vast steppe is the sole cradle for a child
(Keng zhailau zhalghyz besik zhas balagha)
Can a man under the protection of God be starving?
(Alla asyraghan pendesi ash bola ma?)
When you are mature, the whole world will be too narrow for you
(Erzhetken song simaising keng duniege)
You will be longing for quietness and dwelling
(Tynyshtyq pen zar bolarsyng baspanagha)

Who is happy when this is the case: the child or the adult? Apparently, the notion of happiness was not raised as a problem. Moreover, Abai did not use the word "happiness." I do not know how Schiller described it, but Lermontov said, "Life will seem too narrow for him." There is no tragedy here. It is not dangerous if a person sees the world as too narrow because they have a passion for imagination and dreams and a craving for knowledge. The problem is in the minds and actions of such a person. Abai, however, put this openly. He said, "You will be longing for quietness and dwelling." What a tragedy it is that a man could have enough space in the cradle but be unable to find enough space in the whole world. Apparently, this is a matter of a person's essence. A strength that is unrevealed during childhood is revealed in adulthood and empowers the adult with extra energy. Thus, some adults feel the world is narrow and live their life in anxiety. That is how Abai transformed the statement, which Kazakhs understand. The need for repentance is also here. There is no such thing as repentance in Russian people's worldview, so when Lermontov said, "Life will

---

[11] M. Lermontov, Vol. 1, p. 179

seem too narrow for him," he was not talking about the consciousness of repentance.

"Those Who Love the World
Do Not Feel the Same about Judgment Day"

Abai was neither pious nor a Sufi. A pious person will be separate from the world's affairs, and they will be on the path of pure religion. Though Abai was not religious, he was immersed in the piety of thoughts. In his poems, the phrase "dirt of the worlds" is related to the virtue of this thought. It is hard to talk about humanity unless you wash away the dirt of the world from your essence. Similarly, to be "friends with the world" is also a matter of worldly desires. He said the situation of such people will not be the same on the judgment day and their love for this and that world is not the same. The one who is passionately in love with this world will forget the judgment day, which means that his *iman* (faith) is not complete. Is the incompleteness of one's *iman* tested by the Creator only on the Day of Judgment? The answer is no. If Abai approached this issue from that perspective, he would not be Abai. People need a fullness of *iman* in this world. There is another question which comes with being friends with and passionate for the world. Is this existence the truth of life? Presumably, there must be dimensions of friendship with this world in order to be fully human. But to love the world passionately is not a sign of humanity. Abai was obviously talking about the existence of two worlds. One is a false world, and the other is eternal life. He did not deny either of them, but he also did not love either of them passionately. The reality of piety dishonors this world, and those who are "devoted to this world" forget eternal life.

Abai was in search of consciousness, which could be common for both worlds.

"You are a Spouse Sent to Me by Tangri"

The world is mysterious and full of secrets. But two geniuses of two nations came to one conclusion on one issue. It was on the concept of God. Abai translated fragments from the novel *Eugene Onegin* by Alexander Pushkin, a great Russian poet, who became his beloved pen friend. He began his translation of Tatiana's letter as follows: "You were a spouse sent to me by Tangri." Why did Abai say Tangri instead of God or God? Both Pushkin's and Abai's words are understandable. Tatiana cannot say God, because she is Christian. This means Abai had to use a concept that could be common for both a Russian girl and a Kazakh girl—that concept is Tangri. Russian and Turkic people, particularly

Kipchaks, had common ideas, such as Tangri, due to their similar and intersecting historical situations in the past. Abai's genius is that he was able to put historical agreement in his picture of Tatiana. Apparently, wise people utter thoughts not only with their minds but also with their own *natural genius*. However, to discover the essence of that genius, to recognize it, is the work of others. When Abai said something, he said it with its exact meaning. Presumably, this is what is called wisdom.

The concept of the Creator has two meanings in Kazakh. One is Tangri, and the other is God. The first Kazakh concept would suit Tatiana. To use the word "God" would misconstrue the nature of the case, the content of the word, and it would make it seem as if the translator did not care about the content of the letter. Abai was not a poet who used words simply; he was one who made the matter clear. Let me give you one argument for this statement. Before accepting Islam, Turks believed that the sender of fate was Tangri. I found that idea in the works of the Turkic thinker Yollug Tigin. Thus, when Abai has Tatiana use the word "Tangri," he means the scripts of fate. He wanted to express the idea that going against fate is something unacceptable, and therefore, he made the young girl write a letter to the arrogant Eugene and offer him her heart. Eugene was supposed to be Tatiana's spouse, according to her fate. But it never happened. As a result, Tatiana did not have a real life, only an existence, because love was dead. What was left for her after that was only to exist, not to live. Fate is to live in harmony with the universe. This is the truth. The truth beyond fate is the truth that does not make a person a human but makes them just exist in a meaningless life. Abai said desperately, "Even the cattle has such soul and flesh." Indeed, what happened to Tatiana's and Eugene's lives after the collapse of their fates? According to Pushkin, their lives became meaningless.

The content of life is destiny, and the one who gives that destiny is Tangri. Abai figuratively expressed this thought through Tatiana's words.

"A Pure Soul Left the World with No Paint"

These are the thirteenth and fourteenth lines of the poem "Abish, who passed yesterday," which is devoted to the death of Abai's most beloved son.

It is quite understandable that Abai grieved because of his most beloved son, because it is not the natural order. Seeing the death of a father is a matter of justice; when the situation is different, it is a disruption of nature. Abai was a man made up of flesh and soul, and his son's sudden death was a tragic grief for him. Abai went into a deep depression because of his son's death. But the problem I am concerned about here is not a father's lament for his son but Abai's lament for Abish.

Both are historical figures. What is hard for the thinker Abai about his son's death is Abdrahman's (Abish's) pure soul. The concept of pure soul is widely used among Kazakhs. We do not always understand its meaning correctly and use it to describe people's behavior. Most of the time, we do not pay close attention to what it really means. Abai described a "pure soul" as "a soul with no paint." What happens to the original color of the heart that has been painted? That makes us think that a pure soul can have paint. Does this imply that paint is used to conceal the truth and to turn to a different conception? What happens to the original color of the heart that has been painted? Where does the color of the paint go? There is nothing in the world that has no color. So why do we change that first color and put paint on it?

To put on paint is to hide, change, and display the truth for some reason. When Abai says a "pure soul with no paint," he means initial purity. The purity of Abish's soul does not require any paint; this is a quality he inherited from his parents. Abish preserved it; he did not put paint on his heart; he did not need to look different from his nature. That is what makes Abai sad. A precious substance does not need others substances and difference. A precious thing is noticeable itself; it is the law of nature. However, the world does not consist of only precious elements; everything is mixed up in life. Longing for preciousness, missing a person, is respecting humanity. I think that Abai's idea of a pure soul should have been in that direction.

Abai was deeply saddened by Abdrahman's death. Although this is generally understandable, it could have seemed strange that Abai, as a thinker, was deeply immersed in the deepest thoughts about life and death, the body and the soul, and was engaged in leaving his thoughts on paper. A reader may think that Abai was not the only father whose son had died and that it is a common occurrence. However, the issue is in Abai's phrase "a pure soul left the world with no paint."

What makes Abai sad is that Abish did not behave like a child and did not make his father sad with thoughtless actions. The issue would be different if Abai was disappointed with some of his son's deeds. Abish was not the type of son who disappointed his father. All his behavior enriched his father. *Abai saw himself in Abish.* He foresaw the future perspectives. He thought he could continue his life through Abish. That is in his second poem devoted to Abish:

> *He is the beginning of a new year*
> *And I was the end of passing epoch*

There is no doubt that a child who does not disappoint his father is everyone's dream. Indeed, for Abai, Abish was really a dream. That is why Abai's sadness was not just a father's frustration; it was bigger than that. Abish was not just a father's son but a representative of a generation, one that was bigger than him. The sadness, the burden of his death is in this. Whatever Abai wrote, one could see his prints in the poem, and in the last lines of his poem devoted to the death of his son, he gave the following conclusion:

> There is no way to escape a fate
> Except to be patient

There is no way to escape destiny. What kind of power is fate, which makes you bow your head? Fate is not God. What powerful strength is it? Who knows the secrets of this destiny that leaves you no choice, that empties your consciousness and make you accept it? Fate is a mystery. Though its power is unknown to people, it must have its own logic. Thus, there is a consciousness, the name of which is patience. There is no choice except to be patient in the face of destiny. Abai also understood that and was patient, thinking that Abdrahman's death was destiny. Therefore, patience is the consciousness that comes to life after death and that does not extinguish the flame of hope. This is necessary. Otherwise, all things would lose their significance, concepts would become incomprehensible, and thoughts would encounter roadblocks. In this context, the concepts of fate and patience need each other.

Having patience and calmness does not mean being submissive to one's fate; it means having a living consciousness. Adults should take care not to be saddened by the past, by the word "patience," but to be strong in hardships and to not forget their future. Abai was wounded in his heart and was grieving, but he stayed strong by saying, "There is no way to escape fate except to be patient." This is accepting fate, not submitting to it. One can understand destiny and one can accept it. Abai understood the destiny, but he did not accept it; he just demonstrated patience.

"All Without Grief are Rebellious"

On the third line of the third verse of the four-versed poem that begins with the words "My heart has 40 patches," Abai stated that "Everyone without grief is rebellious." Since this thought is very deep, I chose that line as the title for this chapter.

Abai wrote a lot about grief. The sober reader is aware of the poet's main idea: the wise, intelligent person will not be without grief.

Here, I will not discuss common depression. Grief is a sign of thought; grief is the name of the perfect conscience. Undoubtedly, grief is sadness, and it does not bring joy and happiness. Those who say live a happy and joyful life are rebellious people because they do not want to admit that they are grieving, or they do not even notice what grief is. Yes, it is possible to live like that. Not everyone needs to grieve. Having happiness and contentment in life are, of course, a goal and an aim. Though Abai talks about people in general, the main character in his poetry is himself. He said, "Everyone without grief is rebellious; they give no benefit to us." What would a rebel with no grief do, even if they understood Abai? They give no benefit to Abai. Then what does a poet need? Neither Abai nor I know. Unfortunately, people who are not satisfied, who are depressed, who are isolated and alone, are calm. They miss the rebellious state of those who have no grief, even though they understand that there is no meaning in that state. Abai suffered daily, unable to escape his grief. Who put this sadness on him? What is interesting in it for the poet? Why is life not always joyful, why is it abusive? The poet described this situation as follows:

> *My heart has 40 patches*
> *Because of an abusive world.*
> *How can it survive*
> *When it has been disappointed so many times?*

The world is abusive. Abai, who stated this, was dominated by his grief, and he said that those who think the world is full of joy and who have no grief are rebellious. This makes one wonder why all people do not feel that the world is abusive. There are several answers to this. It is obvious that anyone can feel the abusiveness of the world, but no one can express it like Abai. Some people feel that the world is abusive, but they never think about it again. There is a third group of people who do not consider life abusive at all. This is the group that Abai called rebellious.

However, as Abai said, people cannot avoid being disappointed. There are many things in life that disappoint people. And each of these disappointments adds a new patch on one's heart. If we pay attention, we can notice that some people's hearts do not have patches, even if they are disappointed, because they do not suffer. Those are people with no grief; they are similar to children who are still growing up.

Children are mistaken every minute, and their frustration remains the same, but they do not grieve. Mistakes are common things for children; they grow up by gaining experience. There are some adults who feel no grief, like children. They are careless people. Careless people are varmints. The careless rebellious people have a very vulgar understanding of the world. These are people who do not analyze things deeply, who are happy with their possessions; their sorrow is about their belongings. Abai's sadness is the consciousness that appeared because of his thoughts about the world and its essence. As soon as a person starts thinking about it, they realize there is no meaning to life and they feel depressed. If they are captured in such thoughts, they become estranged from life and "carry heavy thoughts." Such thinking would certainly bring someone grief.

Grief's nature originates from justice. If a person understands justice and lives a righteous life, they will soon be disappointed by many things. This is because the path of justice is hard. People who care about justice will encounter many limitations to living in a society.

In every time period, justice has been accompanied by injustice. In most cases, justice and injustice come in turns. Therefore, it is understandable why Abai said:

> *Some people have passed from life*
> *Some of them were my enemies*
> *Some of them were my beloved ones*
> *Some of them had conflicts and quarrels*
> *But in the end, I am all alone with no support*

The problem is the difficulty of identifying and determining the degree of justice and injustice. It is impossible to avoid abuse in times when the degree of justice and injustice is not identified. This problem that Abai raised is common for all epochs. All philosophers and wise people spend their lives in struggle with their epoch. A philosopher is the one who seeks the cause of everything and predicts the future. Therefore, their words do not always coincide with the consciousness of the epoch. This discrepancy was in Abai's thoughts, which made him grieve:

> *Oh, the one who has grief in their heart*
> *Come to my side*
> *Measure the value*
> *Of the soul that is always searching.*

Thus, Abai first criticizes, "Everyone without grief is rebellious." Then he shows respect to grieving people with the words "Oh, the one who has grief in their heart, Come to my side." It makes one think.

"Many are Deceived by This World"

To be deceived by this world is a human weakness. Everyone is subjected to being under the control of life. In the struggle for survival, a person takes various actions and accepts many challenges, and the consequences can be both positive and negative. A person who becomes captured by daily routines will have a sickness of the soul. That is why Abai said that such people often fail. But then, he also said:

Can you say "passed from life" about the person
Who left immortal statements behind?

Those who want to demonstrate Abai's wisdom cite these two lines, not citing the whole verse. The previous two lines are:

Many people are deceived by the world
Deceived and often fail

It may seem like these two lines do not contain deep thoughts. But in my opinion, we just cannot understand the deepness of his thoughts.

The verse has only one problem: the person who will leave statements behind is not an angel but a mere human. If they have not been deceived by the world, if they have not had a sickness of the soul, then how can they leave an immortal statement? Only a person who has experienced tragedy and sickness will be able to leave an eternal statement. The careless person is an ignorant person. Life is not a pleasure but a deep perplexity, agony, and sorrow. The soul who can leave immortal words is, of course, a philosopher. This is the principle that can be applied to people like Abai. This is the case, but there is a big problem.

When I discussed the first verse, I mentioned the lines "Man dies, but not his nature." However, today we do not have immortals, I mean, those who will leave immortal words. Not everyone is like Abai. Then who is mortal and who is immortal?

First, the human flesh (nature) is mortal, and the soul is immortal. We all have a soul. When a soul leaves the flesh, flesh and soul are separated. The soul changes into its eternal form and becomes a mystery, one with its own secrets. This is a common law for people. That is why Abai said that a person's nature does not die.

Second, with the words "Can you say 'passed from life' about the person," Abai emphasized that it is philosophers who leave words after themselves. Therefore, the cases of one's soul and one's word are different. When people say a soul is eternal, they do not know anything more meaningful than that. The only truth they know is that a soul is eternal. They do not go any further than that. However, with one's words, the situation is different. Words are comprehensible, they have meaning and significance. When I say that words are comprehensible, I mean that people can understand them. Of course, concepts have their own possibilities that will be revealed according to the epoch's characteristic. Hence, a person's words live on, so how can that person be regarded as dead? In this context, the fourth line of Abai's verse ends with a question mark: *Who left immortal statements behind?*

"They Who Give Cause for Grief Will Themselves Judge"

This discussion is about "My secret is not easy, young men." The following explanation for this song was published in 1977 in a two-volume work by Ghylym publishing house:

> The text of the poem came from manuscripts from 1909 and 1957 and from the archives of Murseyit Bikeuly. The translation of the poem "I do not want the world to know" consists of sixteen lines in both Lermontov's and Abai's versions. The content of the translation is very close to original.[12]

I add this explanation of Lermontov's poem: It is written on one piece of paper with the poem "Do not laugh at my prophetic anguish," which is presumably dated 1837 in content. It was first published in 1845, after Lermontov's death, with two lines censored:

> *Let me be punished by he,*
> *Who created my torments.*[13]

---

[12] *Abai Qunanbayev*, Vol. 2, (Almaty: Ghylym, 1977), p. 255.

[13] M. Lermontov, *Khudozhetsvennaya literatura*, Vol. 1, (Moscow, 1975), p. 521.

Hence, Abai had access to the full poem without any lines omitted. But this part of the poem is noteworthy:

> *If I have behaved badly or am guilty*
> *The one who sends grief will judge.*

These are the lines, which were omitted by censorship, that made Abai think, and he recited his thoughts exactly as Lermontov did. It is difficult to say that this is a translation. This verse by Abai, who understood Lermontov's thoughts so deeply, can be equated to his own poems. That is why it is quite possible to say that Kazakhs read Lermontov's poem in its authentic version. Lermontov's version:

> *I do not want the world to know*
> *My mysterious story*
> *How I loved, for what I suffered-*
> *Only God and my conscience will judge me!*

Abai's translation:

> *My secret is not easy, young men*
> *It is not for everyone, so stay away!*
> *What I loved and what I suffered from in life*
> *Should be judged only by my conscience and God!*

No single word of Lermontov's has been omitted by Abai; they are all expressed fully in translation. Bilingual people will understand this clearly. My attention was caught by Lermontov's phrase: "Only God and my conscience will judge me!" The translation of God and conscience is *Ar men bir-aq qudai*. The issue of God is clear. The problem is with "conscience." Apparently, the interest in this Russian poet's poem was the issue of conscience. What is conscience, then? How do the two poets use it? Looking at this term from an academic standpoint, its meaning is unclear, because science has a meta concept of morality. In addition, the two poets used this concept in its highest meaning. There is no other absolute concept than God, and the concept of conscience stays equal with it. Therefore, conscience is also an absolute concept. However, conscience is about the nature of each individual, it is one's essence. It is impossible to determine anyone's identity without the concept of conscience. Does this mean that everyone's conscience is his or her consciousness or that their intentions are demonstrated through their actions and behavior? Rather, it is probably a matter of clarification about the various things, the mistakes that are made, and the grief that comes after understanding them. Thus, the question of conscience is related to a person's free will, regardless of God. The Creator is the giver of free will, and the user of this free will is a human being, but the judge of a person's path is their conscience.

A person should not dare to commit actions that will weigh heavy on their conscience. Therefore, a person needs to know and feel the boundaries of their life. Is it possible to demand something from a human being that is difficult for a person's mind and feelings to deal with? Who knows? Maybe it is necessary to make such demands; maybe it is too much.

Here, the heart comes to help. Lermontov:

My heart will open its feelings to them,
And will ask only for their sympathy;
Let me be punished by he
Who created my torments.

Abai understood this correctly and translated it as follows:

My heart will pray to both
It will beg, saying mercy and justice are so hard;
If I have behaved badly or am guilty
The one who sends grief will judge.

The heart prays to God and conscience and asks them to forgive. The two poets have the same thoughts concerning this question, and this continues to be so throughout the verse. So what does the heart ask from God and conscience? Abai said, "Mercy and justice are so hard." Here is a global issue. For the question of why the poets are grieving, the answer is, for their hearts' purity. Abai said this clearly. But Lermontov concluded, "My heart will open its feelings to them." Abai clarified this idea. He added another thought on the third line: "If I have behaved badly or am guilty." In the third line, Lermontov said, "Let me be punished by him." On the fourth line, both poets said, "The one who sends grief will judge."

So, here is the question: Who is the sender? It is the Creator. But why does He send grief? Think about it. Most likely, it is done to stop someone's careless nature. How many people have experienced grief to save their conscience? And those griefs were created by their sender (as a test). Therefore, it is fair that He is also the one who judges.

"Let its Edges be Smooth and Round"

This is the fourth line of the first verse of the poem that begins with the words "The poem is the king and the judge of words." What catches one's attention are the words "smooth" and "round."

According to the philosopher and polymath Ibn Tufail, the most harmonious, advanced combination among geometric shapes is the oval; it does not have any edges, and it is smooth. However, smoothness is not just a concept of smoothness; it can also be used to describe an oval. Abai used the word "smoothness" in this sense. The smoothness of an oval is the best expression of *harmony and artistry*. In other words, it is the advanced form. Abai proposed this best form of harmony and art as the meter of a poem. The verse must not have pauses, so it requires not just the meaning of words but also the meaning of rhymes. The true poem has a meaning and a rhyme, but they are never separated from each other. If they are divided, the poem is not a poem anymore, and that is the difference between a poet and one who is only in search of rhymes. If we look for the geometric figure in a verse, the figure corresponding to the verse is an oval, because its surroundings are both inwardly and outwardly harmonious. The harmony of the things in this world can come from the harmony itself or from the will of the Creator; regardless, it is a figure, which is identified irrespective of human will. Kazakhs use phrases such as "oval earth," "oval head" and "paid great attention to things with an oval figure."

It is known that each thing tries to preserve its own essence, and for that, it searches for a shape that coincides with it. Hence, all things are eager to find advanced shapes, but all are not successful in finding those shapes; they therefore remain in other shapes. Because the urge to search is based on necessity, the search for a shape will never cease. The oval, as a geometric figure, is a symbol of *infinity and limitation*. It has points in the body, but those points lead to both infinity and limitation. If one looks for limitations, one finds numerous triangles in the oval. Triangles mean stamina and firmness. A triangular figure has a very strong, durable property. In addition, there are rectangles in the oval, but after being multiplied, they are changed to triangles, so the rectangle is a geometric figure representing *instability and everlasting* change. People usually rely on the four corners and say west-east-north-south; they do not think that everything is conditional. Since the four corners of the globe are not the basis of the globe, it may change and it is likely to be western-eastern, southern-northern. Since a rectangle is not the basis of an oval, it can change and west can become east, south can become north. But this will not make the oval lose its oval attributes, since the triangular combinations will preserve its oval attributes. In this context,

142

it is understandable that climate and poles change. It would be possible for the earth to live in the form of a globe and change its own corporeal properties, but the stability of its substance would not change.

"The Verse and Hadith are the Beginning of the Word"

Abai valued the poem as the king of words and understood the poem as the beginning of words, since an ayah (verse in the Quran) is a consciousness about the beauty of the world. Abai's phrase "The ayah and the hadith are the beginning of the word" was not said accidentally. The Ayah is the beginning of the word. It is not an invention of humans but a revelation sent in the form of a poem to the Prophet Mohammed. The Ayah is a testimony to Muhammad of his coming prophethood. He declared to the public, "I was sent a revelation from the Creator through ayahs." Those Ayahs were compiled into the Quran. Here, one needs to pay attention to the religious legend about the Quran, which is a religious legend about the Prophet's illiteracy.

Indeed, Muhammad was illiterate. The word "illiterate" is often used to refer to uneducated people. This is an understanding that is used in casual situations. But the case is more complicated than that. Education is usually perceived through learning letters, that is, through the educational system. This is the traditional way. However, there have been times when a person became educated without knowing letters. Only a few people in the history of humankind have been known to become educated without knowing letters. One such person was the Prophet Muhammad. The prophet Jesus also had such knowledge. When the angel commanded Muhammad to recite, Muhammad did not read written letters sent by God; he recited them from memory. As Abai said, "God's word is without letters and without voice." Thus, the ayah remained in the Prophet's memory.

The ayah is the word of God. It is "without letters and without voice." The Ayah is the consciousness that was sent to the Prophet. Later it turned into letters and sounds and became a Quran. The incomprehensibility of the ayah is a sensible issue. Understanding the Creator's "word" is controversial. Language is the treasure of humankind: we cognize it, know it, and use it for our very lives. The ayah is a different "language." It is the Creator's language. It does not have letters. To put it in academic words about energy, the ayah is the reflection of the world energy system. Some people on the planet may well have the power to produce, store, and operate electricity. Plato said, "The essence of human education is to remember." He believed that the knowledge we have learned, has already been known from the beginning, and it comes to human beings as innate information. Modern science and education have a paradigmatic consciousness of "principles," a method that can be used to identify issues that have not yet been discovered. Scholars define the direction through the principles. The direction is a guide. The recognition and selection of the path are based on these ayahs. The ayah, as the Creator's consciousness, was sent to people other than Muhammad as well, but it was misguided in its essence.

The ayahs were always in the same direction as the compass, but there were attempts to change their direction. Therefore, it is understandable why the ayahs were sent repeatedly. This phenomenon will not stop. "Both God and his words are true," Abai said in his poem "Epochs, lifestyles are subject to change daily, there was a messenger for each epoch." The reason why the messengers were sent in a time-based manner is that time is not stable, and there is nothing on the earth that is eternal. Sustainability, eternity are the characteristics specific to the Creator or to a prophet. For humans, finding stability is an unrealizable truth, one that comes true only in dreams.

According to the Islamic worldview, Muhammad is the last prophet. Certainly, using ayahs for clarity and for proof of the word of God does not imply intellect or logic. Would that not cause immediate suspicion in Muhammad's case? It was necessary to speak in such a way that any suspicion would be completely dissipated and strengthened by confidence. The most important proof of this is the fact that the ayahs were sent to Muhammad. However, I think that as time goes by, there will be a need for verses to be sent again, and there will be no barriers to that. This is a topic of discussion for people with specialized education, and it is a different topic than I am discussing here. Indeed, Abai said, "The ayah and hadith are the beginning of the word." To address the question of why the ayah is the beginning of the word, one should pay attention to three things. First, as Abai said, the ayah is the beginning of the word but not the word itself. Words are a human being's quality. The "word" of God is the ayah. Prophets are the ones who turn ayahs into human words. In fact, a prophet is a unique person who can change the Creator's "word" (ayah) into human words. Transformation of the Creator's revealed ayah into human speech requires a messenger between God and humans. When Abai stated that "the Ayah is the beginning of speech," he meant its mystical nature. The beginning of a word is zero, nothing; it has no information, and even if there is information, its secret is unknown to humankind. The meaning of the ayah is that it is a secret of the Creator.

Second, the ayah is the creator's way to be known to humankind; it is His secret. When the Creator wishes to be known to humankind, He reveals the ayahs. The propagation of the ayahs is now a part of being a prophet, so the word after the ayah is the word of the Prophet, which is the hadith.

Many tafsirs (interpretations) of the ayahs in the Quran exist because of people's intentions to understand and explain their meaning. However, if the mystery of the verse can be fully revealed to a person, this is a topic of discussion. If the ayah is the beginning of the word, can it be explained by words? This is worth thinking about.

Third, the ayah is a type of poem. Thus, a human being is a poem, and as such, they will know the miracle of this creation, the mystery of creation. In this sense, the true poet is the Creator, and even poetry is his power. If one says there is an angelic nature to the poetic spirit, they are speaking about goodness; therefore, the beginning of goodness is in the ayah that is in the words of the Creator. Hence, the Creator's language is poetry.

Presumably, this is the reason why Abai said, "The poem is the king of words." Poetry's source is the ayah, because it is the beginning of the word. Now let me quote the poems that are based on these thoughts:

The ayah and hadith are the beginning of the word
It is time to give an example from poetry
If they were not logically interesting regarding that point
Would the Prophet and God say them?

This is the third verse of the fifteen-verse poem that begins with the words "The verse is the king of words, the judge of words." After mentioning ayahs in this verse, Abai said, "If they were not logically interesting regarding that point, Would the Prophet and God say them?" Hence, the topic is interesting. Abai is talking about ayahs and hadiths. This is understandable, but why is the word interesting logically? What is logic? Presumably, the following explanation is close to the truth. Let us think about it. If the word *qisyn* in Kazakh corresponds to logic, then the logic of the ayah and hadith is the beginning of the word. In addition, it should be noted that, here, the logic is not serving a problem. It is a problem itself. The interesting part is in the logic, and that is why the logic of the words is interesting. If the logic of the words were not interesting, then God and His Prophet would not say them. Thus, the logic is interesting. If this is the case, then the concept that draws one's attention is "the state of being interesting." This one word of the Kazakh lexicon has become a concept about discourse because the problem is based on the concept of "the state of being interesting."

The word "interesting" in this case is the most multiplied existence of life. In other words, it is a "soul" of existence. What is interesting? Life is interesting. What is interesting? To live a life is interesting. Is it interesting anywhere else, such as beyond that life? Of course not. That is why a word is interesting within its own logic. Unless we go deeper into this issue, the phrase "an interesting life" is not correct. It is not correct to say an interesting life but rather that the life itself is interesting. Interesting is the concept used instead of life. There is no life that is not interesting. Life is a form of "interesting" that people have learned. The case is not in life, the case is in the state of being interesting. Logic is the way to find out what is interesting. Consequently, it is better to talk about a method than to talk about logic. In that case, the ayah, the "soul" of existence is about being interesting. Thus, we come back to the idea that the ayah is the beginning of the word or that the logically interesting "word," said by the Prophet and God, is the ayah. Abai's verse refers to the view that life is "soul," the beginning of the word, or the logic of the Prophet, and the Prophet is an interesting word.

"Time Drags Everyone Along"

The first line of the three-versed poem that begins with the song "Butterfly with the color of a parrot" begins "Time will drag everyone along." Then, what is an epoch? Where does it get the power to drag everyone? To find out, it is best to know what an epoch is.

An epoch is the time space in which people live. Why did I come to this conclusion? Because Abai did not consider an epoch to be beyond people but neither did he regard it as being together with people. The people and the epoch are things that cannot be separated from each other in Abai's understanding. There is an epoch where people live; there are people where there is an epoch. Alternatively, there are no people without an epoch, and no epoch without people. People call this unity an epoch. If every person is dragged by their epoch, this is their fate, since each individual's action is meaningless in isolation. What, then, is the desire to live in a way that is reasonable? Is each person the constructor of their own fate? Then what happens to the principle that states that a person is the sole author of their own self-destruction and self-construction? There are so many principles. Which ones lead to the truth, and which ones lead away from the truth? Who will know the answer and define it? Does Abai's saying, "Man's epoch will drag him," imply the same meaning? If you are dragged by your epoch and if you do not have enough power to resist it, what will you do? You will follow the stream, and most of us are like that. Abai said, "In the bad times, a bad man's deeds will flourish." Here, he is describing a psychological condition that adapts to one's epoch. The skill of adapting to an epoch is called adaptation in psychology. To adapt to one's epoch is not always the right way. It is a question observed in the pursuit of slavery consciousness. Abai described such people as "bad ones." When he wrote, "In the bad times, a bad man's deeds will flourish," he means an adaptable psychology and a slavery consciousness.

The badness of a bad person is that they have no will; they do not have their own freedom. A bad person is not a citizen. A citizen is an independently formed person. They are a person of great humanity, capable of dwelling in the real world. Abai asks in the second line of this verse, "Who will control the epoch?" Indeed, who will have control over an epoch? If there is no person who controls the epoch, then how is the content of an epoch going to be determined? The content of an epoch is not a self-contained substance but a matter to be determined. Who is the one who determines the time, then? This problem has been topical since the creation of the world, and apparently, it never finds its solution.

Undoubtedly, it is possible to find an answer based on the ready-to-use answers given in the history of humankind. For example, one can approach this question from the perspective of the rulers of an epoch (emperors, khans, judges, kings, prophets, saints, or thinkers, as Abai mentioned), from the perspective of pure religion, one's life with the mighty Creator, from the perspectives of atheists, or from the perspective of the locomotive of history, the masses, and the objective laws. As you can see, there are diverse answers to the question of who must rule an epoch, and the teachings are different based on one's perspective.

When one talks about an epoch one usually means the exact historical period and shape of a time space. Hence, one must not forget the fact that an epoch impacts on an epoch. This is one aspect of the problem. Second, if the result of an impact of one epoch is that the next history is formed, that is a new epoch. In this sense, there is a personality quality in the essence of an epoch, which is similar to the essence of human beings. Then, the epoch is a reflection of a big, vast spectrum of events. The problem is that there is an event. Its main characters are the Creator and His human race. The history was formed from that, and the dialogue between the Creator and the created human became complex. To intensify the story, Eve was created, after an angel forgot his promise and turned into the Devil. The story began. As time went on, the story was passed from epoch to epoch. People now started to call the epoch itself an event. The epoch became rich with events and stories. Then the question arose,

147

what kind of person will rule over an epoch? The reason why there is no concrete answer to that question is that people have come to understand an epoch as an event, and they have forgotten about the meaning of the first big story. When the Creator created humanity, He intended to make him a ruler of an epoch and to make him control himself, but something went wrong with the humane intentions of the time. But what if this was also the Creator's own scenario? Undoubtedly, this is a logic-based hypothesis, but would any teaching be without a hypothesis?

A person does not become bad because they want to; it is because of their fate. If any person has the power to defeat their destiny, then they are not just a mere person, they are an individual. Those who act to become the ruler of an epoch are individuals. Abai spoke of three types of people: prophets, saints, philosophers. These are the ones that rule an epoch. They are supreme people who never become bad people. They are citizens who have their own independence.

A bad person is still a person. Is the person at fault if it is the epoch that makes them bad? That, too, is a matter of concern. Is not the purpose of ruling over the world to take care of those who are dragged by an epoch?

"Yes, Sell Your Labor, But Why Sell Your Conscience?"

This is the second line of the poet's four-versed poem that begins with the lines "The one who is friends with livestock will think only about livestock."

To sell one's labor is a market tradition that has existed in all times. Each person earns their livelihood by selling their goods. There is no special form of practice in this matter. A person studies, grows up, takes care of their health, becomes stronger through daily life and social experience, gets fit, and announces their skills, and all this is so they can work, so others will try to buy their labor. Such people are recognized as professional masters. It is quite logical and natural that a grown person with social skills and a hardworking nature will become a commodity that is in demand.

The problem is how to sell one's labor and through what means? The ways and means of trading labor in civilized countries are accumulated in practice. First, I would like to say that there is a system of services and stages for a person's skills and abilities. Everyone uses their own work and uses it as a source of livelihood and as a way to determine their place in society.

Trading one's labor is a civilized approach. The conflicts that occur are based on the value of that labor. We know from the history of the nineteenth and twentieth centuries that the value of labor has not always been the same. Social upheavals have led to protests which led to political rebellion in the end. This is a special theme. It raises the question of justice in the labor market. There are many doctrines, theories, and experiments on that topic. Abai did not go deep into this issue, and when he said, "sell your labor," he explained it not as a matter of social justice but as the sale of conscience. In understandable language, he said that people should not sell their conscience but their labor. The complexity of the problem is in that statement. How can one know the difference between selling their labor and selling their conscience? Is it not true that in our daily lives, conscience is sold together with labor? That is the issue Abai raised. Both labor and conscience are qualities of a person, but both should not be for sale. It is right to sell labor, but Abai asked why it is necessary to sell conscience. But think, does one's labor itself include one's conscience? Is not the world of a conscientious person valuable? Would the labor of a person without conscience be valuable?

Abai did not know the answer. He considered the sale of labor and sale of conscience separately. Let us go back to the core of the issue. When we talk about conscience, we have two targets: nationality and honor. Abai described this idea in the second part of the poem:

> They gather livestock to show off,
> To point it out to others, and to make others envious.
> He is a pig himself, but thinks of others as dogs,
> To make others love him for his wealth.

Is there a heavier thought than that for the person who understands it? It is clear that to show off and to point one's livestock out to others, to make others value one for one's wealth, were very common things in Abai's time, but in modern times, it is becoming a social disease, which is not a sign of goodness. In a society where the majority of people are poor, the chances that labor can be sold along with one's conscience are becoming more frequent. It is impossible to stop such behavior completely, but how can it be decreased? In my opinion, it is a matter of two parties. First, it is necessary for people to save their conscience while selling their labor, to have the power to save it. Of course, this is easy to say, but it is, in fact, a difficult issue.

Second, those who buy human labor should not make it a habit to exploit that labor. Thus, the consciences of those who buy labor are the way to justice. Abai did not comment on this part, but he concluded, "Not many appreciate people today because of their wisdom, conscience, or goodwill." Such social issues are resolved through the legal system in civilized countries. In a traditional society, they are resolved through tradition. There is a tradition among Kazakhs to protect the community and society from demands for the sale of people's consciences.

However, under certain circumstances, "greedy ones" are not able to sense the difference between selling labor and selling conscience, and they can take on bad deeds. Recalling these facts, Abai raised the issue: "Sell your labor, but why sell your conscience?" It is a matter of concern for everyone in the epoch of the market economy.

When Abai wrote that line, he wanted to underline that conscience can be sold. In addition, he had seen situations in which conscience was sold, and so he wanted to reveal the issue. When can conscience be sold? The answer to that is in Abai's poem. If people do not respect a person with a conscience, if they do not praise that person, and if they do not value the conscience as that person's supreme quality, then one's conscience will lose its value and it will be sold. Hence, when conscience has no value, it will become a kind of labor and will become a commodity in the market. Abai is warning us about that.

****

Abai said that the reason why people collect cattle is to "point them out to others and to make others envious." What burns them is not conscience or shame. Being poor is not shameless; it defiles honor. A person feels dishonored and envious for not having wealth. And the actions of those who point out their wealth to such people and say, "Oh, those poor people, they are not wealthy," are a sign of lacking a conscience. Abai said, "The one who is friends with livestock only cares about livestock." Is this conscience or a lack of conscience? Everyone's inner self is known only to the Creator; one can never rely on another person based only on their words. However, I am convinced that people cannot categorize another's acts as generosity when those acts show off the person's wealth and when the person makes showing off their meaning of life.

Wealth is certainly the result of labor. To earn for one's livelihood is the fruit of human activity. There is no conflict about that. Abai looked for good intentions at that point: "If after praying for their income, they would check their pockets and give others what is left over." Here is the formula for being humane. First, feed yourself, then give *alash* (people) what is left over. This is a good idea, but how can one determine what is left over. Which one of those celebrities would say that they were celebrated? The trouble begins at this point. Since wealth lies on the path of lust, can it ever be satisfied? As the saying goes, Is there a limit to the useless actions (in fact, to the evilness) of the poor who desire to be rich and the rich who desire to be god?

Does that limitation have dimensions? There is an Islamic worldview that addresses this: one should be content, thankful, and repentant; these are the ways to be thankful for God's mercies and blessings. This is a condition of being a real Muslim. It is a waste of time to ask for charity from a person who does not recognize Islam. Certainly, civilized countries have taken decisive legislative measures to regulate the ways and means of limiting wealth. There are systems of antimonopoly legislation; there are taxation orders. In Muslim countries, there are *zakat* policies (a religious obligation to give to charity), but all of this is not enough to keep a person's lust under control; if a person who "prays for their income" does not have the knowledge of conscience, as described by the poet and philosopher Qudaiberdiuly Shakarim, how can that person, prone to sins, know what part of their income should go toward charity?

"What Wisdom Did Not Achieve is not an Ambition"

This is the third line of the fifth verse of a poem that begins "Dirty water will not become oily if sheep cross over it." And this third line does not rhyme with the other lines. In the tradition of *qara oleng* (a traditional Kazakh poetic rhyming system), poets usually try to deliver the main idea of a poem in the third line of the verse. Since this line does not require a rhyme, it is a chance to think freely. Abai used this chance and impressed his deep thought. Two concepts are interdependent with each other in the same line: mind and dreams. The first concept appears frequently in Abai's works. The mind, here, is the concept of a worldview, and scholars have said a lot about it. This time, I am not talking about the mind, but I want to identify a dream through the mind.

The dream is a commonly used concept in art and daily life, more so than in science. The dream is the eternal theme. It applies to a person, often to their future. The word "dream" is often used in Kazakh as a name. This is not the case in Russian. In Abai's poetry, one of the most prominent topics in this regard is, of course, the issue of finding a dream through the mind. Here are two questions that can be addressed. First, why did Abai aim to identify a dream through the mind? Second, is it possible to determine the meaning of a dream without the mind? Now let us try to find answers to these questions.

Abai said that if a mind cannot achieve it, then it is not a dream. Why? What, then, does the mind achieve? How do we perceive that a dream cannot be without a mind? Is not the concept of a dream usually used separately from the concept of the mind? Abai related the dream with the mind; he said that what a mind cannot achieve is not a dream. In this sense, a dream is an extent and space of the mind. Abai seems to be the only Kazakh thinker to raise the issue from this perspective; perhaps there were others, but I am not aware of them. If I encounter such an idea in the future, I can add it; but for now, I have seen this approach only in Abai's work.

Here is another piece of information to add to what I have said and written about the mind. A dream can reveal its content only when its mind can reach it, so the superiority of a dream compared to simple imagination is in its intelligence and even wisdom. Only an object that has been reached by the mind can turn into a dream. A mindless person cannot have a dream. This news has opened a new channel for my thoughts. A mindless person cannot dream; hence, a dream is a model and image of the future.

A person will bring themselves into the future with dreams, and their mind will assist them in doing so. If a person's current life does not have a future, its present day will be meaningless. The content of present life is determined by its dreams.

A dream is not just a picture of the future but its consciousness. What meaningful future and logical consciousness can a mindless person have if they are incapable of analyzing their current situation? Thus, a mindless person has no dream; what they have is meaningless fantasy. Fantasy is different from dreams, and its essence is different. Fantasy and dreams are not synonyms. There is no person without a fantasy, but there might be a person with no dreams, since dreams require intelligence. It is clear that a fantasy does not need intelligence. It is probable that a mere fantasy can give birth to a "forest of dreams," and it is obvious that such a forest of dreams would not lead a person to objective actions but to chaotic, ineffective, and fruitless actions. A person who is imagining with a shortage of intelligence will not be able to reach their dream. Therefore, it seems that imagination is the first step of a dream. It is likely that a person who remains in the forest of fantasy can be lost. In most cases, this seems to be so. But those who are able to find a path out of the forest of fantasy will be found on the path to their dreams, but one's mind must rise to the level of intelligence. Then the dreams will be revealed and one's horizons will be discovered.

A dream is a point that our mind can reach, but how can we determine whether our mind reached it or not? The core of the question is in this: how is a life going to be interesting if one can know an answer in advance? The reason why diverse events occur, develop, and change is that people cannot understand if their minds could reach or could not reach their dreams. The answer is in the hands of each individual. Life, unfortunately, does not have numerical rules;

there are abundant scenarios, phenomena, and situations in life that do not obey the rules of life, and they will change human nature in many ways. This mysterious human nature has never ceased, from the creation of the world up to today, and it will continue until the Day of Judgment. It is the innumerable manifestations of the humility of humanity that are not subject to control.

Returning to the question of whether a dream can be without a mind, my answer is short. There is no consciousness about a dream without a mind. A dream is a high concept. Needless to say, understanding it requires intelligence based on hard work and good intentions and aims. If a dream is not based on good intentions, it is likely that the mind can lead it to actions that go against human nature. There are many examples from the historical experience of humanity and from current experience that show that hard work and purpose do not always lead to good intentions.

****

The sixth line of this verse ends as follows: "Does another purpose fill the mind?" It has two concepts as well: goal and mind. Then, what is the difference between goal and dream? The immediate answer is that it is not wise to be aware of it immediately. A goal is not directly related to the mind. A mindless person can have a goal. When it comes to intelligence, Abai used it in its high meaning. Every person in the world has a mind, but the question is about those whose intelligence is not full. If a mind is filled with a goal, then it might turn into a dream. Perhaps, this is the difference between a goal and a dream.

"Let True Words Not Be Few"

Abai criticized his own time in his third Word of Wisdom. He was not criticizing it out of arrogance but rather because it hurt him. The essence of the criticism was borne out by an attempt to purge, to predict an image of the future. The person who knows their own flaws is a clever person. The person who knows the shortcomings of the people is a wise person. Knowing the deficiency gives one the opportunity to get rid of it. We Kazakhs are well aware of our shortcomings, so the idea that we are a strong country is based on such concepts. Abai said, "Where lies the cause of the estrangement among Kazakhs, of their hostility and ill will towards one another? Why are they insincere in their speech, so lazy, and possessed by a lust for power?"

Indeed, what is the reason for that? I would like to note that Abai's comment was made during a time when there was an absence of Kazakh freedom and the lack of an idea that could unite people. It is a well-known principle that the behavior of enslaved people is due to the loss of their significance.

The ethnic unity formed in the times of the Khanate was destroyed in Abai's time. What was left from the Kazakh Horde (khanate), which existed for 366 years, was the name "Kazakh," a language, and a history in the memory of the people. During Abai's time, being a united state turned into an impossible dream. The only consolation for the spiritual world of the Kazakhs was their folklore (legends, psalms, poems, and so on).

What did the Kazakhs do when were in such a situation? Riding a horse and taking up arms were prohibited. Issues regarding the protection of the state and the land stopped being on the agenda. There was no khanate rule; the election of *bis* (traditional judges) was forgotten. Heroism was transformed into the theft of livestock. Such a weak lifestyle brought a social problem to the Kazakh steppes: namely, laziness. No worthy jobs existed for strong, young men. That is why the epidemic of laziness had risen in daily life. Laziness is the mother of intruders. All forms of intoxication caused this laziness. To save people from laziness, a healer was needed. Does the epidemic of laziness Abai mentioned still exist today? Do current Kazakhs try to harm each other in the same way as those in Abai's epoch did? Let us think about it together. Abai's dream has been fulfilled today. The Kazakh ethnos has achieved its political liberty. The country has the idea of a common state, the basis of which is the Republic of Kazakhstan. Hence, the political roots of laziness have been cut off. The country is entering the market economy. So, are Kazakhs now motivated by their national dignity and civilization? Has there been a decrease in their laziness, insincere speech, malicious intentions, jealous attitudes toward each other, and lust for power? Are there any other opinions on that matter? How will each political party answer these questions? Kazakhs listen to the leaders of each party, read their political programs, and act as representatives of the community as an electorate. Democracy is not just the creation of political parties; it is a breakthrough for and an awakening of everyone.

Well now, let me turn back to the laziness Abai talked about. This is reminiscent of that. When Nikita Khrushchev arrived to the riot of those who participated in the development of virgin lands, he said to them, "The Kazakh people are lazy, and our all hopes are in you." Eyewitnesses reported his words. Then the question arises, why are Kazakhs lazy? Needless to say, that laziness is a natural feature. Consequently, there are "cultural" reasons. I have already mentioned the reason for laziness in Abai's time. Unfortunately, although there was a distinctive feature of the second colonial system, the qualitative difference was insignificant. It was as if Kazakhs, who had begun to build socialism, were able to get rid of laziness, but unfortunately, the economic system was a barrier. Kazakhstan has become an economic region that does not produce final products, only the raw materials; there is also a shortage of professional industries. Unlike in Abai's time, all Kazakhs get involved at work. The former classic form of laziness has been eliminated. Work in cattle-breeding, farming, and factories and plants did not leave space for laziness, but it was replaced by other illnesses. It is a social infantilism. In essence, this means to not take initiative but wait for orders and decisions. In short, only do what one is told. This is a hindrance to professional and social activeness.

Naturally, the naive Kazakh people were too devoted to the idea of socialism. They did not doubt. If there were those who had doubts, their doubts were eradicated by Bolshevist campaigns. The people who were accustomed to such situations were overwhelmed by the market economy that came with independence, and they are only now beginning to accept freethinking and actions. Because of their lack of technological skills and habits, Kazakhs were initially afraid of the market economy, and it is evident that people are still psychologically adapting to the new economic policy.

A more serious problem than the market economy itself is our mentality, which does not seem to be able to adapt to this system. It is surprising that Kazakhs' habits, as Abai said, of being hostile to each other, of having ill will to each other, of having a lust for power have not changed, that these have reached today with no changes. Indeed, they are even increasing and spreading among the citizens of this now sovereign country. What is the reason for this? Are we not a tightly knit Kazakh people, why do we split into pieces? Splitting the united Kazakh ethnos into pieces has been the dream of external enemies since the formation of the Kazakh Horde.

Setting aside the issue of outside enemies, what about the current political parties in Kazakhstan? Are they forces that break up the country or are they powers that group people around the president? Who can answer this? Who can say the true word with no lies? Some people are competing with each other for the lust of power, saying insincere speech, and fighting against each other. Of course, anything is possible in life, but if Abai's remarks are still topical today, such people are a sure sign that there are too few true words!

"Painted Laughter"

In his fourth Word of Wisdom, Abai named one type of laughter among many and said, "There is a painted (or colored) laughter whose only purpose is to look beautiful." When thinking of Abai's painted laughter, it reminds me of the laughter of people who are in politics. Their laughter is a painted, colored laughter. The problem cannot be for any other reason. Once you are in politics, this is your life; your life turns to colored laughter. You are not a politician without colored laughter, because politics is itself colored. Politics is not the face of truth but its colors. When was there ever a policy with no colors? That is why people say that politics is colored truth (Note: this should not be understood to mean "politics is fraud"). From this perspective, then, the laughter of politicians is going to be colored as well.

I understand Abai's words in that way, but what is the truth? Let us think, can those who are professionally engaged in politics be able to have real laughter? No, of course not. Is there a space in politics for a person who reveals their secrets through their laughter? Laughter is a tool that does not reveal the secret but conceals it. The secret of the politician's soul, their final goal, is hidden, and when they turn their secret into laughter, they lose. A person who is engaged in political life cannot be sincere and open; they cannot be too sociable and ready to reveal secrets. People in the field of politics are secrets to one another. What saves them from each other are their secrets. The person whose secret is revealed will have no value. The value of a person is not in their spoken words but in their unspoken words. A person has two kinds of knowledge: one is the knowledge they share with other people and the masses; the other is only for themselves, the knowledge necessary for their personality. People with the second kind of knowledge have both colored character and colored laughter.

Colored laughter comes from practice. There is no color in a baby's laughter. Colors in laughter are a human attribute that gradually begins to emerge. However, such colors are not innate; laughter could generally be without colors. But are not colors the meaning of life? Insects, birds, and other animals use their natural colors to demonstrate their lifestyles; for example, the chameleon ensures its safety by changing its color. I guess people's laughter cannot be colorless because the laughter itself is a color. Laughter is not just a person's mind but also their worldview. People's humanity is in their laughter. Laughter allows one to know what a person is. There is no person who never laughs, and that laughter is what reveals a person's secrets. Therefore, politicians skillfully master that colored laughter and adapt themselves to it. Political leaders practice with special teachers in front of a mirror to master that colored laughter.

One cannot go public without a smile. A non-smiling person is not accepted by the masses.

I mentioned that there is no laughter without color. The role of color, as Abai said, is beauty, that is, a beautiful, attractive laughter. In addition, laughter with color is laughter that can hide secrets, because the second role of color is to change the color of something else. We change a color when we paint. The paint will have the same effect on laughter. To paint laughter is to search for "cultural" methods rather than natural ones. Colored laughter is an art and a culture. Colored laughter is the result of a person mastering laughter. Abai described it as "designing the song of laughter."

Laughter has its own song. That song must be found, and then the laughter will be colored laughter.

Colored laughter is a substance. It is impossible to detect the numerous colors of laughter, just as the melodies of the world's songs cannot be counted. The colors are infinite, and the color of each person's smile is a unique world. The colors of laughter are as infinite as the colors of paint. Paint is not one color. Even the one color has thousands of types. That is why people who have mastered the smile sometimes cannot understand their own smile and get lost, which is very common among politicians. People use colored smiles to avoid problems. In this sense, the colored smile is the most effective method of survival—the mechanism of human protection. That is why Abai called the colored smile artificial.

Let me finish my thoughts with Abai's idea on smiles: "Not all laughter deserves approbation. There is also a kind of laughter that does not come from the heart, that God-given vessel, but bursts out in hollow peals just for the sake of forced jollity."

"People Come into The World Crying"

In his fourth Word, Abai said, "Man comes into this world crying and departs it in sorrow." This is an idea that has come from ancient times. Abai repeated it because it is a word that cannot be denied. Unless people are reminded and warned about what has been heard, read, or learned, they will forget it. They do not forget on purpose, but the joy of life makes it happen. Sometimes, one day's joy can make a person forget many things. They will forget what they know in the process of daily survival. That is why the scholars of every epoch need to repeat their eternal thoughts. Abai repeated that people come into this world crying and depart it in sorrow. Indeed, we are aware that people cry when born. But is that the only time they cry? Will not many of us cry throughout our life? If we think of crying in both physical (that is, with tears) and metaphorical terms, I think people cry not only in birth but also throughout their lives. Life is always full of troubles. People have an inexhaustible dream, which Kazakhs express in one proverb: "The poor man desires to be rich, the rich man desires to be god." The market is a time of competition, and therefore, wealth and power are competing. One's goal is to advance in power or wealth.

The situation of people not being thankful for what they own and making it their goal to collect as much money as possible is described by Abai as follows: "He will burn it up thoughtlessly, squander it in petty quarrels and miserable wrangles, and never know true happiness. He will pause to think only when the sands of life run out. Only then will he realize that no treasure on earth can prolong his life even for a single day." Abai described the end of human life as "when the sands of life run out."

Your life of crying has ended, and now you have no other day than the day "when the sands of life run out." Neither your livestock nor your wealth can give you one extra day. So, Abai asked, "What is the meaning of our past days?" Maybe this is the reason new babies cry. They are crying because they are entering a world full of troubles. When they grow older, they become guilty in front of others and sinful before the Creator (if they confess). There is no other way. A person's passion for life is going to lead only in this direction, and the circumstances of life make a person cry numerous times. There is no person who never cries. Abai said that a person lives "without fully comprehending the value and uniqueness of the life bestowed upon them." It is hard not to agree with this opinion. The thoughtful person knows that there is no pleasure in the world, so if you are human, you can hope for Paradise and remember Hell as a warning. Paradise is hope. It is an idea to keep hopes around. The issue is not in the existence or non-existence of a Paradise but in the truthfulness of Paradise as an idea, in its call to goodness and wisdom, and in its function to help people reach the day "when the sands of life run out" with ease. This is my opinion on the idea that "man comes into the world crying." Now I want to turn to the second half of the sentence: "and departs it in sorrow."

Why and because of whom does a person die in sorrow? Are they angry at life or at death? I think that a person cannot be angry at death, since they do not know what death is. For a live person, death is a mystery. There is no survivor of death in the world. Death is not a matter of experience. Death is something we have never experienced. People only see the death of others. The death of another is knowledge but not actual experience. Therefore, when a person dies, it may be that they are not in death but in the past. Perhaps, they try in vain to see the meaninglessness, instability, and false character of life. Because life is a person's experience; they know how they lived, and they only begin to understand the meaning of their life in that last day "when the sands of life run out."

No matter who a person was or what they have done, it seems like they will come up with special thoughts on the day "when the sands of life run out." There is a great deal of literature on this issue, and it is clear that consciousness in the last days of human life and the consciousness of daily life are different from each other. Who would say that the person who is in the "last station" of life experiences the joy and satisfaction of thinking? No matter how meaningless or insignificant this life, the joy of life is so attractive. Therefore, I think there is no such joy and satisfaction on that last day, but since ancient times, it has been a crucial topic to make that false life unique and to find a solution to make this life just.

"Who is Good?"

Abai described the good man in his thirty-eighth Word. For this, I refer to his thoughts on *hauas salim* (beautiful appearance). Hauas *salim* is an Arabic word, and its meaning in Kazakh refers to the attributes and behavior of a person. Abai explained how a person comes to this attribute. In order to be *hauas salim*, one must meet six conditions: good health, good relatives, good parents, good mother, good fellow, and good teacher. These are the necessary conditions for being a good person. These are the dimensions of goodness. The philosopher Qudaiberdiuly Shakarim asked, "Who is like the best man is?" The answer can again be found in Abai's work. Abai said that after a man has the above-mentioned qualities, "his name will be human," that is, he will become a good person; however, in his actions, a good man must strive "to know God and to understand his own self and the world around him" (Vol. 2, p. 190**). A good person will always encounter these two issues, and as a result, their personality will be determined, that is, they will be known as a good person.

Now, I will briefly address the two issues that make a person good. The first issue is knowing God. Knowing God is not just believing in Him. To recognize God is to recognize His miracles, to understand and to accept Him as the Creator. There is no direct way to know the Creator, except through His creations, which He created with his own power. What did the Creator create? The whole existence is the miracle of the Creator; thus, thinking about the Creator is an attempt to discover the entire creation. Though there are many different types of science—natural sciences, physics, biology, chemistry, and so on—they all study the phenomena and regulations of creation. Therefore, one who recognizes the idea of the Creator will be acquainted with God through His creation. This is the path to knowledge of God, the path of knowledge. Let me give an example of one good person's life. According to later reports, Omar Khayyam died in 1122. On the day of his death, he was carefully reading *The Book of Healing* by Avicenna. Having reached the chapter "Singular and Plural," he put his golden toothbrush between the pages, closed the book, and called people to convey the testimony. On that day, he did not eat anything. After performing the evening prayer, he bent down to the ground and said, "Oh God, verily I have sought to know Thee to the extent of my powers. Forgive me, therefore. My knowledge of Thee is my recommendation to Thee." Then, he passed away.[14]

The second issue is knowing oneself and the world. There are many theories and concepts in psychology and philosophy regarding a human being's "self-knowledge." Of course, how to recognize oneself through others is an essential aspect of the doctrine of humanity. In Russian, there is a word for self-knowledge: *samopoznanyie*. This is a special field of science. The phrase "knowledge of the world" refers to the concept of a worldview. One of the main functions of philosophy is providing a worldview. Abai called it "the beauty of the world" in his poems. Being able to feel, know, and think about the world is a power that gives beauty to a person. One of the noblest qualities mentioned by Abai, a bright mind, is derived from that power as well. Thinking about the world makes a mind bright. Abai was a thinker who did not think inside the frames of religious principles. Would he be a thinker if he only repeated the words of religion? Abai's qualification as a thinker was in his search for the beginning, for the cause of every case. Therefore, he said, "Do not believe, unless your mind believes it." He left every case to the judgment of the mind. The poet questioned neither God Himself, nor His word; his questions were about who God is, what His words are, and how one can think about them. He discussed the problem of recognizing God in his poem "It is easy to say God." It is necessary to feel God in one's heart, not in words but in wisdom; God is recognized through the senses. In addition, Abai said that God exists and it is the truth, and a man has a word too, but there is always a doubt about its truth. Why is that? Again, the answer is in the thirty-eighth Word. Abai said, "God's word is without letters and without voice" (Vol. 2, p. 193**). God's word is a great truth.

The Prophet was illiterate; he could not read. Ayahs were sent to him as revelations from God. The Prophet's knowledge is the knowledge of the

---

[14] *Rubai Omar Khayyam,* (London, 1986), p. 32.

revelation, and our knowledge is knowledge through letters. Thus, it is obvious who is closer to God. Abai said, "The ayah and hadith are the beginning of the word." The ayah is the consciousness of the beauty of the world. The ayah is the beginning of the word, but it was not created from a man's mind. It was a revelation in the form of a poem sent to the Prophet Muhammad. The ayah was a testimony to Muhammad's coming prophethood. Muhammad revealed to the public that an ayah from the Creator had come to him in revelation. There is a legend about the Prophet's illiteracy:

> The angel Gabriel appeared at night as a young man in light before the Prophet Muhammad (peace be upon him). He commanded with his sweet and strict voice: "Read!"

> The Prophet Muhammad (peace be upon him) was frightened. His heart was beating fast. Then he called up his courage and said: "I am unable to read! I cannot read!"

> Gabriel caught hold of the Prophet Muhammad and embraced him strongly: "Read!"

> The knower of the secrets of the two worlds, Muhammad (peace be upon him), repeated his previous answer again: "I am unable to read!"

> Gabriel embraced him strongly, let him go, and said: "Read!"

> This time, Muhammad (peace be upon him) said: "I cannot read." Then he paused for a moment and said: "Tell me, what should I read?"

> The angel read from the beginning of the first verse of the Surah Al-Alaq, which was sent down by God to his messenger: "Recite in the name of your Lord, Who created—created man from a clinging substance. Recite and your Lord is the Most Generous—Who taught by the pen—taught man that which he knew not." (Surah Al-Alaq, 1–5)

> The Prophet Muhammad (peace be upon him), who was exhausted by fear and trembling, repeated the verses in his own language. The verses that have been repeated were at once easy for the prophet to recite and saved in the heart of his heart.

The angel Gabriel, who performed the task, immediately disappeared.[15]

The legend delivers the truth in this way. What did the situation look like? It is true that Muhammad was illiterate. As I mentioned earlier, we often call uneducated people illiterate. This is our understanding, which we use in casual situations. But the case is more complicated than that. In the history of humankind, only a few people have been known who were educated without knowing letters. One of those people was the Prophet Muhammad. The prophet Jesus also had such knowledge. When the angel commanded Muhammad to recite, he did not read the written letters sent by God, but the word was put in his memory. As Abai said, "God's word is without letters and without voice." Thus, the ayah remained in the memory of the Prophet.

The ayah is the word of God. It is "without letters and without voice," as Abai said. The ayah is the consciousness that was sent to the Prophet. Later it turned into letter and sounds and became the Quran. The incomprehensibility of the ayah is a sensible issue. Understanding the Creator's "word" is controversial. Language is the treasure of humankind; we cognize it, know it, and use it for our very lives. The ayah is a different "language." It is the Creator's language. It does not have letters. In the academic lexicon of energy, it is the reflection of the world's energy system. Some people on the planet may well have the power to produce, store, and operate electricity. Plato said, "The essence of human education is to remember." He believed that the knowledge we have learned from the beginning has already been known, and it comes to people as innate information.

In modern science and education, there is a paradigmatic consciousness of "principle," a method that can be used to identify issues that have not yet been discovered. One's direction is defined through principles. This direction is a guide. The recognition and selection of our paths are based on ayahs.

"Knowledge Brings Sorrow"

Knowledge brings sorrow,
Knowledge causes rage.
When sorrow and anger are joined together
Grief pours from my tongue.

---

[15] D. Omirzaqqyzy, *Azamattyng asyl tazhi. Muhammed (s.a.u) paighambarding omiri. Mekke kezengi.* [The Most Valuable Crown of Humanity. The Life of the Prophet Muhammad (peace be upon him). The Meccan Period Book], 1st book, (Almaty, 2003), pp. 124–125.

This poem contains the following concepts: sorrow, teachings, anger, knowledge, and grief. What is grief? It is a characteristic of thought. No matter what the teaching is, it will bring sorrow to a thinker. Since sorrow is deep, it is born from longing for kindness, from the aim to reach it, whereas knowledge is born from ideological necessity. It is hard for teaching to be a kind idea because it serves a certain group's interest. That is why it becomes a source of sorrow. Sorrow is the consciousness that emerges from human kindness. Teaching is the enthusiasm of a political force that is interested in power. In this case, a disagreement between the interests of the individual and the interests of the society is unavoidable, and this makes sorrow appear. Unfortunately, whatever the teaching is, even if it sounds good, it always comes with some part of injustice because it is always hard to find a solution for how to make the interests of a political power accord with the interests of the masses. Authority is not just the means of justice but also the means to achieve it, so the approach to it varies in different groups. Teachings based on the realization of such acts will, of course, bring grief. Human experience in the past and present shows that this has always been the case. Today, to proclaim that authors of teachings are propagators of justice is to understand the level of propagation. This situation was too complicated in Abai's time. Teaching is a sickness of the mind. Teaching is a disease that directly affects your brain. Those who remain healthy will be few, and the rest will be grieved.

One part of the Kazakh intelligentsia, who fell victim to the socialist idea, realized too late that teaching causes sorrow; another group did not understand it until the end of their lives, and they passed away with a "tied" consciousness. It is not easy to recognize and understand the content of a teaching; one needs immunity for that. The teachings of Marx and Lenin's doctrines brought turbulent times among the Kazakh people beginning in the twentieth century. The masses, who did not know whom to follow, were killed by starvation; the intellectuals were punished, and one-third of them were scattered across the globe. It was a tragedy, one which Abai spoke about. That is why it is important to remember that those teachings were the consciousness of the groups that oriented ideologically.

Teaching is artificial human consciousness, so it is not flawless. The flaws of a teaching are the sorrow of the thinkers. Teaching poisons consciousness, restricts freedom of thought, and limits the thinking space. Teaching is a way of making people dependent on something. The creation of teaching will cause tragedy. However, this approach has been transformed into new forms and states, causing new tragedies for humanity.

This is one of the bases for Abai's thoughts that are expressed in the line "Teaching causes sorrow." The innovation here is Abai's idea of relating sorrow to teaching. Sorrow does not happen accidentally; here, Abai speaks not about personal daily sorrows but about a tragedy that is caused by teaching. A sorrow that is not caused by teaching is a natural sorrow, but a sorrow caused by teaching has social content, since teaching is a social phenomenon.

The poet stated in the second line, "Knowledge causes rage." This is, undoubtedly, a surprising thought. Do not people usually say that education is happiness and the light that gives power to a soul? Indeed, knowledge is a matter of pleasure. A lack of knowledge causes ignorance. A literate person will be bright. In short, everything about education is pleasant. Education is the way of humanity, its breath. But Abai said that this knowledge causes rage, how can that be explained?

First, it is an opinion based in Abai's time. Where, how, and in whose interest do you plan to apply your knowledge? This is worth thinking about. Knowledge should serve a person, a country. Do you have such a country or freedom? What happens in this situation if not rage? It is also true that during Abai's epoch, the Kazakh people received education not to become individuals but to become officials; they were educated for the sake of profit. Such knowledge would, of course, cause rage in a thinker. Second, let us consider this issue not only from the perspective of Abai's time but in general. Then, what would the problem be like? Let us consider this question.

****

Kazakhs were brought up believing that "Education is the light of life." That is right. There is nothing is wrong with that claim. There will be darkness without knowledge. We consider the desire for knowledge a quality of hard work. There is a system of stable education in any society. Education is a treasure. Everyone should send their children to get education. Knowledge and passion for knowledge is a sign of goodness. The educated person turns into a citizen; they will get involved in civic works and work for their state. These are unarguable facts.

But what did Abai mean when he said, "Knowledge causes rage"? What is rage? First, rage is human power. One needs energy to become enraged, since it happens when a person does not agree with something. When a person determines that something must not have been this or that way, it will show up as rage. Hence, there are two reasons for rage: one is the realization that something must have been different, and the other is the disagreement with it. Rage awakens in both situations.

Second, rage is an uncontrollable anger. This is not good. One must control one's rage before it causes troubles. Rage is from the devil; its treatment is found in patience.

Third, rage is the consciousness of an educated, intelligent person who aims to change something. Apparently, Abai regarded rage from this perspective. What makes Abai rage is an issue we should think about.

Why does knowledge cause rage? Two issues must be considered. The first issue is in knowledge itself: knowledge itself is a cause of rage, that is, its quality. If the basis of knowledge is the continuous search for knowledge, one must ask whether this knowledge is useful for your epoch and country. Knowledge can be insignificant, countless; is it all needed, or should knowledge be filtered? This is an eternal question. The second issue is high-quality education, which is also a source of rage, because knowledge is like an infinity of doors to be opened. The more a person knows, the more they want to know; it makes them enraged. This is a common thing. In this sense, the rage is the driving force of motivation, the fresh air for a person on the path of knowledge, their passion for knowledge. That is the point. Where is this going to lead after all? It will lead to rage because they will realize that they cannot learn everything in this short life. It is a question with no answer. Presumably, Abai considered rage in that meaning.

Of course, after such a situation, he had no choice but to said, "When sorrow and anger are joined together, Grief pours from my tongue."

Who said that the world is pleasure and paradise? Why, then, does humankind look for a paradise in the other world? Because the thinkers could never find happiness in this life, and Abai was in that state: his tongue was pouring grief.

****

What is a grief? In my opinion, there are three meanings to the word "grief." The first meaning is based on grief's negative effects on the soul. A person's state of being is weakened when they are grieving. Since such situations are a fact of life, they are inescapable. What can a person do when they have problems, when the sadness comes, if not grieve? This is a reflection of one of the many hard states of being human.

The second meaning is used when people desire, when they have a passion to achieve something, and they grieve because of that. In the fairy tale

"Er Tostik," a man and a woman passionately want a child, so they grieve, and eventually their dreams come true, and Er Tostik is born. Grief is used in relation to hope in such situations.

The third meaning of grief has attributes of a worldview. Why do people grieve in such a situation? Here, there are actually two situations. The first is when they are not satisfied. Abai was not satisfied with the sorrow and rage, but they both put pressure on him. This is a situation when one grieves for passed things. The second situation is when one longs for unrealized dreams and for the indefiniteness of the future. This situation is about the future, or in the words of the poet, about the approaching epoch. As Abai said, "The future is a blue mist." The future is uncertain, and the fog does not have precision. No one can say anything for sure, so why does this turn one's consciousness to grief. I suggest that Abai was probably thinking of this last meaning. In my attempt to understand Abai's grief that poured from his thoughts and understandings, I interpret it in this way.

"Goodness Will Not Last Long"

Good and evil are not twins; they are two sides of one thing, and they do not exist without one another. Abai said, "Goodness will not last long." It is logical to ask, "Why is that?" Why does goodness not last long? This is a question that has an answer. For the sake of goodness, humans must abandon their lust and become angels. This is impossible. There were only angels before the human race, but the creation and spread of humans on earth was a natural need. Since we are human, we have lust, and that is why we are sinful. The lust of human beings is interesting; without it there would be no history, no art, and no science. If humans lost their lust, they would become like angels and the Creator's idea would not be realized. Therefore, individuals will not make goodness last for long; they will get quickly bored of it and search for something new, but then they will encounter evil or immerse themselves in it completely. Abai, wanting to describe this situation, said in the second line, "Evil is never out of date." If we again ask why, my answer is that evil dwells in humans' lust, which is their sinfulness.

Evil will never perish; it is the devil in human nature. Wherever the devil appears, it is reflected through a humans' lust. The devil is everywhere because it is in the flesh and blood of humans. Goodness is a moment when a person forgets evil, and it does not have the power to last for long; it is a phenomenon similar to sunshine. Strong people will work hard to make goodness exist and to establish it. It is reflected through the tradition of a past life full of goodness and through present day education and methods of upbringing.

Goodness is the power of the spirit. When the spirit of the country's power is diminished, the good will be darkened and "the devil will create its web." Such times have been experienced by every nation, and it will happen in the future. The succession of generations must not be interrupted so that goodness can stay. When a step-generation grows up, no place is left for goodness, and evil will perform its functions. It is a time when the human race is lost and on the wrong path.

Humanity is too often lost. There is one direct way to avoid getting lost, but sometimes there is no leader who can guide humanity. In times without a Prophet, some people will carry out a prophet's duties. What will be the result of such actions? Therefore:

> Goodness will not last long,
> Evil is never out of date.

****

The following passages of the verse have significant meanings that relate to hope and anxiety. Hope is a sign of the future; in fact, it is the consciousness that future paths exist, which is the light of the future.

Without hope, present life does not matter. Therefore, the content of all this is hope, without which there is no desire for life. If this is the case, then anxieties are a barrier on hope's path. They are a consciousness that takes hope away, destroys it, and announces humanity's infirmity.

The cause of anxiety is evil. Evil creates conditions for its existence with anxiety. Leading hope to anxiety is an action to destroy goodness, to make it not last long. The thinker Abai described this state as follows:

> Hope weakens
> And does not last for long
> No matter how hard you try
> It will not overcome anxiety.

Hope that does not overcome anxiety is not hope. Hope must last a long time and overcome anxiety, and then this hope will sparkle with lights of goodness. Is not a life without goodness a darkness?

****

Since Abai discussed anxiety, he also considered the question of grief. When anxiety turns to grief, the problem becomes more vivid and weightier. What I mean to say by this is that when anxiety turns to grief, one's thoughts are activated. Sorrow is not an anxiety or a problem. It is a thought. Sorrow is a sign of a thought. Many people are deprived of anxiety and sadness, and they feel as if they are stuck in a deadlock. This is the state of grief, and it makes people seek solutions.

Therefore, Abai said, "If you think of one sorrow, it awakens hundreds of others." To think of a hundred sorrows is a sign of wisdom. It is the path that leads to wisdom, and this is the opportunity of clarity. Unless one experiences sorrow, no wisdom is possible.

Now, let us talk about the weight of grief, that is, its burden. It is the state of a person who is left under piles of grief. The state when one sorrow awakens hundreds of griefs is the state when endless sorrows fall on a person as a destiny. So Abai said:

If a man happens to experience many sorrows
That will estrange him anyway.

Who might succeed in overcoming sorrows? The last line of the poem is thought provoking. It relates to concepts of arrogance and praising.

Abai made a special analysis of the term "praise" in one of his Words of Wisdom, so I will not consider it here. Instead, I will focus on what "praising" is. There are many ways of making a person anxious, but what does it mean to make someone anxious because of praising? Praising is usually considered a way of increasing self-confidence, and people usually want to hear praises. So it seems like praising would be a good idea. Indeed, it usually is. However, hope, anxiety, and sorrow are meaningless to the ignorant person, and thus, the ignorant person's consolation is praise. This consolation made Abai anxious, so he concluded, "I became anxious because of praise."

"Banks of Evil"

There is the notion of the "banks of evil" in Abai's Words of Wisdom. What, then, does "banks of evil" mean? Is there anyone who stays away from evil? Apparently, no. Evil is very cautious. If you are not alert, it will cling to you. Evil does not know how to "rest." People like to rest, and evil can stick to people at that moment of rest. What is the power that can resist evil? According to Abai, it is people's humanity. What is that? Human qualities are shame, conscience, and honor.

The banks of evil are related to the lies about this life. People are not angels, and this world is not a paradise. People are on the banks of evil from a young age, so they need education, knowledge, and religion. People are evil savvy, but they cannot distance themselves from the banks completely. People grow up on the banks of evil. It is their destiny. They have no other destiny. The human power of human beings will be determined only when they understand this.

When a person realizes their nature is weak and depends on destiny, they will begin to take action. Now they know what to do and how to do it. They will be on the banks of evil, and they will take actions to become a better person. A good person does not flee the banks of evil but shines their light on them. Others look to the future even though they are on the banks of evil. Hope is a light, a light from a distance, and it gives warmth. Good people will perform the function of light in this world. Then the banks of evil will be full of light and warmth, and the joy, happiness, and hope of the people will grow, and these will be a source of imagination and dreams for the future.

Humans are born on the banks of evil, and they die there. The banks of evil are hardship. The meaning of life is in its hardship. The core meaning of the word "difficulty" is the word "interesting." It is not interesting to live a life without hardships; only interesting things will be hard. I will repeat this once again: hardships make life interesting. This is the core of education. Education is not just a matter of dealing with a problem but a prerequisite for enjoyment. Faith is formed in a person who can handle difficulties.

In order to live, one must identify one's location; it is on the banks of evil.

****

People are born to life to do good deeds. Agreed. This is a high idea. Why, then, are they born on the banks of evil? What is the truth? Why did evil enter the world before people arrived there? First, evil is danger. It involves wildlife, predators, and uncomfortable weather. A newborn does not have enough strength to overcome these, so everything is dangerous to them.

Second, evil comes from human beings. These kinds of evil have been increasing in the history of humanity by using all sorts of maneuvers and teachings and by being continuously "improved." Science labels these as factors—social factors, economic factors, political factors, and so on. Add to these the numerous racial and religious matters and the forms of evil deeds multiply immediately.

Third, evil grows from natural ignorance. It is identified with haughtiness, indifference, ignorance, immorality, and lack of conscience.

The banks of evil are a battlefield for people from the moment they come into this world. It is an inexhaustible eternal theme for art and literature. However, there are some people who do not feel the evil; perhaps they are likely to lead the masses.

There is physical torment and soul suffering. Those who can feel the evil are the ones whose souls will suffer. For those whose souls do not suffer, there are no banks of evil, since there are ways to escape the physical suffering. But to get over the soul's suffering is a difficult issue. The agony of the soul is a source of humanity, which is close to the concept of fate.

****

Let us suppose that there is a good person who is on the verge of badness, and that person realizes their situation. They understood their destiny. So, what is the meaning of their life? This is the thinker Qorqyt Ata's question. Qorqyt's phrase "Wherever you go, there is a grave of Qorqyt" is his worldview, a reflection of his sense of being on the verge of evil.

What, then, is the essence of life? Humans are strange. They suffer trying to find answers for questions with no answers. If everyone understood the essence of life or the meaning of life, would it be interesting to live a life? Would there be the power to live? If everything were clear, why would we live?

Most likely, people find life interesting because the meaning of human life is unknown. Is there any other way out?

Section Three

Words about Words

"You are sick with reason and faith;
Come for a Word."
— Al-Maari

— Word One —

Thoughts That Came to Me[1]

With respect to its content, 'Word One' of Abai was written as a 'Foreword', a 'Preface' to his other "Words." Those who intently read the Words of Abai will, very possibly, wind up having two inexplicable feelings arise in their hearts. On the one hand, we see a man exhausted by perpetual struggle, who has experienced a great many troubles and sufferings, who has grown tired and dissatisfied with life and expresses his faintheartedness as he faces his remaining days, a man run headlong into worry to the point of illness. On the other hand, we meet up with a sage who, with philosophical depth and significance, has drawn wise and measured conclusions from out of the depths of the chaotic affairs he has experienced.

Abai was a man of his time, he analyzed in his poem-songs and Words the matters of chief importance among the main affairs of his day. These were: tending to social-national affairs, tending to livestock, that is, the economy, tending to scholarship and science, tending to religion and tending to the education and upbringing of children.

Eschewing the affairs of government and state[1] while also noting that tending livestock and economic concerns were not his strength, he supplies reasons as to why it is impossible for him to tend to scholarly-scientific pursuits. There simply was no one in his midst to converse with on an academic level and, if that be the case, then from whom can you inquire concerning the things you do not know and to whom will the knowledge you do have be 'medicinal', that is, beneficial? Since such was the state of things, scholarly-scientific pursuit itself was a distress of soul for him.

Abai said that in order to follow the path of Sufi asceticism and tend to religion, peace of heart was needed. But there was no peace, neither in his own heart nor in the days in which he lived. How, then, he intimated, shall one tend to religion or pursue the ascetic life? Abai ponders over the matter of the ascetic Sufi life more deeply in Word Thirty-eight. But as for this first, opening Word, he does not expound his thoughts fully. Again, the poet-sage tells us that in order to tend to religion, peace of heart is needed. And in the plain truth of it, is not religion one of the spiritual forces which should bring peace to the nation? Be that as it may, this issue is addressed, but not fully expounded upon in Abai's Words.

---

[1] An English translation of the 'Words' of Abai can be found at: http://www.leneshmidt-translations.com/book_of_words_abai_kunanbaev_english/index.htm

His reasons for not being able to tend to the education and upbringing of children are clear, however. He says, "I have not come to the place where I am convinced of the benefits of progressive life and education for my children; where those benefits are and what the children should do with them I am not sure. In tending to their education, what should I tell them to become?"[2]

Pondering deeply over these thoughts, we cannot conclude that they are an indication of the poet-sage's feeling of despair from life. Rather, they are grievances toward the social conditions of his day, conditions which had become like a narrow cage, leaving no space for people to carry on their lives and activities. Convinced that his efforts in the face of such circumstances were futile, Abai decides: "I will take paper and pen as my companions and start writing down all my thoughts. Should anyone find my words useful and copy them down or memorize them, let it so be; and if no one needs my words, they will remain with me anyway. As for me, I have no concern now other than writing."

To express his thoughts freely, Abai introduced a new, original genre: the Word. The poet's Words are the genre of free thinking expressed in appropriate form. Fortunately Abai avoided the lot of many well-known philosophers who tried with less success to find an appropriate form in which to express their thoughts. Unfortunately, however, the genre created by Abai was not developed further in his own native Kazakh culture. But, the culprit of such misfortune must be – to put it in the words of Shakerim Kudaiberdi-uhli, one of the most well-known of Abai's disciples – the time of "clear, precise thought," that is, the era when 'free thought' was choked out and restricted by 'clear, precise thought', namely that of 'the party line' in the late Tsarist, early Soviet period. In a day and age when one became a transgressor for expressing their own thoughts, it was of course impossible for the genre of 'the Word' to be developed, and thus for the tradition of Abai to be continued on. It is hoped that this genre can be renewed and continued in our day, since the foundations have been laid for it. That which we call 'pluralism' today was reflected in the method of thought which Abai employed in his own time.

The careful reader will certainly notice some inconsistency in the poet's own statements. But this does not mean that Abai actually contradicts himself, it is rather a manifestation and evidence of how his thoughts successively develop. On certain occasions, Abai, who ever-develops his thoughts each time he writes, delves deep into various details and throws the solution of a matter back onto the reader. He puts questions to the reader. This is how he engages his generation. Abai never attempted to give ready-made answers to all life's happenings. He spoke about difficult challenges, about the contradictions and paradoxes of life. It is my hope that the reader, after making their way through and familiarizing themselves with all forty-five of Abai's 'Words', will become thoroughly convinced of the excellence and enduring value of Abai's philosophical reflections.

— Word Two —

Knowing Yourself
Through the Eyes of Others

In his second 'Word', Abai clearly demonstrates that the Kazakh's own understanding of themselves can be glimpsed from the estimates they make of other peoples. The fact that coarse, uncomplimentary ideas, which were rather far from the truth, had spread widely among the nation was due to the poverty of the Kazakh's own familiarity with and conception of themselves. Saying that 'we are the soundest people in this world' is a crude form of understanding which leads to ethnocentrism. Abai offers the way of cleansing from this overly simplistic mentality. The poet-sage tells us that "in my childhood I used to hear the Kazakhs looking upon the Tajiks, Nogais (as well as Tatars) and Russians and mocking them, turning them into an object of joking. I thought then: 'Oh, dear God, it turns out that, besides us, all other peoples are worthless scoundrels, they come out on bottom when compared with us, we are the soundest of all peoples'."

"If I myself stop to think about it though," says Abai, "there is no crop which the Sarts (that is, Uzbeks)[3] have not planted, no technical skill or profession which they do not engage in, mastering quickly for themselves even the skills of the Russians. They do not live in enmity with one another, even providing the Kazakhs with burial robes for their dead and clothes for their living."

"As for the Nogai-Tatars, they endure both poverty and military duty, they uphold their mullahs and medreses (that is, mosque-based religious schools) as well as observe their religion. They know how to work hard and make a profit, maintaining purity before both God and society as well. As for us Kazakhs, in order to obtain our daily bread, one of us serves them as a hired-hand, and another is a receiver of their benevolence."

"As for the Russians, there is not even a word to be said, we are not even worthy of their male or female servants."[4] What, then, is this boasting that we are the most sound people, except empty vanity?

Abai is speaking this word, not to humiliate the Kazakh people, but to intentionally touch their very souls, their sense of honor and dignity. No one desires to see the good qualities found among the people fall by the wayside. Thus addressing their inappropriate and unbecoming ways and deeds is the path to overcoming them. Why not plant crops like the Uzbek-Sart, why not observe religion and engage in trade like the Nogai-Tatar, why not embrace the knowledge of the Russians and expand their own horizons on an equal plane with them?

These are the thoughts which are troubling Abai. What is it that the Kazakhs need to do in order to be delivered from this predicament? They must first look at themselves through the eyes of others. In order to be lifted to that kind of level, they have to pursue work, find and develop a skill and prosper economically and then, if they excel in these things, they will be delivered from reproach. Only under those circumstances will the Kazakhs' conception of other peoples change.

In this brief word, Abai has set forth the essential path for cultural and national development. There is no option but to confess that the ideas of the poet-sage are still to this day not being put fully into practice. If the Kazakh community had, in due season, given heed to the teaching of Abai, one can only wonder whether there would have been any who perished in the famine of the 1930s? When the Uzbek-Sarts and Tatars remained substantially healthy and whole, nearly half the Kazakh population ran headlong into bloodshed and slaughter. Abai's declaration, "work and make a living, develop a skill and become someone significant," remains the order of life for our day.

— Word Three —
"If There are Two Judges, There Will Surely Be Four Disputes"
(Kazakh proverb)

In this third 'Word', Abai addresses the problems of authority and government. In the time of the poet-sage, the Kazakh people, who had lost the former freedom they enjoyed in their own homeland, had begun to sink into decline. Earlier, when their khans and judges, heroes and *zhiraus* (that is, poet-musicians and counselors to the khans) were around, there was no historical-social ground upon which behavior might take root and grow that might lead to enmity or mistreatment or any other unwholesome attitudes between people. People deemed by the larger community to be lacking in human dignity were entirely excluded from the great meetings and councils, they were not even invited to participate in the community meetings. In those days, every Kazakh leader served the people in accordance with the purpose and best interest of the people in mind. Today if we stop and evaluate our Kazakh people's history, the young Kazakh men mainly passed their days atop of a horse. For one of the most important contributions of a citizen at that time was in defense of their nation against the enemy.

Afterwards, once our people had passed into subordination to Russia, the need for the Kazakhs to be soldiers, taking the reigns of their horses and flying like birds at top speed across the steppe in order to defend their vast, rich fatherland fell from the order of the day, which is to say, it simply lost its importance. Trivial life pursuits took root and unhealthy, negative character traits and actions started to take pasture. Khans to rule the nation, judges to speak wise counsel, the service of the *zhiraus* within the community – these all disappeared, falling into ruin. Their places were occupied instead by Russian officials, whose religion, language and worldview were foreign. The Kazakhs were left only the right to elect the chiefs of the administrative districts established by the Tsarist government, which, according to Abai, was for a three-year term.

But over the span of this three-year term, the first year was spent listening to all kinds of grievances and complaints from the people, declaring "We elected you!" The second year was given over to seeking candidate status for re-election, while in the last year, the election draws near and their whole life is consumed with the desire to being re-elected as an administrative chief again.

Abai expresses his bitter opinion regarding this particular "exacting authority" of the Russian Tsar. With the situation like this, it would be more appropriate for the authorities of the larger Tsarist administrative territories and the military governors to appoint the chiefs of the administrative districts from among those who have had a Russian education. This is because, like a bone tossed to dogs, the very idea itself of becoming an administrative chief is a cause for contention among the people.

Seeing his fellow countrymen, out of their want to become administrative chiefs, disputing with one another and breaking off into political parties to the degree that their eager attempts were creating consternation among the people, Abai insisted that they should acquaint themselves with the earlier codes of Kazakh national law: Kasim khan's (1511-1520) 'Straight Path', Esim khan's (1598-1643) 'Ancient Pathway' and Az Tauke khan's (1680-1715) 'Seven Decrees'. Of course Abai, yearning for those who could take from these national treasures the things which conformed to previous lifeways and substitute for them something more suitable for the present day, ached in his heart at the fact that there was no one in his day able to carry out such a task.

Abai notes that those who knew the Kazakhs well said: "If there are two judges, there will surely be four disputes." Therefore, the number of judges needs to be odd, not even. That is to say, if three people are elected to authority in every administrative region, then it would not take such a long time to reach agreement on various matters. Abai knew well that as long as the situation remained as it was, the disputes among the Kazakhs would not come to an end. This is because authority had passed from the former judges known from Kazakh history, with their places now controlled by those eager for their own gain who had just enough Russian to pass themselves off as candidates for the task.

Since no justice had been established and no good came forth from their service for the people, Abai considered it appropriate that the ratification of administrative chiefs should come from above, that is, from the Russian colonial powers themselves. The poet-sage noted two good things which would issue forth from this: One, Kazakh children would strive to become educated and that also is a necessary, beneficial thing. Second, those appointed as administrative chiefs would have no obligation to those who elected them, but to the Russian officials.

Some of course might go so far as to say that this means Abai was lending support to the Russian colonial political system. But if we get right down to the essence of the issue, in Abai's eyes, those among the Kazakhs who undertake the planting of crops, work at finding ways to increase their livestock and thus develop the Kazakh economy and those who go down the path of education – all these are far more profitable than those who vainly burden themselves and their people with disputes over administrative authority. This is how Abai set forth the problem. Abai said many things about political authority in his other words as well as his poem-songs. The sense and essence of all of them fits with the opinion expressed here.

The content of these words of wisdom from Abai have value for our own day. The poet-sage has spoken his own thoughts regarding the socio-political foundations of administrative civil service and offered cutting-edge suggestions. But, you say, who was there in that time who thought about the Kazakhs? It of course was very profitable for the Russian officials that the Kazakhs fought among themselves over administrative positions, allowing their character to be broken down and dilapidated, coming to the point of impatience, falsely accusing one another and ultimately giving bribes to the powers-that-be, that is, the Russian authorities. Abai brings to life a vivid description of this spectacle in his writing.

"People are Born Crying, and Die in Sorrow"

Human nature is a mystery. Human beings are creatures which tend to go through continual change throughout their lives. Abai explains that the two main states of human existence are joy and sorrow, laughter and tears. Is there anyone on earth who has not experienced joy, not known sorrow? Laughter and tears each come in turn, do they not?

But Abai also speaks of something else here. There are people who spend their lives in idleness and wanton pleasures. They think life is a continuous feast. Others are always despondent. They are not able to find joy in life. They see everything in dark colors. Abai thinks that senseless laughter resembles drunkenness. But drunkenness leads to misbehavior; a conversation with a drunkard gives one a headache. Anyone who constantly indulges in senseless merriment neglects his responsibilities in a slipshod manner.

Others, being depressed, are prepared in advance for all kinds of misfortunes and troubles, providing themselves even with burial robes long before their appointed day. But should a person always be downcast? A person who is in constant sorrow can fall seriously ill. Laughter and joy are as the rain which comes during a drought in summer; they feed the soul with life-giving moisture. Everything, as much as possible, should be done with joy, smiles and good spirits.

Abai tells how to achieve that: "Laugh at the absurdities of a fool, and do it with a feeling of righteous anger. But such laughter should not be indulged in too often, for it is bitter. When you see someone who leads a good life, whose kind deeds are worthy of emulation, laugh with a glad heart, with sincere joy." A good example teaches you many useful things.

Human beings are born into this world crying and they depart from it in sorrow. The person who lives without thinking of the purpose of life simply vegetates and 'exists' or 'survives'. Life spent in idleness is useless and futile. The rich console themselves with the thought that they can buy everything that pleases the eye and flesh, but when the time of death comes all their wealth will seem worthless compared to life, the only thing that could not be bought. And the understanding of this truth is a sad awakening for those searching out the purpose of their earthy existence, is it not?

Death is inevitable for every living creature, even our famous forefather Korkit-ata, the great Turkic mystic philosopher and poet-musician of the 9-10th century, could not avoid it. If a man works hard, trusting in his own powers, he can learn to value both joy and sorrow.

Summarizing his thoughts about the purpose of life, Abai says: "Put your faith in God and trust in your powers and abilities. Even the hardest land will yield good crops to honest and selfless toil."

— *Word Five* —

"Is This the Nation We Were Seeking?"

In 'Word Five', Abai analyzes the philosophy of backwardness which has been thoroughly absorbed into the mind of his people. He explains how we can understand the petition of the Kazakhs which says: "Oh, God, make us as troublefree as babes." What is their idea of being like little children? To the point, it is making no effort to engage in industrious activity, being satisfied with what one has, that is, complacency, taking no thought of what is lacking, living with the understanding and mentality of a child.

Abai discovers this mentality in common Kazakh proverbs and sayings: "A heroic person and a wolf will both find their food along the way," "My hand which takes also gives," "Not being able to count on the judge is like not being able to count on God," "If you are famished, drop by a home in mourning, for there you will find a feast,"[5] "When in the 'noonday' of your life, gather daily the flocks and herds," "A rich man has a countenance full of light, a poor man as hard as stone," and others.

Based on these proverbs, the poet concludes that the troublesome sorrow of the Kazakhs is in their livestock, but they take no concern for them. They do not know how to make the most of their livestock. For them, deceiving those who are rich in cattle or turning on them as enemies, doing crafty, treacherous things are of no shame or trouble. But to think about how they themselves can increase their own livestock and then make a diligent effort toward that end, this is trouble and sorrow. And for that reason they love being troublefree as babes.

Abai seeks to move the people from their traditional pastoral economy to other vocational activities. The zeal of the Kazakhs is only in their livestock. But increasing one's livestock and thinking together as a community of ways to go about that task requires well-thought-out action. The fact that the people are still unable to deal with such problems and, instead, desire to be only carefree as babes vexes the poet-sage.

Abai is struggling from the heart in this 'Word' with advanced, vital issues. That the Kazakhs take no thought for scientific inquiry, education and justice and instead only weep and moan over livestock is a sad state of affairs. Abai says that the way to wealth, property and power comes through knowledge and education. Only education can help get rid of evil vices and the habit of seeking to live care-free, being complacent. The people must awake and realize that a different age is upon them. The time of Abai was the time of domination by Russian officials. Kazakhs ceased from being one nation united by their own leaders.

Abai comprehended clearly that people were sinking down into petty living, that their morals and manners had taken a turn for the worse. Feeling that he could not change much of anything, Abai addressed words of reproach and compassion to his enslaved people: "Is this the people whom I love with all my heart?"

— *Word Six* —

The Unity of Wisdom

In this 'Word', Abai offers philosophical reflections upon the Kazakh proverb: "The beginning of skill is unity, the beginning of prosperity is life." All of us use proverbs at times, but do we ever stop to reflect upon their inner meaning? Abai raises the problem of just what kind of people or nation can have unity. What kind of unity can there be among a people who have fallen into subjection to another power and who, as a nation, no longer rule themselves?

The Kazakhs do not fully understand unity, they think that if they share a horse, a meal, clothing and wealth, they have unity. Abai critiques such trivial ideas, this narrow pastureland of Kazakh thoughtlife. Who can guarantee that such people will, being neither rich or poor, not turn into lazy bums who lie around drinking all day until their common prosperity disappears instead of working to increase their livestock, that is, to make an honest profit? That kind of 'unity' spans only a brief, passing moment, like snow melting and flowing away like water. If someone's relative comes and seeks some kind of unity based in such things, he is only flirting with disaster, since in the end he winds up pursuing his own cause, finding no profit. Such unity breaks down when their common prosperity dries up and withers away.

Abai tosses out all such ideas of unity and says that true unity is the unity of reason and wisdom. The poet-sage has not come upon this idea in vain. There are many angles from which it can be developed. For example, to consider the well-being of the nation, putting the matter to mutual counsel by reason and wisdom, this is true unity. Abai must surely be indicating this direction at the root of all that he is saying in this Word.

Then Abai, after having shared these kinds of thoughts regarding "unity," delves into the meaning of the term "life" or "existence" which occurs in the second part of the proverb. He says that life is the source of well-being. What kind of life do we lead? Is it only about commonplace living, for the soul not to give up its body, that is, to avoid death for as long as possible? Even an animal can lead such a life. Is that life? No, it is about life lived through intelligence with one's heart and soul. If you are alive but your soul is dead, words of reason will not reach you.

There is no strength of heart along the road which knows not how to increase livestock with good, honest hard work and, instead, has fallen prey to some parasitic way of making one's living:

> *A loafer and a servile self-seeking flatterer,*
> *One who barely scrapes out their existence,*
> *Living one meal at a time, hand-to-mouth.*
> *Outwardly they appear energetic,*
> *but they are craven in their heart,*
> *With no sense of shame,*
> *taking no thought of their end.*

Abai thinks that it would be better to die a righteous death than lead such a life. Meditating on the meaning of life, he urges not just mere 'existence', but dignity and pure conscience. "Can one forgo dignity, conscience and principles for a crust of bread?" Abai's opinion is confirmed in his words from the verse dedicated to the death of his brother Ospan: "Your death is blessed, for you did not have to abase yourself for a piece of bread, you did not experience the corruptibility of others."

In such a case death seems better than life when life does not make one happy, but instead becomes a dreadful burden which thoroughly tears down and corrupts the soul. The proverb "work is the beginning of success" is true because work is the source of all benefits. By working hard with your own developed skills and abilities, you can earn a living fairly.

Concerning the Desires of Flesh and Spirit

'Desire' is a broad concept. This quality given us by nature makes us different from animals. There are desires of the flesh and desires of the soul. Born into this world a person inherits two essential needs. These are the need of the flesh to eat, drink and sleep, without which the body cannot be the house of the soul and will not grow in height and strength. Once they have become accustomed to living in comfort a person will not want to live under any other circumstances.

I think Abai aptly depicts the reason why upon growing up a person likes the pleasures of the flesh more than of the soul in the following words:

> Subjugating our souls to our bodies, we have contemplated everything around us with our eyes, but not with our hearts and minds. We do not trust the impulses of our soul. Satisfied with outward appearances, we make no attempt to uncover inner mysteries in the vain belief that we shall lose nothing by remaining in the dark. In what way, then, do we differ from animals if we perceive things only with our eyes? We know nothing, but will defend our ignorance and try to pass off our ignorance as knowledge.
>
> It seems we were better off in our childhood. We were human then, for we sought to learn as much as possible. If, after childhood, the desire of the soul overrides the desire of flesh, then a person has the right to be called an adult, a full-grown person. What is the desire of the soul? It is the wish to know, to see and to learn. A child, when he or she sees unknown objects or hears unknown sounds, asks numerous questions: 'What's that? Why? How?' Why, then, upon growing up and supposedly gaining in wisdom, do we not seek to satisfy our curiosity? Why do we not tread in the path of those who seek knowledge?

This Word contains more questions than answers. And it is clear why. Intellectual aspiration is not just a wish to know, see and learn. It is a gift from God, and not everyone is given it. Everyone has abilities given them by nature. Most people do not go deep into the root of the matter. They are satisfied with simple surface contemplation. Abai says: "A person becomes firmly established on the earth by learning the mysteries of nature and drawing sound conclusions. That sets humans apart from animals. They have reason, will and soul."

The nature of a human and an animal are different. An animal knows nothing and has no aim in life, but the potential of human beings is inexhaustible because they have perception and discernment. Their conscious activity is the evidence of their intellect. But people do not think about food for their soul, they are satisfied with what they have learned, though their knowledge is rather limited. Abai called them people without light in their soul.

Who Needs Wisdom and Instruction?

Abai starts his eighth Word with a question: "Who will heed our advice and listen to our counsel?" Indeed, who needs it? Abai enumerates and discusses those who may need wise advice.

> One man may be a regional administrative chief, another a judge. Do they need wisdom and advice? No, because these people consider themselves quite clever enough and seek power so as to teach and give guidance to others. Are they the kind who would spare time to listen to us? Their minds are filled with other concerns: not to offend their superiors inadvertently, not to provoke the anger of the thief, not to cause trouble and confusion among the people, and not to wind up on the losing side, but gain some personal advantage. No, judges and district administrative chiefs are too busy.

Well, then, maybe the rich? But no, says Abai!

> They think they possess the treasures of almost half the world. They can pay in (cash or) livestock for whatever they lack. They are certain that if they own livestock they will be able to bribe even the Most High. Their herds take the place of everything else for them – their native land, people, religion, family and learning. They must feed and water their livestock, protect it from thieves and wolves and shelter it from the cold. No, the rich are too busy to heed good counsel.
>
> As for thieves and scoundrels, they obviously would not listen anyway. The poor are only concerned about getting their daily bread. What good are advice, wisdom and learning to them when even the rich do not want it? If a wise mind is not honored by people, is there any need of a wise man?

With such questions, Abai draws Word Eight to a close.

"This is Who I Am, I am a Kazakh"

Abai starts Word Nine with these words: "If I am a Kazakh and must love my people, then which of the Kazakhs ways should I affirm and support, determined to love them, and which ones should I despise and determine to hate?" He then further meditates on the qualities of his people which are close to his heart and those in which he should find cause for blame.

But he does not offer answers to the questions he poses. He does not believe that his people will correct their misguided ways. Abai says in bitterness: "Even though I live, I do not consider myself alive. Outwardly I am alive, but I am dead within." These words of Abai should not be interpreted in the manner which the great Asan Kaigi, musical poet-philospher and counselor to Zhanibek khan in the 15th century, interpreted similar words in his own time. To give an impartial assessment of oneself, to look for the cause of evil in oneself, to find and cure it – these are the main views and aims of Abai's philosophy.

Since the times of Korkit-ata and Asan Kaigi, philosophical outlooks on life and death went hand-in-hand. In Western Europe this trend was called 'existentialism'. The Kazakhs have a custom of pondering life and death, of reflecting on the transience of earthly existence and the inevitability of death. That is why they did not take death as something unexpected, but took it quite naturally and made preparations for it in advance. As a part of Kazakh lifeways, it was customary to leave behind thoughts about death which themselves would never die. It is for this reason that Abai, without sorrow, desires that which he first desired, and holding no regret for the past, says: "This also is good, that in the time of dying, alas, those, yes those cares of mine have been left behind!"

Does not such an attitude toward death reveal a deep understanding of its meaning? On the other hand, to accept death without any regret, is that not a recognition of the uselessness of life? For many thousands of years people have been asking this question, but there is still no answer because no one has yet understood entirely the meaning of life and death. Indeed, no one can possibly understand this great mystery of nature. We bow our heads to it.

— Word Ten —
On Parents and Children

This Word speaks of the relationship between a parent and a child. "People pray to God to send them a child. What does a person need a child for?," asks the poet-sage. Is there any greater love than the love of parents for their children? The parents see the child as their support. According to the Kazakhs, a home with children is a *bazaar*, that is, a marketplace.

But Abai considers this matter from a different angle. The poet-sage pays attention to the fact that most of those praying to God to send them a child do not think about their responsibility for that child:

What kind of statement is it to say 'Let my child fill my place when I am gone'? Are you concerned that the vast store of wealth and achievement which you leave behind may wind up with no one to inherit or take possession of it? ...Is this something you say out of jealousy for others while you are heading off to your death bed? You who cannot cut yourself loose from jealousy of others, what sort of superior place would you have? The good of a child is your desire and good pleasure, the bad is your grief and sorrow. Did you inquire and learn what kind of child they would be? Were the dog-like vile deeds you yourself committed few in number? So now why are you so eager like this to have a child, making them a dog and causing them to experience humiliation as well?[6]

The poet-sage states that people are responsible for their descendants. Who has not dreamed of having children? This is the sacred duty of parents. But if your child is bad, then your life will become a living hell. A good child can make your life happy. Is there anyone who has never experienced hardships and troubles? Life passes in the struggle for survival. A person always lacks something or faces difficulty and tries to find a way out. Are you sure your child will avoid such a lot? What should they come into this world for? To live the years fatefully given them in suffering?

These problems should be well thought out. But there is no time or opportunity for that. When children are born, the parents' problems come together with them. And no one can avoid these problems. This is the law of life. There has always existed a conflict between parents and their children. So, as a parent, you should be ready for that if you wish to have a child.

Abai does not say how to establish good relations between parents and their children. He considers the matter of an individual's responsibility to society, reflecting upon the issue of descendants and the problems they may face in their lifetime.

The parents want to have a child who can pray for them after their death. This is one of the main postulates of Muslim law. And in our opinion, reading verses of the Qur'an in commemoration of the diseased is not only a privilege of a pious Muslim, but also a tribute to the ancestors. Abai, however, says:

You say 'Let my child have the Qur'an read for me after I am gone', but if the people you have done good to are many, who will not have the Qur'an read for you? If, on the other hand, you have done much evil, then what will your child's Qur'an readings accomplish? The things which you yourself have not accomplished in this life, can your child, after you have died, undertake a trade and accomplish them for you? Your desire for a child in order to use them as a cover over you like a burial shroud is nothing other than your wishing your death to haunt your child in the prime of their years. If you say 'Let them grow up and become adults', then is there any child born of the Kazakhs who themselves reaches adulthood and is able to save their father and mother from hell? I can only wonder whether there is any father like you or nation like yours who can raise up such a child?

These are extremely wise thoughts. A good person is good in both this life and in death. The entire nation will respect such a person as if all of them together were such a person's child. Therefore we can only wonder whether your child will ever be able to accomplish in your stead the good things you yourself were never able to achieve.

Pondering the matter in this way, Abai comes to the conclusion that the parents should use their wealth to give their children an education. There will be neither faith nor well-being without an education, that is why every child should study and learn.

In this Word, Abai again repeats his thought that the sense of life is to be sought in an education, not in wealth. This idea is met up with regularly in the poet-sage's poem-songs, as for example his well-known poem-song "Having not yet discovered knowledge and learning, be not proud..." Abai interpreted the word "knowledge" in a broad sense, not simply in rationalistic terms. According to the poet-sage, 'knowledge' is a synthesis of wisdom and sense-intuition. He used 'knowledge' in the sense in which it underlies one's entire outlook and worldview.

— *Word Eleven* —
No Way Out?!

The colonial policy of Tsarism brought stealing, pillage and plunder to the Kazakh Steppe. This does not mean that these things were unknown before. As long as humans have existed, theft and plunder have accompanied them throughout the entire span of their lives. But in Abai's time these vices became an incurable disease of the society and, as a result, it was the ordinary people who suffered most of all. The reason for this is that not only was it the thieves who stole, but also those in authority by promising the former they would assist them in evading justice.

How could this happen? The explanation was quite simple: theft remained unpunished because it was good for the regional administrative chiefs and other officials. They took bribes from both the thief who was trying to avoid punishment and the plaintiff who hoped to win a case. Therefore, if each case of theft is an opportunity for our judges to make money, then why be in a hurry to punish criminals? The crooks also contribute to the enrichment of the authorities because the ordinary people will make request of the latter, and not empty-handed of course.

Before, the thieves and robbers were afraid of the respected figures of the clan. Since Russian officials took over authority, however, the rich were also infected with this disease. They squandered their property and lived 'hard and fast', not understanding that they were creating new heartaches and pains for people. These two vices, theft and bribery, are a pair which together breed trouble in Abai's opinion. If everyone starts stealing, who will correct them? Will such moral qualities as honor and commitment, loyalty and conscience sink into oblivion? The rich have the opportunity to help guide people down the right path because they have power and money, but instead they cast prudence to the wind.

What could be expected from a people who had lost its freedom and unity? Understanding that the situation was critical, Abai desperately sought a way out.

The Kozha Akhmet Yasawi Mausoleum, Turkistan, Kazakhstan.

Built by Amir Timur (Tamerlane) in honor of the 11th century Sufi saint who helped spread Islam among the Turkic peoples. Yasawi's Mausoleum remains one of the most sacred pilgrimage sites in Central Asia to this day. Photo © R. Charles Weller

— Word Twelve —

On Faith and Devotion

Although the term *iman*, that is, "faith," entered Kazakh vocabulary and thinking via the religion of Islam, it became in time the primary term for honor and dignity as well as good etiquette. This is why the Kazakhs call 'a good soul' a person of faith. In Muslim understanding, a person of faith cannot be 'devotionless', that is, they must live a life of worship and devotion. What we mean by 'devotion' is a Muslim's fulfillment of their duties and obligations. Abai says that anyone who has faith and goes about engaged accordingly in a life of devotion should receive affirmation. This is because people do what they have learned; you cannot expect someone to do what they have no knowledge of.

However, says Abai, if that person thinks to themselves that their knowledge is sufficient and they have no further need of learning, then God has stricken them, for their 'devotion' is not true 'devotion'. Having no passion for knowledge and learning, for developing and exercising one's talents, such is faithlessness. This is how Abai goes about reforming the religion of Islam. He insists that the eagerness to learn and be educated is the essence of faith and devotion, it is a high and admirable idea, a word of confession by the person themselves regarding their limitless potential for personal growth and development. If you have faith, do not look carelessly upon your undertakings, for carelessness blinds the eyes.

Abai attempted to clarify the nature of being human through faith. He used the concept of faith not just in a religious sense, but in another sense as well. Here one can observe clearly the tremendous influence of Sufi philosophy upon the poet-sage's worldview. Analyzing and explaining 'faith' from a perspective not just of religious faith, but of knowledge and education is a tradition in Islamic philosophy. Abai here observes that the idea of faith as a strictly religious concept is not limited to mere repetition in their careless religious practices, but has also taken a foothold and manifested itself in their daily lifeways and activities.[7] In this way, he sets forth his thoughts, born out of inner turmoil, in plain view.

— Word Thirteen —

What is True Faith?

*Kozha Akhmet Yasawi
Mausoleum, side view.*

Abai in this Word continues the subject of devotion and faith which was spoken of in Word Twelve. Offering a definition of "faith," he says there are two kinds of things one needs in order to have 'faith' and attain to a state of belief: Namely, the first is to believe by demonstrating the veracity of that which one places their faith in. This Abai calls '*yakini*' faith or a faith which is 'tried and true'. To attain to this state of belief is not an easy undertaking. One must study deeply, being a scholar of sorts. Among the Kazakhs there are very few, if any such people to be found.

Second are those who hear from others and believe based on the words of the religious leader. This he calls '*taklidi*' faith or faith which is placed in something by simply following along behind another, a 'blind faith' of sorts. Even if someone threatens to kill such a one, their mind and heart is set immovable and steadfast. Abai sums things up by saying that to defend this kind of faith one needs a fearless heart, they must be unyielding, remaining true to their convictions. As the main body of believers within the nation holds to a '*taklidi*' faith, that is, a 'blind faith', having no solid foundation on which to stand, they will not forsake calling a lie the truth in the face of life's pressures. These kind of people have the understanding that "there is no sin which God Almighty will not forgive."

But if that be so, then what kind of faith can we speak of? Abai gave no answer to this problem, but he exposed it, lifting its veil. Thinking over and pondering the issue of faith and then coming to a decision as to whether one should live a life of faith and devotion – this is no else's business but each person's alone. It is only right that there be no force or coercion employed with respect to a person's faith. In order to arrive at '*yakini*' faith, or a faith which is 'tried and true', one must come to personally know that God exists through some kind of logical method. But if your own wisdom and intellect is not sufficient for that, if you have no proof to offer yourself or others, then what is left except to believe in God.

Abai's conclusion regarding faith comes to us along these lines of thought. He was unable to find these two types of faith among the people. "There is no scholarly basis for saying that anyone has 'yakini' faith, and there is no solid foundation for saying that anyone has 'taklidi' faith...," says Abai. The seemingly goodhearted Kazakhs who refuse to accept his ideas look upon the false proverb "there is no sin which God Almighty will not forgive" as a powerful truth. Try, then, to understand this kind of Kazakh! Even Abai has not attempted to transcend such limited bounds of reflection in pondering the matter. He says nothing by way of clear demonstration about why the Kazakhs of his day were not acquainted with true faith.

— Word Fourteen —
"If the Tongue Obeys the Heart..."

The Kazakhs talk a great deal about the heart, but they do not understand that the best human qualities such as mercy, compassion and philanthropy are commands of the heart. Calling someone 'a person of brave heart', people respect them as a *batir*, that is, a courageous person or 'hero'. People say a *batir* is *'zhurekti'*, or 'one with heart', which again means brave, just or courageous. These qualities are attributable to a person who can listen to wise counsel, control their emotions, who has a strong will and can be patient. The problem with the Kazakh people is that they cannot listen to the lectures or speeches of learned people and that some of them, upon hearing them, are unable to do away readily with their mistaken ways or ideas.

Abai's words remind us of the people's tragedy in the 1930s when many were put to death under Stalin. We regret the poet's words were not heard by the rulers of that time. Who knows, maybe numerous deaths could have been avoided.

Strong will and conviction should be in every great action. The worst qualities of a human being are boastfulness, weakness of will and laziness. Such a person obeys destiny like a dog that follows a caravan lost in the desert sands. If a person is able to free themselves from the vices which control them, then they can be counted a healthy person.

This is the main quality in the definition of the word *'zhurekti'*, that is, 'one who has heart'. "A mind that obeys the heart will tell no lie."

— *Word Fifteen* —
Take Account of Yourself

In life, there are both wise and unwise people. "Every person is 'a child of humanity'." Coming into this world, a person cannot live without being attracted to and excited by the fascinating things around them. Those days of questioning and of passionate interests remain in a person's memory as the brightest period of life.

The difference between people is discerned through their deeds and actions. A person will live a good life if they have a genuine interest in this life, that is, a passion to live. That interest stirs up the imagination, it reveals the person's capabilities. Upon growing up, a person will recall the unforgettable time of their first searching and discoveries. It is at this age when the difference between wise and unwise people comes to light. A sensible person will interest themselves in worthy and serious matters. Those who are unwise will frivol away their time in worthless, futile and absurd undertakings. Having indulged in delights, when they come to their senses, they realize that their best years have swiftly passed in vain. In these younger days, they behave as if youth is eternal. Yet too soon they lose their former strength and become good for nothing.

To achieve a goal you need wisdom and volition. Our wisdom is determined by our choice of useful undertakings. These are values a person chooses for themselves. What do human values include? According to the philosophical sense of Abai, it is these kinds of activities, these kinds of useful undertakings, which help a person to unearth new qualities, merits and opportunities, as for example, the joy of having a child and raising them.

Taking stock in youth is a delight. Aspiration for knowledge is also good and natural. But to make one's life meaningful, aspirations themselves are not enough. You should have a strong enough volition to carry them out and not everyone is able to achieve that. Life is full of temptations. Temptations destroy a weak person. The poet says: "And yet another temptation lurks in the path of passionate souls." Success intoxicates their feelings, clouds their reason and causes them to commit blunders. It also poses a great trial for those who attain it and not everyone can pass the test because it is such an intoxicating feeling; you feel you are a champion, a conqueror of the universe. When you come to your senses, you recall how many boastful claims you made and how many blunders you committed.

"If you wish to be counted among the intelligent, then ask yourself once a day, once a week, or at least once a month: "How have I lived? Have I done anything to improve my learning, my worldly life or my life hereafter? Will I swallow the bitter dregs of regret in my latter days?" Or perhaps you do not know or remember how you have lived and why?

In the philosophical sense, Abai's precepts here are of great importance.

— Word Sixteen —

Submission to God

A sense of devotion to God has not been absorbed to any strong degree in the Kazakh mentality, but in many circumstances has become a habit or custom. Does anything happen in the world without reason or cause? No. There are surely two reasons for the Kazakhs' looking upon the matter of religion in a carefree way. In the first place, the religion of Islam did not fully penetrate into the midst of our people.[8] What we call mosques, which spread religion and safeguard its purity, were mostly in the city areas and, even then, Tatars were in charge of them. Within the nation, other than the community mullahs, those trained in the teaching and spread of religion as well as religious books were insufficient in number.

In the second place, the need for the religion of Islam in Kazakh life was not that great in those times. For a people who went about moving and settling, that is, a nomadic people, the only things necessary were those which could quickly be placed on camels and hung on horses and then carried off on their way. Throughout these centuries what took shape and formed as a custom and lifeway was defending themselves against their enemies.

In the third place, many of the beliefs and practices belonging to the Kazakh worldview continued serving also the function of a religious worldview. To the point, Islam was not necessary for the Kazakhs, rather the Kazakhs took from Islam that which they needed for themselves. For example, while the Sufi monastic tradition in the sedentary oasis regions of Central Asia took to itself orthodoxy as one of its characteristics, Sufism in the Kazakh land found fertile soil within the folk poetry tradition. What I am speaking of here is the impact of the Sufi worldview upon the historic development of mystic love poems and songs within Kazakh culture.

To sum things up, the Kazakh people did not, for the most part, serve God as those sold-out — certainly not to the point of death — or those given over wholly and completely to Islam. This unique aspect of devotion is observed only when people are genuinely in submission to God. The wide-open space of the Kazakh steppe land bequeathed unto them a freedom to act and engage in their own affairs. A person who is free steers clear of even servitude to God and safeguards their freedom.

"I Will Give Preference to My Heart"

"I will give preference to my heart," say the Eastern philosophers. Such trends as rationalism and sensualism prevail in Western philosophy. Reason is the most important thing in rationalism. Feeling is the basis of sensualism. Eastern philosophy does not have such a contrast. That is why we cannot assign it to any certain trend, because when speaking of reason the poet-sage, that is, Abai, always adds heart and will to it.

Reason, Heart and Will are inseparable in his poetry and other writings. These three notions stand together as a whole in Abai's Word. It is not important for us whether the dispute between 'Reason, Heart and Will' which the poet-sage speaks of in this Word actually took place or not. It is not important to know the story's source. Abai's thoughts about Reason, Heart and Will are much more interesting for us than finding out whether the dispute actually occurred.

In Word Seventeen, Reason, Will and Heart argue about who was the most important among them. At the beginning of life they are all equally important to a person. The sensitive reader will discover a good many new things for themselves in the definitions of these notions. First of all, each of them speaks of themselves; secondly, Knowledge, to whom they all appeal to settle their argument, has her own opinion of each of them.

Thus, Knowledge unites Will, Reason and Heart. What is Knowledge, then? Abai does not explain it in simplistic terms. He says that it is a 'bookish' word, that is, a word connected with the reading and study of books. There is nothing more important in the world than knowledge. Abai considers reason separately. He says reason is 'the tongue' of knowledge. Abai does not deny his mystical attitude toward knowledge.

When Abai says knowledge is a bookish word he does not mean secular books, he means God's Word. A scholar tells ordinary people the essence of this or that book, and explains it to them. Abai calls such work *naklia*. In such cases, a scholar tells of knowledge which has been attained beforehand by others. If a scholar tries in their writings to get to the root of known truths, to find an explanation for them, then these works will be called *gaklia*.

Based on these definitions, Abai's Word here is *naklia* because it does not contain new truth(s). Will, Heart and Reason are considered from the point of view of objective ideas. The Greek philosopher Plato was the founder of this point of view. Consideration of these notions as separate ideas was traditional in Eastern philosophy. There is no need to search for the meaning of these notions in Western philosophy because this Eastern approach is one of the methods of the epistemological search for truth in Islam.

— *Word Eighteen* —
On Beauty and Vanity[9]

It is a part of human nature to dress in beautiful clothes, which stimulates a warm mood and makes a person attractive in the eyes of others. The skill to dress beautifully speaks of good taste. Abai, approving of a person's desire to look beautiful, at the same time criticizes beauty when it is taken to extreme measures.

There are two types of beauty, says Abai. One is in paying attention to the face, cultivating one's moustache and beard, pinching out and painting brows, pampering the body and trying to make a show of good manners. Another goes out of their way, finding no greater pleasure than to arouse envy among the people with their rich apparel and Arabian horse. "But this is absurd and shameful," notes Abai. " No one should get carried away by such desire for beauty, otherwise they will find it hard to look like a normal human being again. A person should distinguish themselves by virtue of their reason, knowledge, conscience and goodness. Only a fool thinks they can gain distinction by other means."

In this Word then, Abai gives the definition of the word "beauty." There is nothing bad in this word. Beauty is only bad if a person is so caught up with it that they take no concern for reason or knowledge. Our famous judges and leaders showed off their manners and sharp thinking, not their stylish clothing.

"Poetry is the ruler of language, the genius that carves marvelous things out of stone." Are not Abai's words here true beauty flowing forth from the poet-sage's figurative thought! It is in this sense we say that Abai is *the* embodiment of beauty itself. Having studied carefully his heritage, I came to this conclusion because he wrote down and left behind a full explanation of the nature of beauty. 'Beauty' is a lofty word. No one should underestimate its significance because, in its essence, it indicates not just beauty itself, but the human search and longing for beauty.

Being Attentive

The Kazakhs have a proverb: "Observing much you will become a prince, ever speaking good words of counsel you will become an orator of wisdom." What we mean by 'attentiveness' is not, as is said in the proverb, an innate ability of people that comes with merely being born. It comes as a result of intentional familiarity with the world. In order to be attentive, the poet-sage says you must bear in mind the words of those who themselves have paid careful attention in life. But being attentive by itself, in general, does not come to anything. What counts is bearing in mind the good things which one has heard and gained knowledge of from those who are attentive, while at the same time taking care to steer clear of evil. Abai grieves over the deficiency of people who do nothing other than simply bear in mind the words of those who are sober-minded and attentive in life. Abai informs us that a certain scholar of special knowledge and insight, that is, a *hakim* scholar, once said: It is better to tend pigs which can at least recognize you as opposed to wasting your time speaking to the crowds who cannot recognize or understand the word which is being imparted to them.

Those who listened and understood 'the word' which was spoken to them were few in Abai's day, and it is still so now. They do not concern themselves with the words of those who are attentive, with those who count knowledge their chief obligation and calling, which is why attentiveness itself is one measurement of a people's social mentality and outlook.

— *Word Twenty* —
Growing Weary

Abai did not acknowledge asceticism as a way of life. He stood for a life filled with work, everyday concerns and cares. The poet thinks that asceticism does not allow a person to fully enjoy life, to realize the joy of existence as he or she properly should. An ascetic person does not value life in this world; it seems senseless and useless to them.

Without denying the philosophy of asceticism altogether, Abai in this Word thinks of weariness, moments when life seems a burden. A good many things cause people to be filled to the point of saturation. For the most part, there is nothing with which a person cannot be satieted: food, amusements, fashion, feasts and parties, the desire to excel beyond others, sexual pleasure, etc. Sooner or later, discovering the vanity and viciousness of all that, a person will become disenchanted and indifferent.

"Weariness is the lot of clever people who seek perfection in life, who know the worth of many things, who are meticulous and discerning and can perceive the vanity of human existence. Those who have realized the transitory nature of earthly joys will grow weary of life," says Abai.

A wise person is accustomed to thinking over everything and drawing sound conclusions. The life of a careless person is full amusements and cloudless happiness. In this context, the poet-sage ironically notes that thoughtlessness and carelessness are also the qualities of human nature.

The questions Abai asks in Word Twenty find their answers only with the passing of much time. The question is: How to live a good life, the right life? Whether to spend time in thinking and searching for the purpose of life, to have a partial attitude toward everything or to indulge in amusements? The answers to these questions can be found in Abai's poetry. A person has one life and it is short. Therefore it makes no sense to be in constant sorrow, burdening the soul with grave thoughts. Those who are sated with pleasures and disappointed with the shortness of earthly existence finally reject the earthly things and come to God. The world is unstable; human life is subject to change. With age a person becomes weak, they feel their end near at hand. Therefore they change their views, habits and undertakings. But I think a person should never tire of searching for truth, nor be satisfied with the level of knowledge they have attained.

— *Word Twenty One* —

Maturity and Pride

Abai identifies two kinds of self-satisfaction or, to say it in another way, complacency: they are pride and boastfulness. "A person of dignity and honor has a high estimation of their own worth. They will do the utmost to ensure they are not regarded as an ignorant and unreliable person who does not keep their promises, as ill-mannered, arrogant, a shameless liar, a spiteful critic or a crook. Aware of the baseness of these vices, they will aspire to be above them. This quality is unique to a person of conscience, who is reasonable and high-minded. Such a person dislikes hearing people sing praises about them but, on the other hand, they will allow no one to tarnish or defile their name."

To identify who is who, and appreciate them fairly, to speak openly about them is not boastfulness, rather it is the only real opportunity there is to determine who can rule or who might be capable of accomplishing something heroic, said the poet-sage. Praising those who deserve it is a concept which has not yet found its proper place in Kazakh ethics yet.

The role of worthy elders and overseers in Kazakh society was special. Respect and recognition from the people came not only with age. A worthy person was known by their qualities, such as decency and honesty. The status of a worthy person played an important role in the life of the Kazakhs. What people of high repute said was taken as fact. A person could achieve a respected status even in youth. Kazibek biy, former judge of the Senior or Great *Zhuz*,[10] was called *Kaz Dauistuh*, that is, Kaz, the one with a strong, commanding voice. He received that nickname when he was young.

Abai speaks of three types of braggarts. The first is eager to gain fame abroad, among strangers. This is an ignorant and unwise person, but they still retain some human virtues. Wishing to be praised by strangers, they hope to be famous among their own people. They do not care whether they have done any good deeds. Though such a person is unwise, still they retain their humanity. As a rule, that concerns especially the elders and leaders.

The second type of braggart wants to be famous among their own kin. They wait for praise but do not know what it should be for. This kind of person is a complete ignoramus.

The third is a notorious braggart who shows off before their family or in their native village. This type is the most ignorant of all, losing all grasp on their humaneness, which is why they seek after the praise of their family. However, the one who is praised by their family is shameless because they are master in their family. They are sure they will get the praise they desire by extolling and praising themselves to the skies. This type of braggart is lazy, unwise and weak-willed.

Bragging will give rise to a great many vices: disgrace, ill gain, licentiousness, vanity, falsehood, guile, baseness. The worst thing is that a braggart, seeing these vices, does not try to correct them. They care only of hearing praise for themselves, whether deserved or not.

Abai in this Word explains the meaning of three ideas: praise, praising the one who deserves it and bragging. Each one serves a person differently. "It is difficult to protect oneself from praises," says Abai. There are many proverbs about it. "Praise is half the work," "Praise the worthy, let them be joyful, blame the unworthy, let them turn pale." Abai said praising the one who deserves it is an example to follow. To reprove a braggart for their ignorance is to educate others.

— Word Twenty-Two —
The Poor Rich Ones

When reading the Twenty-Second Word of Abai we will not find his usual accusations of the rich and expressions of sympathy for the humiliated and offended. To the contrary, it is for this Word Abai was marked out as a mouthpiece of the rich people's ideology. But the thoughtful reader will understand that it has a much deeper sense. In this Word, Abai gives a thorough analysis of the social system and all the layers of Kazakh society. He speaks of his attitude toward each of them.

He says he would have respected a rich person, but there are no truly rich people anymore. "He is not the master of his will and wealth and worthless people of every kind live at his expense." He would have respected a *myrza* – that is, a 'sir' or 'lord' in the traditional British sense – but now you cannot find a truly generous one. "Their own personal well-being is their main concern. They do not care about the people." If we come to the regional administrative chiefs and judges, their power has been purchased not through God's will, but with livestock, thus they are unstable, like the snow which melts and runs off as water.

"I could have respected a strong man but I see that everyone among us has the strength to do evil deeds; one cannot find anyone prepared to do good," continues Abai. There is no wise person to honor, for there is none ready to use their intelligence to serve the cause of good conscience and justice. One and all rush off to guile and treachery. Who else is left? Only feeble beggars whom I might have respected, but they are so lazy they cannot even climb on the back of a camel. And their cunning and grasping at all they can possibly get their hands on will not stop until they ruin others completely.

"Whom shall I love and believe on this earth?," asks Abai with bitterness. His conclusion is that we shall pity a peaceable rich person who by virtue of his meekness lives by the saying: "If you want to prosper, avoid discord." Life taught them a lesson: to give away half of their wealth to protect the other half. Yes, they are the victims, but they are meek. Maybe it is them we should pray for?

In these words of Abai we find the answer to the question about those who were rich among our Kazakh ancestors. There was no state mechanism to protect their wealth. They had no rights, only duties. 'Rich people are a calamity waiting to happen', concludes Abai. He thinks that Kazakhs should live relying on the mercy of rich people who have wealth. The role of the rich in the life of nomads was special. They decided their fate, united them into *auyls*, that is, communities, and coordinated their actions. That is why Abai supports them and feels sympathy for them.

— Word Twenty-Three —

"Given Over to Evil, Can There Be Any Good?"

The Kazakhs are a meek and plain people. The simplicity of Abai's countrymen was that they could rejoice when there was no reason to rejoice or find consolation in things which otherwise would not be counted consolation at all. But this simplicity can play a nasty trick on some of them, developing into such qualities as laziness, weak will and lack of initiative.

It is not important if other peoples have similar vices. Abai does not take note of that. He says some of his countrymen console themselves irrespective of whatever grief has come upon them. The poet writes:

> They rejoice when they meet a wicked person or see a wicked deed, saying: 'May God preserve us from that!' But did God say that it is enough for them to be better than such-and-such a person? Or perhaps clever people promised they would not be counted among the wicked if they could find someone more ignorant and vicious than themselves? But can you become better by comparing yourself with a scoundrel?

To laugh at a person you think is worse off in some way than you is a sign of ignorance and you should avoid showing such feelings. You should not try to compare yourself with those who are weaker than you, rather compare yourself with the best and then your joy will be justified. The thought that you are better than someone, that you surpass someone should not be cause for rejoicing. Joy should accompany things which are connected with risk.

You should also remember that joy only lasts for a brief moment in time. It can stop a person half way, dim their enthusiasm and even consume their energy. Joy is evidence of some sort of victory, but if you dwell on what is achieved and 'rest on your laurels' you will soon be sick at heart.

Intoxicated with the joy of victory, forgetting that new heights are awaiting them, and thus becoming complacent, this is what hampers people in their lives. There were many people in Abai's time and afterwards who had this kind of 'psychology of complacency'. It is wide-spread nowadays as well. You should get rid of it because there is nothing good in it.

Looking for the right way to live, Abai considered joy from this point of view. Joy cannot serve as the foundation for serious matters, it is a passing feeling a person experiences when they dream and see the dream come true. Joy quickly wanes. A person experiencing such a feeling should know that and be ready to press on to do new good deeds.

"Company in distress makes trouble less"; a powerful argument can be made for this popular saying. The social system of the Kazakhs assumed that people should stick together, but this principle had the potential to invalidate the uniqueness of each individual. A multitude does not distinguish between people; it is a crowd. The highest knowledge cannot be attained by everyone, it is accessible only to a chosen few. Only one in a thousand will be found who is endowed with genius. A crowd cannot feel it; it obediently follows the person who tells the truth. The problem is that the crowd often does not listen to the words of a wise person, but on the contrary is ready to throw stones at them.[11]

Abai finishes the Word as follows: "Will one who courts a woman win his intended bride if he tells her that all his family suffers from bad breath? Will his betrothed be comforted by the thought that he alone is hers?"

Speaking of consolation Abai expressed his thoughts in the form of questions. He gives the reader an opportunity to think. The poet sees that the old patriarchal way of life among the Kazakhs is dying out, coming increasingly into conflict with the new age. This is the age which puts an individual in the forefront, along with development of the individual capabilities of each person. Word Twenty-Three is confirmation of that.

— *Word Twenty-Four* —

Kazakh-ness

Abai thinks not about his own welfare, but about the life of his people, the Kazakhs, and despairs as he looks to their future. He says that our Kazakh hospitality or inhospitality toward other peoples, our pride and strength, our quest for development of economy and technical skills, and our familiarity with the larger social world around us are unlike that of any other people. Which is to say, we do not 'measure up' with respect to these matters in comparison with other peoples.[12]

So then, in what way are the Kazakhs special, going beyond what others have already achieved?[13] Abai suggests they are distinguished in their manner of spying upon and lying in wait for one another, being habitual thieves and slaves of petty living. This is nothing but the going about of two hundred people, following behind one hundred in search of calamity. If it continues on like this, then the Kazakhs are bent upon destroying one another. Who will profit from it, who will win? There is not one soul who can make sense of it. Do we plan, then, on continuing to go about as the scum of the earth. This is a question left to the future generation, one which demands an answer.

The primary reason that the Kazakhs have wound up in this kind of predicament is to be found in the failure of their national vision. It has not taken shape or solidified. This is due to their self-centeredness, the way they live out their lives meaninglessly in every conceivable way. It is clear that the idea of the Kazakhs becoming a civilized people is strange and foreign to the Tsarist officials. But there is not even one citizen from within the nation who will loose the sash around his waste and rise up to call the Kazakhs to become a nation. Those considered in their right minds and full of strength say they want to be administrative officials and judges within the Tsarist system of government. This is why the poet-sage is troubled in heart, saying there is not a courageous person of strength to be found who takes seriously the welfare of the nation.

— *Word Twenty-Five* —

"The Path I Spoke of was not the Path of Sparing Your Wealth"

Abai says that for those among the Kazakhs who have received an education in the Russian schools, the knowledge of a foreign language and culture makes their life much easier. The Russian language and culture are keys to riches and knowledge which nurture the human soul and spirit. They will help the Kazakhs understand the world and adopt the achievements of the Russian people because it is by learning foreign languages and assimilating world cultures that the Russians have become what they are.

But do the Kazakhs educate their children for this purpose? Or do they try to use their literacy as a proof of their own superiority when quarrelling with their kinfolk? Parents, you know, can spoil their children and lead them astray. But even if that be the case, such children are far better off than those who have not received an education at all, for their potential is great. That is why the poet-sage offers this piece of advice:

> You do not have to get a wife for your son or leave him ample wealth. But you must give him an education, even if you have to part with all you have earned. For if he remains an unlettered scoundrel, who will benefit? He will not be a solace for you. Neither will he be happy himself. He will be of no good to his own people.

"The future of the Kazakhs is in education. Don't begrudge the expense! If you want your child to become a genuinely healthy human being, give them an education!," says the humanist Abai.

202

In this Word, Abai expresses a great many deep thoughts. According to him, Russian language and culture learning opens our eyes to the world. By learning the Russian language, we study the culture and knowledge of other peoples, we become acquainted with Western European culture, we even learn French, German and English through Russian.

Abai is a realist and looks at the world realistically. Learning the Russian language and culture are keys to a world heritage. And that is the most important thing. "For the one who knows this, the world will be brought within reach at much less expense." The problem is that it is necessary to set aside petty things, forget squabbles and petty quarrels. Such are Abai's thoughts in this Word.

— Word Twenty-Six —
"The Kazakhs Have No Other Enemies Besides the Kazakhs"

This Word speaks of irresponsible, care-free living. Abai criticizes those who become elated like children at the more trivial matters of life. The Kazakhs are elated if their horse wins a race, if a wrestler of their community wins a match, or if their hound or falcon does well in a chase. Is there is anything that gives them greater joy?

Of course, to some extent we can understand the joy of such a person, but those things should not suffice. Abai speaks about the narrow-mindedness of his countrymen, about their tunnel-vision. Their world does not go beyond the limits of their own community. They are satisfied with their scarce knowledge, not perceiving the importance of life, that it is full of meaning and significance. This is difficult to comprehend. He pours out his bitterness on paper seeing that, in comparison with the Kazakhs, other national peoples excel more in building cities, educating their children and developing higher education as well as technical skills and crafts.

"The Kazakh is an enemy to himself," says Abai with annoyance. If they engage in anything, they do so to provoke the envy of others. But to stir up other peoples' animosity is contrary to the Shari'a law of Islam as well as one's own interests and sound reason.

Abai approaches this problem from the perspective of a humanist. The fact is, fast horses are here today, but gone tomorrow. In the same way, young men of great strength come forth from one community or nation today and another tomorrow. One triumphs, one suffers defeat, but they will not always go on that way. So in what are they rejoicing beyond measure, and in what are they finding such shame? "They feel ashamed of what is not shameful, but sense no shame in that which is disgraceful. In all of this they manifest their ignorance and foolishness."

Of course Abai is correct in what he says. But if a Kazakh cannot rejoice in a swift horse, a capable hunting bird and the strength of his own forearms, in what shall they rejoice? The problem is in the measure of their rejoicing, in the limits of that joy, and in the absence of other useful activities besides these. There are "interesting" things in the world, and there are "joyous" things. A fast horse, dog, an eagle, these are all interesting. These also comprise legitimate forms of skill and artistic expression. But there are other things of interest in the world as well and Abai, who longs to see some effort being made in that direction, says: "Regardless of how bad something might be, if they turn it into a habit, only in great fear or death will a Kazakh bring it to an end, and unwillingly at that. If that not be the case, it is doubtful that you will find anyone who is won over by their reason and, of their own accord, admitting that their habit is not good, puts it to an end."

What the poet-sage has said here is fitting. Obstinacy comes from the inability to think through and analyze one's actions. The habit of thinking over words and actions is a necessary quality of human beings, but simply declaring 'this is something which my forefathers passed down to me', unwilling to move beyond their traditional ways when necessary, often leads to irresponsible care-free living.

— *Word Twenty-Seven* —
Great, Boundless Wisdom

This Word is a conversation between the great thinker Socrates and his pupil Aristodemus.

Much was written about this famous ancient Greek philosopher, especially by Plato. Socrates was a great thinker who said that the basis for our humanity was knowledge and learning. He gave preference to reason and expressed certain brave ideas which undermined the authority of God, something for which he was punished. Socrates ridiculed those who worshiped God. He discussed with Aristodemus people's serving the Most High in order to understand the meaning of worshiping God.

Ancient Greek philosophers shaped their thoughts in dialogues. They never offered ready-made truths. They started seeking the truth by exchanging their opinions and, thus, seeking advice from each other. They always reserved the right for the hearer or reader to think, discuss and choose their own point of view.

At the beginning of their conversation, Socrates and Aristodemus spoke of worshiping God and of admiring things created by human hands.

"Well, Aristodemus, do you think there are people in the world whose creations are worthy of admiration?," asked Socrates.

"There are many of them, master," replied Aristodemus.

"Name at least one of them."

"I admire the greatness of Homer's poetry, the tragedies of Sophocles, the ability of some people to appear in other forms. I admire the paintings of Zeuxis."

"If it is so, who then, do you think, is more worthy of admiration: the Most High who created people endowed with reason and a living soul, or one who creates a lifeless human image?," asked Socrates.

"The Most High, certainly. But only if His creations are the product of reason, not pure chance."

In saying this, Aristodemus reveals his lack of faith in the omnipotence of God. He thinks there are many things which God has not created by means of reason. Why should we worship God then? What God has created for people causes admiration. But human creations also cause admiration because an artist is also a creator, a creator of new things. For example, the poems of Homer, the tragedies of Sophocles and the paintings of Zeuxis depict not only what exists in life, but also what should exist or take place. That is why their creations cause admiration.

Socrates asks Aristodemus: "The world has many useful things. The purpose of some are obvious, while the purpose of others cannot be discerned by their appearance. What do you think: which of them have been wrought by chance and which by reason?"

"Certainly, the things of which the purpose is obvious are created by reason," replied Aristodemus.

"Good," said Socrates. "Creating humans, the Most High endowed them with five senses, knowing they would be useful for them."

Pondering for a while, Aristodemus acknowledged this. He had no doubt that the Creator made His works with great love and care. Then Socrates and Aristodemus talked about different types of reason.

"How can you believe, Aristodemus, that none save yourself, a human being, can possess reason? How have you become the master of reason? I know you will say: first comes a soul and then comes reason."

Abai, with these words of Socrates, expresses some deep thoughts about reason. First, he believed that human beings did not possess reason alone. Reason comes to humans together with a soul. A soul is the vessel for reason. "It is thanks to the soul granted to you that you have become a vessel of such high intelligence." The soul lives in the heart. So to become reasonable, you should first of all have a heart. If this is true, that is, that reason comes to the soul of human beings, then it means that reason is outside a person. This should be pondered.

Secondly, if the soul is a vessel for reason, then what is the soul? Why does it enter a person? What is the reason? The animal also has a soul, but it does not have reason.

Third, a human being cannot comprehend the sublime intelligence of the Creator, but they can perceive His greatness and worship Him.

Wise Socrates went on: "You possess a soul and reason. And what of it? You perceive the harmony of the law whereby nature is created, but you cannot comprehend what you see. You are amazed with its greatness and the inaccessibility of its truth only because our reason is limited. That is why you try to understand it. Where does nature come from? What is its origin? What do you think, is nature the purposeless outcome of chance or is it given birth by the possessor of infinite reason, by the force of immutable laws, which wisely coordinated the purpose of all creation?"

Abai often used such words as the Arabic term *falam*, which refers to limitlessness or boundlessness. Human beings with their limited knowledge cannot understand limitlessness. This idea could be compared only with an idea of limitless Reason, which a person cannot comprehend.

Aristodemus, having agreed with his teacher's arguments, said: "I do not doubt the omnipotence of the Creator. Yet I do not cease to wonder why the almighty Creator should need my prayers?"

"You are mistaken, Aristodemus. If there is someone who cares for your well-being, you are indebted to that person," Socrates replied.

"But I do not know whether God cares about me or not," said Aristodemus.

"Then observe the animals and look at yourself. Do we perceive reality in the same way? An animal cannot build a town, make tools or weapons and become a skilled artisan. Even if animals possessed human intelligence, their outward form would have hardly matched the capacity to toil, to teach arts and virtue. The fact that God endowed humans with high intelligence and placed this intelligence in such a perfect body, combining both spiritual and moral beauty, is proof that God made human beings with loving care. All that considered, is not humankind obliged to worship him?"

Two significant things should be given attention here. First, a human being and an animal perceive reality differently. Second, the outward form of a person matches the form which reason needs. It is this harmony which places people in debt to God. This debt can be paid only by offering God worship.

At the beginning of this Word there is a phrase: "Socrates ridiculed those who worshiped God." It surprises us that Socrates, not being pious himself, convinces Aristodemus that it is necessary to worship God. Abai does not offer any explanations. He simply throws the problem open for the reader to consider. And he is right in doing so. For the problem is not submission to God, it is in great, limitless reason. Our submission is in acknowledging this great reason, not who says what about it. Whatever the case, great reason exits in the world. This is a fact. There are many disputes over the truth, and many understandings and explanations of it. Abai does not waste his time analyzing them. Through a *hakim* word, that is, a special, wise word, Socrates relates a magnificent story about reason.

— Word Twenty-Eight —
"Are Poverty and Sickness Really 'the Will of God'?"

In the world nothing happens without a cause. One is rich, one is impoverished, one is healthy, one is sick, and so on. What is it that causes people to wind up in all kinds of contrasting conditions?

There is a ready-made answer for this: It is all the will of God, the sovereign one. From the beginning everything that comes to pass was written upon the forehead of each person. People call this 'fate' or 'destiny'. When put like this, what other conclusion can we come to except to say that it is the sovereign God who holds the fate of people in his hands. But this is not simply faithlessness, it turns whatever faith in God we may have entirely around.

We placed faith in God, believing him to be without reproach or flaw. According to Abai:

> God, the sovereign one, evidently turns a profit in livestock for a worthless scoundrel, one who does no work. Yet he does not bless the work of a person who has placed his hope in God and sought a fair profit through an honest hard day's work, not even making it possible for him to sustain and provide for his wife and children, but instead makes him poor. He, likewise, causes a quiet, cooperative person who has done no harm to anyone to become sick, making them evidently a disgrace. Meanwhile, one who is a thief, who does evil, he makes healthy and sound. He makes one of the children of a father and mother to be of sound mind and the other to have no sense... Is all of this worthy of the sovereign God's blameless and faultless mercy and justice?

Yes, if it is all by decree of the Creator, what profit comes from our feeble human strivings to accomplish anything? 'God is not moved by his feeble human creatures, all is through his power as creator'. This theory is called 'fatalism' in the West. Abai does not agree with it, he does not think that binding up and casting aside human freedom is the will of God. What he says is that "the worship of God is a duty for those who possess any reason."

That is, in order to place faith in God, one needs reason. Without reason there is no faith and no knowledge of or familiarity with God. Only for those with reason is the worship of God a duty, which means that reason is a characteristic personally possessed by every soul. Surely God must say to people: "Let those who would know me, know me through reason." What profit is there from religion if it puts an end to reason? If our religion is false, is the matter resolved by declaring that we as feeble human beings should not concern ourselves with that side of the question? Of course not, thus Abai puts forth the following cutting summary of the matter:

> ...God is the one who makes good and evil possible, but God is not the one who causes people to be careless in choosing between the two, God is the one who makes illness possible, but God is not the one who causes illness, God is the one who makes wealth and poverty possible, but God is not the one who makes one rich or poor.

How should we understand this? In my opinion, there are two problems here: One is that when God created humans he gave them freewill. Humans have used it in multiple ways. The point being, lazy people became poor, hard working people achieved riches and success. Thus God gave freedom to people to use the freewill which he bestowed upon them. The one who gives freedom is God, the one who executes it is the human being. How people will use their freewill is something only they themselves can know.

Second, in order to make people ponder matters for themselves, God made both good and evil possible. Whether you are good or bad is in your own hands. God has nothing to do with it. If you follow after evil temptations, you will be enticed to evil, if angelic ones, your undertaking will be directed toward the good and you will prosper. The world is under this kind of spiritual struggle. 'Life's attractions are satan's sustenance'. If you do not follow good reason, if you do not curb your fleshly desires, if you do not fulfill your obligations, God is not the one to blame for it. The sin is on your own head. There is no sin with God, he is pure, he is the forgiver of human sin.

Knowing the essence of the sovereign God and believing in him, this is called faith. And we have already stated above that faith is the obligation of people who possess reason.

— *Word Twenty-Nine* —

Words Spoken in Ignorance

We are accustomed to thinking that proverbs and sayings contain people's wisdom. We piously believe that they contain infallible truth. Abai scrutinizes some these proverbs.

Indeed, a foolish word uttered once remains in our memory by chance and is presented as a pearl of wisdom from the people. Abai says that "the Kazakhs have a lot of sayings that merit attention, but there are some that do not." He then gives some sayings as an example. Of course, we can agree with Abai's opinion or we can choose not to accept his arguments. We should not agree simply because it was Abai who said it. We speak here of the proverbs and sayings that are widely used among our people. We must apply wisdom in deciding what to take and what to leave from Abai's ideas. Abai did the same. He has never blindly believed the scholars. Abai took only what was useful from them. He could openly express his opinion if he did not agree.

In this Word, he speaks of seven sayings: "If you live in need, forget your shame," "A clever fellow can set even the snow on fire," "You can get anything if you know how to ask," "If your name is unknown, set the field on fire," "Better one day as a stallion than a hundred days as a gelding,"[14] "A treasure chest is dearer than father and mother, but your own life is dearer than a palace of gold."

We might have agreed with Abai's opinions about these proverbs, but we think he interprets them rather narrowly, understanding them too literally.

— Word Thirty —

"Tireless Cheeks Make for a Shameless Face"

In Word Twenty-One, Abai spoke of two types of praising: Praising that which is worthy and boasting. In Word Thirty he writes about "boastful windbags." What are they? Abai says: "They lack self-esteem, they are narrow-minded and shallow, without valor, humaneness or conscience." There is an abyss between their deeds and words as that between heaven and earth.

Most often braggarts prove to be ordinary cowards, windbags and pretenders. According to them, there is no one braver than themselves, they do not bow their heads to anyone. But you should not entrust even a minor task to them. The people came up with a saying about them: "Tireless cheeks make for a shameless face." You should not take boastful windbags seriously. They are shallow-minded, thoughtless and unreliable people. They are useless. Squabbles, gossips and scandals arise where they appear. Abai called them unscrupulous, dishonest people.

— Word Thirty-One —

Hinderances of Thought

Abai tells us that in order not to forget the things we hear, there are four things we must set our minds to do:

> First, your heart and mind must be fixed, ready to take things in; second, when you hear or see whatever it is that you need to remember, you must note it, trying to make some example of it, pondering it deeply, getting a feel for it, making an earnest effort to grasp it; third, you must review it, reflecting upon it several times over in your heart, absorbing it until it becomes a part of you; fourthly, you must avoid any thoughts which would distract or hinder you.

The second and the third pieces of advice out of these four do not require any explanation. We should ponder over the first and the fourth ones.

With respect to the first one, we can say that a person has a sincere aspiration for truth if they have purpose in their life and strive for knowledge. Purposefulness assumes a fixed and sound heart and mind. Secondly, if you have a purpose, you should believe in it. Thirdly, firmness of purpose is a sign of virtue, adherence to principle and conviction. A person lacking these qualities does not experience the impulse to seek after and learn truth. Such is the conclusion we come to after reading the sense of Abai's first piece of advice.

The fourth piece of advice is very deep in its sense. The states of mind defined by Abai are: careless sloth, indifference, senseless argument, the inclination to morose reflection and destructive passion. Defining ignorance, Abai speaks of careless sloth and indifference. He says elsewhere that: "The salvation of the people lies in a reasonable person who cares about their future." A careless person is an irresponsible person. They are indifferent to what is going on around them. Those who believe in God should not be indifferent and passive, but active, for they come into this world to live through faith in God. Life is given to them to live in joy and God endows them with power to believe for such. The fate of a person is in their own hands, therefore they should not be indifferent about things. This is what Abai declares.

Abai condemned senseless amusement in all of his works. According to Abai, it is a sign of ignorance. The motto of the people who revel in senseless amusements is "dining and amusements." There is a place for fun, laughter and amusement in life, but you should be moderate. To overstep the bounds of decency is ignorance; to stay within the bounds of decency is a sign of reasonableness. A person often errs when they fail to determine the bounds of decency.

Abai wrote much about human sorrow. You should not give way to despair until you are completely exhausted. You should be able to resist the pull of sorrow, keeping firmness of spirit while comprehending the bitterness of loss. Not to lose your dignity is a courageous act. To give way to despair when you are in sorrow is not sound or reasonable. To be always careless is not good either. Grief should have reasonable limits, states Abai.

Another important subject is passion. Love and tenderness are accompanied by passion. One should know when to stop. If you are a slave of your passion, you will come to nothing. If you can overcome it and gain victory, you will achieve much.

"These four vices can destroy both your mind and your talent." With such words Abai finishes Word Thirty-One. A very deep thought, and there is nothing to add or subtract.

— Word Thirty-Two —
The Requisites of Learning

Abai considers the word "aspiration" in terms of a philosophical category. Those who seek to learn should understand certain essential conditions without which they cannot achieve their goal. We can consider each of them one-by-one.

First, if you value knowledge as the greatest gift in life, each new truth you uncover will bring peace and satisfaction to your soul. You should love learning for its own sake and strive for it. "If you have another purpose in mind, such as seeking knowledge with no other aim than getting rich, your attitude toward learning will be the same as that of a person toward something which is not their own." If your heart and soul are set well upon learning, it will bear its fruit in season, it will surrender it riches to you readily." Your attitude to learning should be as that of a mother toward her own children.

Second, study with clear and noble aims, not seeking to acquire learning so as to be able to argue with other people. Now, arguments within reason help to strengthen one's convictions, but excessive zeal for them can only spoil a person. It is true that disputation is one of the paths to knowledge. Beyond mere disputation, however, there are people who give themselves entirely to learning. Such people will not stoop to slander, backbiting and reproach. Abai called them *hakims*, that is, elite scholars who gain special knowledge and insight.

Third, Abai insists: "If you have succeeded in discovering some truth, do not turn back from it even on pain of death. If you do not value your own knowledge, how can you expect recognition from utter strangers?" If you are not confident of your own knowledge, do not imagine that someone else will respect or appreciate it. But if you count what you say an inflexible dogma, not listening to someone else's opinion, that also is wrong. It is not shameful to learn from others what you do not know. This is one of the conditions for people who want to learn.

Fourth, there are two tools that aid the acquisition of knowledge. One is exchange of opinions or 'debate' and the other is firmness in defense of one's views. The poet does not go into details because these ideas are taken from Muslim philosophy and when interpreting them you should attentively study their place and role within Muslim philosophical discourse.

Fifth, the poet says to beware of evils such as careless sloth or idleness, which he mentions in Word Thirty-One. Abai also mentions them in Word Nineteen when he speaks about indifference.

And finally, Abai says to develop character because human character is a vessel containing knowledge and intelligence. "To attain your goal you should foster constancy of purpose, determination and strong will." Determination and strong will are the basis of genuine character.

— Word Thirty-Three —

Behavior that Hinders the Kazakhs

Wealth diminishes with time, but trade does not. The one who sells the fruit of their labor without trying to deceive is considered a saint of sorts by the people. Yet "those on whom God has bestowed some skills will not avoid certain vices either," says Abai. He lists them in this Word. They are:

1. Lack of initiative: Complacent people do not improve their skills. They do not seek to learn from better artisans. This is their main vice.

2. Laziness: This vice is connected with the first one. There are people who imagine themselves to be rich and successful and so become lazy, boastful and careless in their work.

3. Bragging: By succumbing to flattery and exaggerated self-confidence a person wastes their valuable time and lets a sly flatterer take advantage of them.

4. Over-eagerness to make friends: There are certain people who are overly eager to make friends of any kind. Trying to please others, they will waste their time and run into debts, they will get into quarrels because of these debts. They will live in want and disgrace.

Reading Abai's words about an over-eagerness to make friends among the Kazakhs, you automatically recall their former lifestyle. Hospitality was always a notable quality of the Kazakhs. Certainly hospitality is a good thing, but only when it is kept within reasonable limits. How else can one understand the beginnings of mastery over our nation, over our land except through foreigners who, eager to be guests, came flowing to the Kazakh nation as "guests" and, little-by-little, began saying "the place of honor is mine." And the Kazakh's rightful trust and acceptance of the sentiments of those who were well-meaning, or the intention to be so, was this 'respect'? If not, what did the Kazakh people do that they themselves should be respected, apart from the claim that 'we hosted those who came', though in numbers too great to applaud.

We can also speak here of one other manifestation of hospitality among the nation's people. They will share their food and clothes with a guest; they will feed them and offer presents to them. Now imagine the same herdsman as a guest in the city. The poor wretch will not even find a place in a hotel, not to mention a hearty meal. These are our morals. Following the old traditions and customs, the people in the village and other community settlements do not typically build hotels or canteens. It seems this problem should be given some attention.

Abai completes his thoughts with the following words: "Why does all this happen? Because those inclined to deceive others often themselves fall prey to deception." More than a century has passed since the time when these words were penned. But have we in our day gotten rid of these vices mentioned by Abai? We, still like children, can be deceived. Is there some way we can be spared from our naivety and simple-mindedness?

— Word Thirty-Four —

Matters of Life and Death

This Word touches upon the philosophy of life and death (see also Word Nine). Everyone knows that death is a reality, that it comes not only to those thoroughly decrepit and advanced in years, but that it may even be met up with suddenly, from out of nowhere, and that once God has taken the soul of a person they will never return from that place. Everyone believes these things. But they do not arrive at this belief by putting the matter to reason and passing it through their filters of thought. They accept it because they have no choice, no option. Abai sought an answer to this eternal question.

Every human being, as much as possible, strives to know the mystery of life and death, but it will never be fully revealed. Therefore Abai expresses doubt in the claim of the people that they believe in the power of the Creator. He is saying that there is an act of believing whole-heartedly in the truth and, at the same time, a belief which thinks the fate of things is written or predetermined by the Creator. People believe that the will of the Creator is that the soul who comes into this world dies and goes to heaven and, for that reason, they should steer clear of evil and stay close to good. This is still not to believe as one who is fully convinced of the truth. It is only the mere acknowledgement that this is a person's ordained course in life, their fate. There is blind submission which acknowledges the fate of something in the mind, saying 'it was the will of God'. But there is another kind of faith as well which is attained by a genuine comprehension of the truth. Abai is doubtful about the existence of the latter among the people.

If people believed, thoroughly convinced of the truth, they would be spared a great deal of the world's sorrow. They would turn down the path of the saint, forsaking this false and deceitful world, and enter upon a concern for the afterlife and eternal faith, turning all at once, fully and completely, down the Muslim path. According to Abai's understanding, the faith of people in both the afterlife and the present world is uncertain. When such a problem exists, what is it that can we make the people believe in? The poet-sage's response to this problem is clear: Abai says:

214

Whoever thinks they will not be left empty-handed in the afterlife as well as in the world, that they will 'have their cake and eat it to', should know this: there cannot be two equal joys in one person's heart, there cannot be two burning passions, just as there cannot be two fears or two sorrows; these too cannot be one and the same, they cannot be equal within the same heart. It is impossible to say that these two different kinds of things can be one and the same. If such is the case, then in whoever's heart the sorrow and joy of the world surpasses the sorrow and joy of the afterlife, they are not Muslim. Now go ahead and consider it, even our Kazakhs are Muslims apparently.

So then, are Kazakhs true Muslims? As for the one who ignores that which beckons them – namely their duty toward God – while saying to themselves that God in his vast graciousness will surely forgive, instead giving themselves over to the world's pleasures, is there faith among such a one?

Abai sets forth the idea that all children of humanity are friends one with another, and if that be the case, then they are all guests one of another in this fleeting life and guests themselves, likewise, in the world. And yet, in spite of that, can we say that the one just lying around who cannot share the joy of the world itself, and instead turns people against one another, making them enemies of one another, enticed by whatever happens to come along, can we say that this is something worthy of God? Abai is not content with this kind of behavior. When he brings together the main point of both words, he is saying that such people have neither refined skill nor knowledge. He asks concerning the one who goes on arguing divisively without end, saying as one merely full of hot air, "Oh, dear God!" – what is it of theirs that we can call a worthwhile 'word', that can be considered genuinely 'human' in the sense that God intended it to be?

When we speak of Abai's idea of being Muslim, it reveals a thinker who goes beyond the mere sphere of religious orthodoxy. The poet-sage is not depending solely upon the religion of Islam for his understanding of 'the way of God'. He depends upon the central Muslim doctrine that "people are friends one of another," be they Muslim or not. Abai demonstrates this in his 'Words'. Human essence is common to all, the pleasures and sorrows that all will see are between these two worlds, the present world and the one to come. Life and death are one and the same to all of us. And if that be the case, then Muslim-ness and faith – these are what a person needs, but how shall they attain them?

There is no answer to this question because a true Muslim does not place his own happiness or the world's sorrow above the joy and sorrow of the afterlife. If so, they are not truly Muslim. What then shall a person do? What people need is to sense that they are guests, pilgrims in this world, realizing that they are not eternal, and thus, for the sake of this fleeting life, people must become accustomed to doing good deeds without constantly quarreling with one another.

Here then is the path which Abai has proffered. But Abai cannot see any who have turned down this path. He sees instead those who have turned the world's pleasures into a 'highway to hell' and laments what of this can be called 'human' in the true sense of the term? Thus has the spiritual nature of human beings revealed secrets about the philosophy of life from the depths of the poet-sage's heart. The eternal topics of this world's philosophy and their resolution are extremely complex. There are, for the time being, no clear answers to these issues. They move a person's spirit to reflect upon such matters and mature it through eternal philosophical questions.

— Word Thirty-Five —
To Call to Account

The one who will receive an accounting from human beings for their actions is the one and only Most High God. All people will give an account for their lives when they go before God, but God will also receive an accounting from the hajjis (that is, those who have successfully completed the hajj to Mecca), mullahs, sufis, martyrs and *zhomarts* (lit. 'generous ones'), lining them up and setting them aside in a special way to appear before him. He will set aside those among them who, during their lifetime, served him and did good deeds only to receive respect and the good things of life. He will separate them from those who desired only to serve and please God with a pure heart.

To those in the first group the Most High will say: "You made a show of yourselves in the world in order to receive praise as hajjis, mullahs, sufis, respected leaders and heroes. There is no such place for that kind of lifestyle here on this side of heaven. That world of yours to which you were so devoted was empty, and the show which you all made of yourselves has come to an end. Now it is time to receive in full what is due you for what you have done, give an accounting for yourselves! I gave you wealth and life, and for what? To hold eternity before your faces while you wasted away your wealth and your lives, deceiving the people as you lived in the world under false pretense?"

It is difficult to answer these questions because people need to live in both this world and the next. A person comes into this fleeting world, grows up, raises children and enjoys earthly pleasures. There is no eternal life without life first in this world. That is why it is a difficult task no matter who it might be to steer entirely clear of worldly pleasures. For this fleeting world has been created by God with honor. Life in this world is a privilege which God has given to people.

216

So then, if people do not value the privilege which they have been given by living out their lives to the fullest, are they not guilty of some sin or crime? By all means, they are guilty. Therefore, to punish someone for doing something on behalf of life in this world is not right, the problem is when someone is so given over to worldly pleasure that they forget God. Such is a sin.

Abai says in this Word that the hajjis, mullahs and others frivolously spent the treasures which God entrusted to them, deceiving the people who were entrusted into their care along the way. Indeed, this issue is one which needs to be reflected upon deeply. What kind of truth are people in need of? What even is truth?

In Word Thirty-Eight Abai expresses the view that 'life itself is truth'. If the hajjis, sufis and mullahs had explained to the people how to live, would this not have been truth? But the world is full of deceptive pleasures, and there are those among the mullahs and sufis and others who, even though speaking about such truth and teaching it, nonetheless in pursuit of their own selfish lives turn away from righteousness and wind up being given over to less noble things.

Concerning the second group, this is what God has to say: "You sought nothing else but to please me, offering up your wealth and your lives, and I am well-pleased with you. I have a place of honor prepared which is worthy of you, enter in! And besides the places which are yours to enjoy, among those here in the afterworld, if there be beloved, dedicated friends who, although not achieving what you have achieved, nonetheless followed along and supported you in their hearts, then perhaps they will ask for your favor as well!" Who exactly belongs to this second group is, however, unclear. Obviously they are few in number. There may be hajjis, mullahs, sufis and others among them.

But when all is said and done, we wonder if perhaps God will not, even more than such 'holy ones', exalt those among the common folk who toiled by the sweat of their brow, those who raised children, those simple souls who thus lived out their lives ever mindful of God as opposed to those who lived a monastic lifestyle forsaking all of life's pleasures. The heart of the story, when you get right down to it, must be about these hardworking people. In living out their lives in this world, it is only those righteous people who lived a life full of suffering who must surely be greater than the mullahs and sufis and others like them. It is clear that they will receive their due portion of God's genuine satisfaction.

When Abai took this Word from the books of religious philosophy which he studied, he did not alter or undo their basic premises. And when he added words reflecting his own perspective on the matter, he stated his own opinion clearly. But he left the ultimate resolution of the issues in the reader's hands, so it is possible that readers might be of varying views with respect to this Word.

217

First of all, it is possible to conclude that in Abai's criticism of the hajjis, mullahs, sufis, *zhomarts* and martyrs he is saying something in opposition to religion because those who are named are the ones upholding religion and without them religion comes to nothing.

Second, the poet-sage is not casting to the wayside religion in general nor, with it, hajjis, mullahs, sufis, *zhomarts* or martyrs. He has only spoken about those among them who have done things in the name of religion for sheer personal recognition, that is to say, he has defended the purity of religion.

Third, Abai's placing of hajjis, mullahs, sufis, *zhomarts* and martyrs all on the same level is not an accurate representation of reality. This is because hajjis and mullahs are quite different from one another. Not everyone's wealth is sufficient for the hajj and not everyone's training is sufficient to become a mullah. And it is quite impossible to compare sufis with mullahs. A true sufi is one who has forsaken the world's pleasures. Their aim is not acquiring a place in heaven, it is solely to behold and experience communion with God. As for *zhomarts*, they do not spare their wealth, but give up their best to the way of God. In the religious books, generosity is spoken of in a special way, even above martyrdom. A generous soul in the religion of Islam does not wind up in hell because generous ones are those counted as being on the path of God. The truest and most generous one is God himself. The person who has been generous is a person doing deeds in conformity with the character of God. Therefore, God watches over generous people.

Fourth, Abai has spoken about the purity of religion. When one worships before God they should not do so seeking there own selfish profit, but be given over to him in their hearts without ulterior motive, aiming to achieve his satisfaction and favor. Abai calls this being a true Muslim.

Drawing an overall conclusion from this Word of Abai, there is no great need to search for some systematic treatise of the issues raised. He has shared the thoughts which have come to him, and whatever conclusion one might arrive at from that is each one's own matter to decide. Abai has set forth all these various problems concerning hajjis, mullahs, sufis, *zhomarts* and martyrs because, even if not all of them exist in exactly the way the poet-sage has spoken about them, there are surely those who live for the world as opposed to God. And this, according to Abai, is evident not only to people, but to God himself as well. Therefore, God will certainly call them to account, putting before them the questions which have been highlighted above.

— Word Thirty-Six —
"What Exactly Is Shame?"

In the Hadith of our prophet (that is, the officially recorded tradition of Muhammed's life and sayings outside the Qur'an), it is stated: "He who is without shame is also without faith." Kazakhs also have a saying: "He who has shame has faith." Abai notes these sayings and then sets before himself the task of trying to understand just what shame is. We referred to Abai as a *hakim*, by which we mean one who searches out the reasons for all things, an elite scholar of special knowledge and insight. When we look at the way in which Abai searches out the cause of shame and offers an analysis of it, we would place Word Thirty-Six, not within the Islamic tradition of narration (that is, *naklia*), but in its tradition of research (that is, *gaklia*).

Indeed, then, what is shame? Abai reflects on shame as follows: "There is shame which arises from ignorance. It is like the timidity of a young child who is shy in uttering a word or approaching and greeting a good person even when the child has done nothing wrong. It is doing something in ignorance contrary to one's own desires which one never intended to do, which is neither against the Shari'a law of Islam nor contrary to good reason, and then feeling ashamed over it when there is no reason to feel ashamed. Such people feel troubled and make their life complicated.

It seems to me that the kind of shame which is born out of ignorance is connected with a person's own limited understanding, with the state of their mind and emotions. As Abai says, a person of limited reason and shallow thinking, of restricted emotion and feeling, is not a healthy one. The essential meaning of shame is not to cover one's face and get uptight over something which should not be done. It is to find one's own place in the world, living a productive and active life, saying the things you intend to say without being intimidated, leaving behind a trail of deeds which neither you nor your descendents will regret. Actions and behavior such as laziness, reluctance, cowardice, unbridled behavior and irresponsibility are the things which shame, born out of ignorance, is made of.

Therefore, accepting the rule of the Prophet that "where there is no shame there is no faith," and the Kazakh proverb "whoever has shame has faith," it cannot be said that shame is strictly something negative. There is also shame of shame, that is, the need to be ashamed for feeling such a false sense of shame. The shame born of ignorance which Abai speaks of has nothing to do with faith. On the contrary, the two are mutually set in opposition to one another.

With respect to faith, Abai encouraged an understanding of true shame. According to him, "such shame is of two kinds. One is when you are ashamed, not of anything you yourself have done, but upon witnessing the shameful conduct of someone else, a stranger. The reason for this is because you are sympathetic toward the person who has committed the shameful act." The ability to be ashamed of someone else's deed is a genuine human quality. It means that you love people and have high moral qualities. It is true that any person can commit wrong actions, but the observation of this wrongdoing by others and the shame which they feel should be a warning and a lesson for them in the future.

"The other kind of shame comes from your own wrongdoing before your own conscience, something you may have done in error or inadvertently."

Abai, defining shame, says that you should forgive a person who repents of their wrongdoing and is ashamed. Only a magnanimous person can do that, one who has experienced such feelings themselves. Abai said he did not see such people around him. People who do not have a sense of shame, appropriately understood, cannot be called true believers. Shame and faith are indivisible in Abai's opinion. Values common to all humankind form the basis of Abai's humanistic reflections and poetry.

— *Word Thirty-Seven* —

The Fidelity of a Loving Heart

This Word, unlike the others, does not have a specific subject. Word Thirty-Seven consists of twenty-three axioms, most of which have become popular expressions and are used in everyday life as proverbs and sayings. For instance: "However good a thought, it is tarnished by passing through human lips," "A father's child is an enemy to others, but a child of humankind is your dear brother or sister," "A good person may ask much, but will be content with little; a despicable one will ask much, but will not be satisfied even if they get more than they asked for," "Those who work for their own benefit alone are like animals that graze to fill their stomach; but those who work to fulfill their human duty, the Most High will distinguish by His love," "If you want your labors to be successful, start the job in hand wisely," "High office is like a high cliff; the slow snake will crawl up it and the hawk will swoop down on it," "A common person renowned for their wisdom is greater than a king who has been raised up by good fortune," "A youth who sells their handiwork is worthier than an old man selling his beard," "A beggar with a full belly is the devil incarnate," "A false friend is like a shadow; when the sun shines on you, you can't get rid of them, but when clouds gather over you, they are nowhere to be seen," "Be frank with those without friends; keep on good terms with those who have many," "Beware of the careless person; be a shield to the destitute," "There is no use of anger without power, love without fidelity and a teacher without pupils."

Proverbs and sayings make our thoughts and speech more colorful. By using them a person can make their arguments more convincing. Time-tested proverbs acquire a sense of common truth and become axiomatic. Not everyone can produce such proverbs.

People express their inner thoughts in the form of proverbs. We use those sayings which are simpler in meaning and more readily understood more often than those which are not. Thus, the proverb "There is no use of a teacher without pupils" is widely used among the Kazakhs. But we do not often use the proverb "A beggar with a full belly is the devil incarnate." If a person is satisfied, if they have clothes and shoes to put on, but like to complain about their poverty in order to get something more for themselves, they lack of spiritual principles. They cannot be counted as servants of God. Such people lived in the time of Abai; there are such people among us these days as well.

"Beware of the careless person," says the poet-sage. And he is right because only a careless person can be ever free of trouble and worry. But how can they know the price of genuine joy if they have not known sorrow? Joy and sorrow are inseparable. One cannot exist without the other. Abai warns elsewhere about excessive joy and unbounded sorrow (see Word Four). A person should know how to control these emotions and frames of mind, otherwise they can become crafty designs of the devil.

Abai is a psychologist of sorts, an expert on human nature. He writes: "Love without fidelity is of no use." He does not speak of the feeling of love, he ponders over the notion of love. Where there is no fidelity, there is no love. But to know true love, one should have an idea of infidelity. A person has love for God; a girl loves a young man; a child loves his father and mother and so on. Love is born in the heart. Cold rationality and reason kill love. If love were based in reason it would have lost its main feature – fidelity.

It is impossible to comprehend the sources of human thought. Reason makes a thought ingenuous. Intuition gives constancy to reason. We believe that reason is constant; reason is boundless. The wise compare it with an ocean. I would compare reason with a river. Static reason cannot be called reason; scholars would call it a 'dogma' or 'doctrine'. If yesterday's truth appears to be a lie today it is not real truth. In this case, intuition comes before reason because reason is restricted without intuition. Abai's words "there is no use of love without fidelity" can be likened to reason based on intuition.

Besides these proverbs and sayings, Abai lays the foundation for certain philosophic terminology. He speaks of the term "multitude," saying "all of the evil in the world is in the multitude, but the most interesting and entertaining things are with the multitude as well." When he speaks of the "multitude," it is in the sense of a "mass" or "throng" or "crowd" of people. "Who poisoned Socrates and crucified Jesus? The masses, the multitude. The multitude is devoid of reason. Seek to direct them onto the path of truth."

Abai raises a problem here, one which is important in our day as well. If you thoughtlessly follow the multitude, ultimately it will not result in anything good. The Soviet Empire established its political authority declaring that its policy was the policy of the masses, but the legs of such a policy were not stable. If reason is God's light, it does not shine on everyone, only those chosen. And God's chosen then bring light to the multitude. This has occurred in all time periods; it is a law of history. (It is not, therefore, the multitude we should follow, but those endowed with good reason, that is, wisdom and understanding.)

Abai expresses another idea of deep reflection: "Until your garden is grown, everyone desires what you desire, and you desire it too; after your garden is grown, you alone desire it." Indeed, while you are working to achieve your success, most people feel for you and are compassionate. But that only continues until you achieve what you wanted. Then their attitude changes because you have outdone the masses. The one who is dragging behind in the caravan envies you. This is one part of it.

Second, to be envious of a person who is happy and successful is part of human nature. Envy is like black and white, it has its good side and its bad side. The good is that the person upon whom happiness has rested is motivated to take heed to themselves and be responsible for their actions. The bad is that, for the one who is envious, a binding rope, as upon a horse's two front feet, is placed upon the pastures of their mind and a wound is placed upon their soul. That is why, if you have achieved something in your life, you must rely mainly upon yourself, on your own reason and will. Your destiny is your own hands and you should keep a firm hold on it.

This is how Abai understands and explains one of the more complicated aspects of human relations.

— Word Thirty-Eight —
Life Itself is Truth

The Thirty-Eighth Word is noted among the Words of Abai as being the most difficult to understand. We meet with many thoughts of this Word in Abai's other poem-songs and Words. For example, the ideas expressed in his poem-songs, such as "Both God himself and His word are true" and "It's easy to say the word 'God'," are repeated in Words Forty-Three and Forty-Five. But the poet's discourse about God and humanity expressed in those other Words comes across more clearly and convincingly here in Word Thirty-Eight.

The 'Word' is a special genre which requires very accurate interpretation. In its form and content it is close to a philosophical treatise. Therefore, it is built upon the foundations of the laws of logic, not poetic expression or figurative speech.

To comment briefly on this Word, we should first understand the main idea which it seeks to express. Concerning the main idea, Abai declares: "Life itself is truth. Where there is no life, there is no consciousness." This is a clear idea. The key of all issues is life. Only after we have life is it possible to have a meaningful discussion about other things. Notions about God and humanity are not separate from life, the truth about those notions is directly connected with our lives here and now. In general, we can say that the term "life" expresses the totality of existence. Because there is life, we have an understanding of God and are able to reflect upon humankind. And there is love, which represents the very essence of being human.

Thus having clarified the basis for the fields of multiple branches of knowledge and academic inquiry about God, humanity, love and other such things, Abai sets forth his ideas regarding those who instruct us in the way of truth: prophets, saints and *hakim* scholars, that is, elite scholars whom he considers to have special knowledge and insight.

His first word on these subjects is dedicated to addressing the essence of the Most High God. In Abai's understanding, God is the sum of all existence. "For God himself is the way of truth," said Abai. The object of human inquiry into the arts and sciences is to know the veracity of this truth, to evidence a passion for it. This is not the mere study of theology. Inquiry into the arts and sciences which seeks to clearly know and understand the wisdom of all things is what constitutes the knowledge of God. Human inquiry into the arts and sciences makes one passionate for knowledge of God. It is this passion itself which gives substance to the scholarly and scientific pursuits of humanity.

But for that, one must have a love for God. For knowledge and inquiry are a characteristic of God. He is truth, and love for him is what makes people characteristically human. Abai considers those who have given themselves to the pursuit of knowledge via human inquiry into the arts and sciences to be those pursuing truth, that is, those pursuing the way of God. Thus, for example, for those who have gone the way of seeking earthly riches, love for God, which again should be the true fruit of human knowledge and inquiry, will not be found.

Abai starts off his thought regarding the truth with the idea of placing faith in God Most High. He says, "Do you believe in God for his sake?... God will not suffer any loss from your lack of faith." God has no need that we should place faith in him, it is for our own sakes that we do such. Abai spoke of faith in Word Thirteen, that is why there is no need to ponder it here in great detail. What has been said in Word Thirteen still holds true.

But in this Word, that is, Word Thirty-Eight, Abai's thoughts run along these lines: "Do not despise the foolish idea that you can be like God. The idea of being like him is not about being exactly the same as him, but consists of following after him." This is a rich idea which has not, up to this point, been encountered. Here we have God himself standing in the place of what the poet-sage formerly referred to as human inquiry into the arts and sciences. "Make it your aim to be like God," says Abai. "You, O child of humanity, are a servant of God, but if you are truly a Muslim and given over to God, then make it your aim to become like Him."

It is clear that the Islamic religious leaders will not like or accept such a statement. In this respect, Abai goes beyond the bounds of Islamic religion on two points. First, in Islam, there is no permission granted for anyone to liken themselves to God. The Prophet, Rasul, that is, Muhammed, is a mediator between God and humankind. If you are going to be like someone, be like the Prophet. As for Abai, he did not offer any such injunction. According to religion, a human being's free will is restricted. The activities of people should be carried out in accordance with the commands of God. Abai discards this idea that human beings are so bound by their differentiation from and dependence upon God that they have no capacity to be like him. When he says that a person can strive to become like God, he shifts the discussion to one about the limitless opportunities and capabilities of humans.

It is in this light that Abai reflects upon eight of the attributes of God: Life, Knowledge, Power, Will, Sight, Hearing, Word (or Speech) and Creation. Abai says: "The Creator has endowed human beings with these eight attributes of himself, according to each one's condition, though not in the same absolute perfection. Therefore, the idea of likening oneself to God is not a cause for shock or amazement." Once again, in this case, Abai speaks the views of a reformer.

Are we, then, Muslims if we possess these eight attributes in significant measure? Of course not, because God has no need of such attributes, it is we who need them; they are necessary for our knowledge and understanding of who he is. We can never know God completely, but through these eight attributes we know only that he himself has been known. From its very sources the essence of God is perfect, there is not one among the scholars who can, by their wisdom, grasp God in all his perfection.

Abai explains this by saying that: "the Most High is without measure, that is, infinite, but our wisdom is finite. It is impossible for the finite to know the infinite fully." We say: 'God exists, God is one', but the declaration that 'God is one' is but one aspect of the concept of God spoken for the sake of our understanding. Otherwise, the declaration of God's oneness is not worthy of the Most High, that is, it cannot be taken to fully express his nature and being.

To the point: we cannot comprehend God with our own wisdom or our scholarly inquiries because our mind and understanding of nature are finite. Finite reason and unbounded truth, these two notions make it impossible to fully perceive God. 'God exists' and 'God is one' are not ideas which disclose for us the fullness of God. They are used because of our finite understanding. They are terms conceived by humans themselves. Otherwise, his 'existence' and 'oneness' would be unknown to us.

Similarly, we cannot say that any one of the eight attributes of God is greater than the others because he manifests them all equally. Besides these attributes, God also has the following names (or attributes): Merciful (*Rakhman*), Compassionate (*Rakhim*), Forgiving (*Gafur*), Loving (*Uadud*), Protecting (*Hafiz*), Coverer of Guilt (*Sattar*), Doer of Good (*Rasak*), The One Who Prospers (*Nafig*), Representer, Advocate (*Uakil*) and, finally, Beneficent, Lowly (*Latif*).

In knowing God, Abai used two methods: a method of demonstrating truth called *naklia*, which relies upon previously fixed expressions or declarations that have been passed down from former times, and *gaklia*, which relies upon human thought, that is, reason and wisdom. Enumeration of God's names is *naklia*. As for *gaklia*, it is knowledge of God's power through wisdom and reason. According to Abai himself: "My evidence of *gaklia* is that the Most High created this world interdependent, so that one thing follows from another, from things other than those created that human wisdom cannot comprehend. He created those things which have a soul, that is, which have life, from those which have no soul or life, and, likewise, created those souls endowed with wisdom and reason from those things possessing none. The beasts are exempt from the Last Judgment, while humans are endowed with wisdom and reason and their dominion is over everything upon the earth. That God has created humankind capable of answering for their deeds on the Day of Judgment bears witness to His justice and love for humankind."

Abai thinks this is just because God created humans in love and has given them dominion over nature, endowing them with special characteristics which reflect their Creator. "The Creator put human beings on two legs, he has placed their head high so as to enable them to behold the surrounding world, and not let them crawl on all fours, as the beasts do to get their food. He endowed humans with two arms and two hands in the service of their heads. He gave them a nose to enjoy fragrant scents. He provided them with eyes so as to see and behold, eyelids to protect the eyes, lashes to stop the eyelids from rubbing together, and eyebrows to stop the sweat from trickling down into the eyes from the forehead. The tongue has been given to allow humans to communicate, to understand one another and work together. Does all this not testify to God's love for humankind?

But if someone loves you, are you not obliged to reply in kind, that is, to love them in return?" To the point: what we mean by faith (*iman*), that is, what we mean by being 'a servant of God', is to pay one's debt of love. Human beings are indebted to God to love and serve him. Those who do not understand this have no faith and no wisdom. A wise person has faith.

But how should we understand such an idea? There are a lot of people in the world who are endowed with wisdom and yet profess a different religion. They worship another God and proclaim another faith besides Islam. Abai explains this in his own way. He demands something different from Muslims who profess Islam. He explains Muslim faith through the notions of love and justice. Where there is violation, there can be no Muslim faith says Abai. In order to demonstrate his proposition, he quotes several verses from the Hadith tradition: "Think of what God has given to us," "If you love God, he also will love you," "Command people to do good deeds, to practice doing good, for God loves those who do good," "Such people have faith in God, they do good deeds, their place will be forever in Paradise."

And so, Abai explains that whatever is outside of justice is a departure from the way of God, it is faithlessness. When we come to know God, our eyes are opened to the fact that he is compassionate, just and powerful. Humans possess knowledge, compassion and justice – Abai said nothing about human 'power' – and their three attributes. Those three attributes are discipline, Muslim faith and philanthropic humanitarianism. And in the heart of a good person three additional qualities will also dwell, namely truthfulness, purity and wisdom. Abai calls this 'abundance'.

Those who possess these qualities are the prophets, the saints, the *hakim* scholars (that is, elite scholars of special knowledge and insight), and mature Muslims. Abai delves into the activities of these three, that is, the prophets, saints and *hakim* scholars. The prophets venture down the path of religious devotion, submitting themselves to the service of God. They assist people in discerning truth from falsehood. People should not be passionate about the attractions of this deceptive, fleeting world, but about the world to come, rejecting worldly things. As for the saints, they make love for God their teaching, forbidding themselves lustful longings and distancing themselves from the pleasures of this world. The *hakim* scholars reflect upon the usefulness of (life in) the world, and speak of being an example.

Of these three, whom then should we heed and follow? When it comes to the question of who possesses the three qualities listed above, Abai has already expressed his opinion about who he intends to follow. He does not uphold the way of asceticism nor of those who renounce earthly joys. He says: "If such were the case, who then would have grazed the livestock? Who would have protected us from our enemies? Who would have knitted things to wear? Who would have raised crops in the fields? Who would have searched out the riches of the world which God created for the sake of humankind?"

Abai likes to speak clearly. Renouncing the pleasures of this world is not God's path because earthly desires were given to people by the Creator himself as a special part of what makes them human. If we do not use the human desires we have to enjoy the good things of this world, then we are opposed to God's intention. It is a different matter if we suppress our desires when and where it is necessary. But complete rejection of the pleasures of this world is not the way of believers. It is not fitting to Muslims to try to escape from life in this world, to attempt to avoid the good and profitable things of this world. God gave people animals to satisfy their needs. To breed them and take care of them, to make good use of them is an act approved of God. If there is no thought of living in this world, the people and nation would have been cut off from their nationhood and become an easy prey for unbelievers. The world would have fallen into complete desolation. For this reason, Abai declares: "Life itself is truth."

Abai notes in passing that not all of the saints abandoned the world in the same way. He then offers some examples from the world of Islam. But, in preference to the prophets and saints, Abai's passion remains fixed upon the *hakim* scholars:

Had there been no elite scholars of special knowledge and insight who remained on the straight and narrow path, the whole world would have gone to rack and ruin. Most of their activities are directed towards well-being in this world, for the things which they have accomplished and the teachings they have spread which have been spoken of so highly, they all contribute to the world to come, for as it is said, earthly life is a field tilled for the hereafter.

227

To profess that the *hakim* scholars are superior to the prophets and saints is counted a departure from traditional religious dogma. Such a view of things does not stand in agreement with the tenet of Islam which declares: "God is one, the Prophet is (the bearer of) truth." It is possible that the religion of the scholars winds up multiplying into various branches. Such an idea leaves one bewildered. Can the scholars be of one faith, one religion?

To the point: If we recognize Abai as a *hakim* scholar, then doubt can be cast upon his Muslim faith in the traditional sense of that term. He counted himself a Muslim and gave several proofs for that fact. First, in Word Thirteen, we noted that there was something said regarding 'conscious faith' (*yakini* faith). According to what the scholars say, we call the simple act of faith *taklidi* faith. That is, we say that these ordinary scholars believe in God through *naklia*-type proofs, while the belief in God through *gaklia*-type proofs by the *hakim* scholars we call *yakini* faith (see Word Seventeen on *naklia* and *gaklia*). In other words, that which we call *yakini* faith is to believe in him with a very deep level of understanding.

Abai distinguished between ordinary 'scholars' and '*hakim*' scholars. In his opinion, "Not every scholar is a *hakim*, but every *hakim* is a scholar." With respect to 'scholar', Abai gives the following explanation: "In the world, there is 'outer scholarship', which is dependent upon the sayings and quotes of other scholars, or *naklia*, and through which scholars can swiftly attain a good reputation. That which the scholar (routinely) says is *naklia*. An ordinary scholar is one who knows and understands the world, one who speaks from that frame of mind, in accordance with his or her knowledge and understanding.

But Abai has spoken differently about *hakim* scholars. God has not created anything in the world without a reason. Therefore Abai says: "(only) those who search out the reason and cause of each and every thing are worthy to have the title *hakim* applied to them."

And thus we see wherein lies the strong-point and uniqueness of the *hakim* scholar which places them above and beyond not only the ordinary scholar, but the prophet and saint as well. The *hakim* scholar is one who will stop at nothing to search out the cause and significance of every kind of matter under the sun, regardless of what it might be. Nonetheless, this does not mean that they are able to completely unveil the mystery of everything, for such mysteries belong to God.

Thus the Muslim faith of Abai requires special study and contemplation. He has, in clarity, given concrete understanding to the idea of being 'Muslim'. His Muslim faith does not, in some simplistic manner, coincide with 'orthodoxy'. Searching out the cause of things causes a person to transcend their faith.[15] In traditional religion, you must (simply) believe in God, there is hardly a need to search anything out. As for Abai, he searches out the very cause and purpose of faith itself.

Second, Abai offers the following assessment of Muslim faith: "It is said that, in religion, our foremost example is that of our prophet, the ambassador of God, as recorded in the Hadith, and good people are those of charity." It is this kind of person that Abai calls *hakim*. So true 'mature Muslims' are *hakim*. And what is their religion called? The truth of the matter is that even until this very day the answer to this question has still not been found. Each one is dedicated to his or her own religion, searching both from within and without for some complaint about the other, some reason to believe in their own supremacy and dominance. Which religion brings only good to humankind? Abai was on the side of those wishing to reform religion. And in saying that about him, we are calling him a *hakim*, that is, one who searches out the cause and meaning of everything. He is not one to simply believe on and follow along blindly that which someone claims. He himself searched things out, a sage of great wisdom who went to the point clarifying the true cause and purpose of everything.

But when Abai speaks of the prophets and saints, he never entirely dismisses or refutes them. There is a special need for both the prophetic mediators between God and humankind and the saints who esteem the purity of both body and soul. If we did not have them, the attractions and beauty of the world might well turn people into animals. In Abai's understanding, "the attractions and beauty of the world enlighten only one side of our understanding." But it is nothing to be marveled at when those attractions turn people astray from 'the straight and narrow path'.

Although everyone is (born as) a person and given a name, each is unique. But Abai seeks to guard against 'uniqueness' being turned into a simple synonym for 'difference', for when a person begins to think they are different, they start to descend into pride. That gives birth to envy. Of course, wishing to excel beyond others is not a bad thing, but if it turns to pride and causes you to agonize in vain, it is nothing but pure folly.

Abai reflects upon moral issues at the end of this Word, and in doing so what he himself intends to express is communicated as *naklia*, that is, something set forth in dependence upon others who have expressed their views on these subjects before him. For example, he speaks of three things that spoil a person: ignorance, laziness and wickedness. He offers clarification of each. In such scholarship there is no great revelation of anything new, but he does speak inspiring words, in particular he gives the following profound explanation of laziness: "Laziness is the enemy of all artistic talent and skill in the world. It is a lack of discipline, of inspiration, and of honor. All poverty comes forth from it."

In conclusion, Abai speaks of worship. In doing so, there are no thoughts based upon *gaklia*, that is, no real effort to get to the root of the matter, only *naklia*. Abai himself senses this and ends by exclaiming: "Alright then, perhaps we can be satisfied with what we have said here?!"

— Word Thirty-Nine —

Two Merits of Our Forefathers

This Word contains deep reflections on the national character of the Kazakhs. Abai, comparing the character of his forefathers with his contemporaries, confesses that the Kazakhs of his day are more advanced than their forefathers, but says they lack two characteristics, or merits, which their forefathers possessed. And because they lack these two merits, the uprightness and integrity of the Kazakh community is hindered from advancing any further. We are departing farther and farther from the foundations of nationhood and have started to succumb to destructive ways.

What kind of characteristics, or merits, were they? One of them is national and community leadership. National and community leaders set in order and oversaw all the affairs among the people and nation. The people placed trust in their national leaders, enabling them to go about their own business with peace of mind. A proverb was often quoted: "When everyone is his own judge, people cannot live together in a spacious mountain; when a community has a competent chief, no one will get burned even though a fire is set aflame." Likewise, the people would declare to their rulers 'we have given you two bridle reins and one tethering rein for the horses'. Once these words had been spoken, the national and community leaders never lost the respect of the people, but were held in esteem by the nation from that time forward.

In addressing this matter, Abai exposes the roots of a major problem. It concerns the social structure of the Kazakh *auyl*, that is, the community grouping into which Kazakhs were arranged. The Kazakh *auyl* was based on blood relations, therefore if the *auyl* (or community) leader was not out of his mind, he was certain to repent whenever he failed to take the well-being of the community to heart. If he failed to be integral in his dealings, there was no easy or quick way out, sooner or later he would have to face his own relatives and answer to them.

But why did the Kazakhs find themselves cut off from these two merits in Abai's day? Because now on Kazakh soil the authority of national affairs was no longer in the hands of the Kazakh national leaders. It was in the hands of the orchestrator who was proposed and elected by those over them through the participation of Russian officials. Thus, the trial and punishment of people, along with other civic affairs, was subject to the will of the Russian officials. Since they were no longer a nation who ruled over themselves, inhumane ways began to infiltrate the Kazakhs. The number of people who were able to comprehend 'the Word', those who were able to reflect upon 'the Word' decreased. In place of national and community leaders those eager for their own gain, cunning and crooked ones, sprang up in clusters like mushrooms after the rain. The character of the people was broken into pieces.

For this reason, the word 'honor' (or 'dignity') which was associated with the Kazakh ancestors fell by the wayside and lost its meaning. This is the second characteristic, or merit, which has fallen into decay in the present time. But when the names of the ancestors are called upon, says Abai, the Kazakhs do not quarrel with their kin or remember offenses, but give themselves for the sake of their people. This is honor and dignity. For this reason the people say: "Even if there is a dispute among brothers, they will not forsake one another."

The poet-sage grieves that these two merits have started falling into decay among his contemporaries. You can only be amazed at this reflection of Abai, the wise one, for it is a window on the Kazakh world of that time. It was a time when, in an age precisely as the present, unwavering and unchanged, these merits did not exist. Under such circumstances, the act of calling them to mind itself was an item of news, like something previously unheard, as in the present day. Most of those who are national and community leaders today, as in Abai's day, are officials appointed and elected from above. Those coming forth by virtue of their own wisdom in support of the cause of the people are few. There is hardly any honor or dignity left to be found, we have been cut off from them: "The friendship of those in the present time is not sincere, it is deceptive. Their status as enemies is not merely an annoyance, it reflects their inability to sit together, whether in rivalry or peace," says Abai.

— Word Forty —

Questions

"Who will answer my questions?," says Abai. He then proceeds to ask twenty-one questions. Instead of taking time to list each of these questions, I have pondered why Abai chose this way of addressing his readers. Asking questions and answering them is one of the ways of ascertaining the truth. Abai poses questions, but he does not answer them. That is a traditional method of getting to the root of the matter because sometimes the content of the question is more important than the answer to it. We can consider here some of the examples.

First, a person who tries to learn what they do not know asks questions. A child starts learning about the world by asking questions and getting answers to them. A question gives rise to truth; that means the person asking the questions understands the thought-provoking nature of life. Second, a question is given as a test. In this case, the person who asks the question knows the answer. This technique is used in education. A teacher asks a pupil; a parent asks their child. Third, there are questions that assume a great many answers.

Abai asks questions which do not require clear-cut answers, but rather cause discussion, meditation and healthy forms of debate. It is important to be able to demonstrate what you are saying, to convince others that you are correct in what you say. The Kazakhs say: "Only a dishonest person can dispute a great word." A great word, in this case, is a convincing argument within a dispute in which the truth can be proven.

Very often the answers to the questions can be very short, consisting of one or two words. The Kazakhs have questions intended for one-word answers. People have given preference to brevity. They think it is more accurate and colorful.

Abai's questions could be answered in accordance with the present time and situation, but in general it is impossible to give irrefragable answers to them.

There is a Kazakh word 'surak' (that is, 'question', which is a noun) and a word 'surau' (that is, 'to ask', 'to call to account', which is its corresponding verb). A person asks questions, but God calls to account. The first condition of understanding life is to know how to ask questions. When God calls a person to account, his task is to determine that person's humaneness. Watching people's vices, Abai asks questions in order to expose their wrongdoings and deficits, and to reveal discrepancies between their ideals and actions.

The importance of these questions is in the ability to answer them by thinking deeply and developing formidable arguments.

— *Word Forty-One* —

Power and Wealth

According to Abai, a person who is concerned about the future of the Kazakhs must possess two positive traits. Without these traits it is impossible to persuade a Kazakh that there are more useful things in life than their daily concerns, to convince them of something unless you frighten or bribe them.

First of all, a person must wield great power and immense influence, enough to inspire an awe of education in adults to the point that they release their children to go to school. Second, they must possess enormous riches, so as to bribe parents into sending their children to school. Yet no one has sufficient power and no one has enough wealth to win the parents, therefore their children remain ignorant. So regrets Abai. "The ignorance inherited from their forefathers and imbibed through their mother's milk has reached their marrow and killed all the humanity in them," said Abai in bitter despair, realizing the hopelessness of the situation. And we understand his bitterness and sad thoughts. Having lost their independence and former greatness, and having no ruler who would be concerned about their future, the Kazakh people were doomed to stay ignorant.

To become enlightened, first of all, means to become free. The growth of social contradictions marks the start of a people's struggle for independence. But Abai does not raise such problems in this Word.

— Word Forty-Two —
The Lack of Work

According to Abai, "One of the causes of the Kazakh's inclination to vice is the lack of work." This is a very appropriate word. As that which reduces a person in stature and diginity, Abai wrote a great deal about the lack of work in his poems and songs. If a person worked the land or engaged in commerce would they live an idle life? No, they would not have free time. But the Kazakhs neither work the land nor engage in commerce. Instead, convinced of the insane and mindless idea that "Livestock belong to the wealthy, the soul belongs to God," they ride from community settlement to community settlement hoping to eat and drink and enjoy themselves at someone's wedding; they drift about and do nothing. Abai thus blames the Kazakhs for idleness.

If we consider the reasons for their indolence we face a big problem. The Kazakh society in Abai's time was in a state of confusion. First, having become a Russian colony and lost its sovereignty, the Kazakhs did not need to defend their land. They led a peaceful life. But if in previous ages daily laborers, women and children were engaged in cattle breeding, now the former warriors, the defenders of the homeland, also became the masters in their households and had to join the others in the same tasks. A lot of free hands appeared. The young people had nothing to do in their community settlements. The elder people tended herds; they were not accustomed to working the land; they did not know commerce and they were not experienced at it. Surely there were people who tried to work the land and learn commerce, but they were few. That is why "they leave their livestock to the care of their neighbors asking them to keep an eye on them. They are unable to overcome the temptation of taking part in secret plots, gossip and petty squabbles. They will engage in all kinds of nasty intrigues and dirty tricks. They give themselves up to idle chatter, scrounging and roaming around." It became their habit because bad habits have a tendency to spread quickly among the multitude. You cannot but believe the truth of Abai's words.

"Today people do not value high intelligence, a good reputation or wealth; the ability to scribble complaints and the cunning to twist somebody around one's little finger – these are the things which are respected." According to Abai's caustic remark such a scoundrel can easily ingratiate themselves with the simple-hearted rich person by a bit of sweet talk:

> 'You just say the word, and I'll go through the fire for you!' And then, sometime later, without lifting a finger, they will be well fed and clothed and enjoy general respect. The rich person does not attach importance to what is going on under their nose, fully confiding in the scoundrel, because they seek to gain insight from them, to keep themselves informed. They want to be aware of everything, to know the prices at the market, etc. And when the scoundrel bows and scrapes for fear of losing the rich person's confidence, the rich person takes at face value whatever they say, because they have become accustomed to using them as an informant on whatever occasion they may have need.

Although aware of such circumstances, the authorities were not in a hurry to change anything. To the contrary, it suited them well. It was easy to manage people who wallowed in squabbles, enmity and complaints. This is a favorite method of imperializers and colonizers. Knowing that, scoundrels and rogues feel freedom to support the flame of enmity and incite people against each other. Parties at enmity seek justice from a tsar; they scribble complaints to the officials. This was the worst trait of the Kazakhs; it was soaked into their heart and soul.

It should be noted that there are two aspects of idleness. First, when the number of people exceeds the volume of existing work. That happens even to more developed countries; it is a law of nature. Second, when there is no steady work. Abai speaks of two aspects of idleness, but he speaks in more detail about the second one.

— Word Forty-Three —

On Soul and Body

Human beings are endowed by nature with a body and a soul. That, of course, has been known since well before the time of Abai. The poet says one should know which of their properties are innate and which are acquired by toil. The need for food, drink and sleep is natural, instinctive. The desire to see and learn something comes from a natural instinct as well. Intelligence and learning are gained through hard work. The sensations received by the five organs of the senses are ordered in the human mind according to a definite pattern and produce a certain imagery.

Mental aptitudes occupy a special place. Abai calls them the vigor of the human soul. At first these shoots are very frail. People must cultivate and amplify these aptitudes, for without due care and attention, they wither and become useless or die. But the Kazakh has a ready excuse for this: "What can I do if God has not made me a rocket scientist?" Or, "God has not made us equal, you and me." That is how they try to justify themselves. Such people want to justify their ignorance and passiveness. They try to shift the blame for their idleness onto God. But such only reveals the weakness of their heart and spirit. People should satisfy not only their biological needs but also think of their spiritual and mental health, that is, develop their memory and strengthen their mind.

Abai says the power of the human soul possesses three special properties which must be treasured and cherished, for without them a person becomes an animal. Regarding the first, he seems to have read literature about it in Russian, which would explain why he calls it a 'driving element', that is, a force which helps us not only comprehend what is seen and heard, but also to vividly perceive cause and effect. Second is 'the attractive force of similarity', because when learning something new, people often begin to compare it to other similar things. The third property is called 'sensibility of heart'. You should manage to keep your heart from four vices: conceit, covetousness, frivolity and carelessness. The impressions that you receive of this world will be clearly reflected in the mirror-like chastity of your heart. These impressions will be long remembered. But if you do not preserve the purity of your heart, the mirror of your soul will grow dim, and everything will be blurred and distorted in it. All of these ideals are related to psychology, so we can say that Abai was familiar with psychological works.

Pondering the power of the human soul, Abai thinks that everything gained through effort, that is, all that lies outside you, should be called wealth. Unless you know all the problems and details of managing a household, you will find it hard to keep your goods. Wealth is an external sign. That is why people say: "Riches are a calamity waiting to happen." But it is equally hard to keep the spiritual wealth that you have gained — intelligence and learning, which, incidentally, may cause considerable harm as well. Unaware of that, you may easily forfeit what has been acquired. Abai also warns of excessive enthusiasm for scholarly-scientific inquiry. There should be balance in everything. All that is excessive is evil. The wise men of old used to say: "In what we seek too persistently we find evil." To have a sense of balance is to avoid such evils as lust for power, uncontrolled anger, etc.

Reason distinguishes that which is beneficial from that which is harmful; yet even the force of reason cannot vanquish evil. Only those who unite in themselves the force of reason and the force of will can succeed at that. Those who possess these two qualities have spiritual and physical power, says Abai.

— *Word Forty-Four* —

Berikeldi!
On Admiration and Approval

In Word Thirty-Two Abai noted the requisites for learning. In the same Word, he spoke about idleness, inactivity and passivity with respect to learning. Learning has various forms and they are not always profitable in relation to one another. According to the poet's explanation: "Whether a person is learned or unlearned, it still does not render unnecessary the need for praise, approval or acceptance, the kind which is indicated, for example, by the Kazakh expression *berikeldi*, meaning 'so nice of you to drop by' or 'welcome, so good to see you! It thus indicates warmth, acceptance and approval. Whether merited or not, a person will always search for encouragement through someone who will say to them '*berikeldi*'. Regardless of which path in life one takes or where one chooses to live out their lives, they will be companions or partners with others on the same path, with those dwelling in the same area. They are not interested in hearing *berikeldi* from those on a different road in life. If someone says *berikeldi* to me, it those who are with me as companions or partners.

What, then, is the meaning of the world *berikeldi*? Abai has used it as a distinct term. *Berikeldi* is essentially praise. Abai spoke of praise in Word Twenty-One. There he laid bare two types of praise. They are 'greatness' and 'arrogant pride'. If a person does something genuinely good and desires to hear some sort of praise or words of approval for it, then you cannot really blame them; what they have done is praiseworthy. If, on the other hand, a person sits around waiting for

236

praise, but does not know what they should be praised for, then this is called arrogant pride. Abai considers the idea of *berikeldi* in the light of the deeds which people do. People are valued by their actions. If they are respected and honored among the company they keep, then this is the highest form of recognition one could hope to achieve for their merits. And it is this value of which Abai speaks. Thus, praise and approval from the people who walk alongside you in life indicate the recognition of your professional and human qualities. The praise coming from the flatterer or fawning subordinate, that is, from a 'brown-noser' or 'bootlicker', will do nothing but deceive and harm.

According to Abai, the majority of people in the world desire to possess power or wealth at any cost. But we cannot say their intentions are good because good intentions are born out of a pure soul. When Abai speaks of the purity of the soul, he means not only the thirst for knowledge, but also our common human qualities. A person of high moral standards strives for things of pure and noble aim. To praise such people for purity of thought is not flattery and servility, only a fair assessment of things; welcoming the worthy with praise is an expression of our admiration and approval – *berikeldi*!

— *Word Forty-Five* —

A Sense of Justice and Love

Abai interprets the notion of 'God' very broadly. Abai says that although people have, for thousands of years, believed in various religions, all of them have known the one 'Great God' and rendered him service. For this reason, all the various religions are merely ways and means of finding the one 'Great God'. But for all religions, the issues which they must grapple with are Justice and Love.

The true way of God is recognition of the 'Great God'. For that, we should not just acknowledge the Creator, we must be a lover and passionate desirer of him, we must have a sense of his wisdom and knowledge.

What makes one person greater than the other is not the kind of riches or power which they have, but a sense of God's wisdom. God's wisdom is justice and love. Without a sense of such qualities, there is no life. If one possesses a sense of these attributes in fuller measure, then they will be learned and wise. Abai says knowledge and learning cannot issue forth from the human soul. Knowledge and learning come about by having a sense of the world beyond and then observing with the eyes and perceiving through reason the things of this world.

This kind of philosophy is sometimes considered a type of 'pantheism' in the West, but the 'pantheism' of Abai has its own special character. In this case, the concept of God is taken as a quality, with his wisdom being the precept of humaneness, while the one in the world who senses him explicitly, who is familiar with him and acts on his behalf is a human being. When put this way, the issue is not about God, but about the nature of human beings. It is not a person's servanthood to God, but the wisdom of God which has been given to human beings which is important – this is what is taken as the foundation of all things in Abai's worldview. With respect to human beings, they must sense God's wisdom, this will free them from their servitude to God. To sense God's wisdom is to walk in the way of God. And for that, the senses necessary for people are justice and love. These are the primary precepts of humanism, that is, of being human.

With these thoughts, Abai transcends far beyond the bounds of one religion or of one religious worldview and embarks upon a system of thought which is fit for all of humanity. When Abai says "Love all humanity, calling them your brothers and sisters," it reveals the loftiness of the thoughts he speaks.

ENDNOTES

---

[1] This statement should be understood within the larger context of Abai's life, namely that he did *not* 'eschew the affairs of government and state' in his earlier years, but served as an administrative government official between 1875-78, that is, ages 30-34. The entire first 'Word' is describing Abai in his later years.

[2] Compare-contrast Abai's thoughts here on education with those near the end of Word Five as well as with the whole of Word Twenty-Five and Word Forty-Three.

[3] There has been much debate over the meaning of 'Sart' as used in Abai's day. Abai himself, however, clarifies his intended usage of the term as 'Uzbek'.

[4] See Word Twenty-Five where, in Abai's view, "learning Russian language and culture are keys to a world heritage."

[5] The socio-cultural context of this proverb is one in which the funerary-memorial meal tradition is observed which, in the Kazakh case, consists of memorial meals in honor of the deceased on the third, seventh and 40th days as well as at the one-year mark. The 100th day is also observed on occasion while among the Uzbeks the 6-month mark is also traditionally observed.

[6] D. Aitkyn's translation of this passage from Abai in Russian reads: "Leaving an heir, what does it mean? Are you afraid there will be no one to look after your property? What kind of treasures have you gained to regret so much? A good child is a joy, but a bad one is a burden. Who knows what kind of a child God will bestow upon you? Why do you ask to shift your sufferings and dreams that have not been realized onto the weak shoulders of your child? Will he or she be able to bear such a load?" Perhaps the difference is not that great, but it reveals the 'loose' nature of a translation derived from Russian instead of Kazakh.

[7] The sense of the original Kazakh here is a bit difficult to follow. I have transposed the phrase "in their careless religious practices" and connected it with "mere repetition," leaving "lifeways and activities" to stand on its own, though still of course properly connected within the overall context.

[8] More literally: "the religion of Islam did (or possibly has) not entered into our people with its full essence/substance/nature/content."

[9] This 'Word' should be understood within its Islamic context as elucidated by S.H. Nasr (2003:87-8), who notes that: "To understand …the Islamic tradition better, we turn to the terms *islam*, *imam*, and *ihsan*, all of which are used in the text of the Quran and the *Hadith*. The first means "surrender," the second, "faith," and the third, "virtue" or "beauty."

[10] The Kazakhs historically were grouped into three 'zhuz,' with the term 'zhuz' often being translated as 'tribe' or 'horde' in English works. Such translations offer some limited help in moving toward a better understanding of Kazakh society and its structure and organization into three traditional 'zhuz,' but they are loaded with Western cultural ideas and values closely connected with concepts of 'primitive', 'barbarian', etc., which themselves are too closely associated with European interpretations of African, American Indian and Australasian 'primitive tribal peoples'. Cf. M. Khodarkovsky, "'Ignoble Savages and Unfaithful Subjects': Constructing Non-Christian Identity in Early Modern Russia" and B. Grant, "Empire and Savagery: The Politics of Primitivism in Late Imperial Russia," both of which are contained in Brower and Lazzerini (1997), *Russia's Orient: Imperial Borderlands and Peoples, 1700-1917.*

[11] See also on 'the multitude' in Word Thirty-Seven.

[12] I am supplying the clarifying phrase "we do not 'measure up' with respect to these matters in comparison with other peoples" due to the context.

[13] "Going beyond what others have already achieved" is not in the original Kazakh, but is justified by the use of "special" in this context.

[14] A 'gelding' is a castrated male horse.

[15] Kzk. 'adamdi senimnen shigaradi', which might be translated more literally as 'to cast out or expel a person from out of (the) faith', which might then be interepreted as 'causing them to lose faith'. But, based on my extensive personal conversations with the author, this would by no means be his intended meaning. Rather, he spoke on numerous occasions of "transcending one's faith" in such a manner as to retain it, and yet view things from angles which went above and beyond the boundaries and limitations of that particular faith, whether it be Islam, Christianity, Judaism or otherwise.

Glossary of Names

Abai (Ibrahim) Qunanbaiuly (1845–1904) – Great Kazakh poet, composer, philosopher

Abu al-Ghazi Bahadur (1603–1664) – Historian

Abu ʾl-Qasim Ferdowsi (940–1020) – Eastern thinker

Adam Bernard Mickiewicz (1798–1855) – Polish poet, political publicist, activist of national civic movement

Ahmad Yugnaky (12th–13th c.) – Medieval poet, scholar, thinker

Ahmet Baitursynuly (1873–1937/38) – Kazakh great enlightener, great scholar-linguist, scholar in Turkology, poet

Aiteke bi Baibekuly (Aityq) (1644–1700) – Kazakh state and public activist, member of *Biler kengesi* (Soviet judges), famous orator, top judge of junior *zhuz*, one of the founders of the Law Codex called *Zheti zhargi* (Seven laws)

Alain Resnais (1668–1747) – French satirist and novelist

al-Basṭāmī (Abū Yazīd Ṭayfūr b. ʿĪsā b. Surūshān al-Bisṭāmī) (year of birth unknown – 875) – Famous Persian mythicist

Albert Camus (1913–1960) – French writer, philosopher, owner of the Nobel Prize in literature (1957)

Aleksei Fedorovich Losev (1893–1988) – Russian philosopher, philologist

Alexander Sergeyevich Pushkin (1799–1837) – Russian poet, playwright, prose writer

Alexander the Great (356–323 BC) – Ancient Greek commander

Alexandre Dumas (1824–1895) – French playwright, son of Thomas-Alexandre Dumas

al-Farabi (Abū Naṣr Muḥammad ibn Muḥammad al Fārābī) (870–950) – Philosopher, encyclopedic scholar who was known as the second teacher of world education and culture after Aristotle

al-Ghazali (Abū Ḥāmid Muḥammad ibn Muḥammad al-Ghazālī) (1058/59–1111) – Arabian theologist and thinker

Alighieri Dante (1265–1321) – Italian poet

Alikhan Bukeikhanov (1866–1937) – Well-known Kazakh public figure, scholar, leader, and a founder of the theory of national civic movement

Alisher Navoi (1441–1501) – Poet of Turkic (Uzbek) nations, Sufi philosopher, state activist

Allah – Creator's name, God, absolute

al-Tabari (Abū Jaʿfar Muḥammad ibn Jarīr al-Ṭabarī) (839–923) – Islamic historian

Amasis II, King (Ahmose II) (6ᵗʰ c. BC) – Ancient Egyptian pharaoh

Anacharsis (605–545 BC) – Scythian thinker and philosopher, one of the Seven Sages of the antique world

Anaxagoras (500–428 BC) – Ancient Greek philosopher

Andrey Nikolayevich Kononov (1906–1986) – Soviet philologist, linguist of Turkic studies

Auelbek Qongyratbaiuly Qongyratbayev (1905–1986) – Kazakh scholar, Turkologist, doctor of philology, professor

Auguste Comte (Isidore Marie Auguste François Xavier Comte) (1798–1857) – French philosopher, founder of positivism, founder of sociology.

Aristodemus (11ᵗʰ c. BC) – Legendary Spartan king

Aristotle (384–322 BC) – Ancient Greek philosopher

Asan qaighy Sabituly (14ᵗʰ–15ᵗʰ c. Politician who founded the Kazakh Horde, *zhyrau*

Attar of Nishappur (Abū Ḥamīd bin Abū Bakr Ibrāhīm) (1119–1234) – Persian poet

Avicenna (Ibn Sīnā) (980–1037) – Medieval scholar, philosopher

Babur (Zahīr ud-Dīn Muhammad) (1483–1530) – Uzbek and Indian ruler, commander, founder of the Great Mughal empire, poet and writer

Barshylyghi (Husam al-din Barshylyghi, Husamaddin Barshynkenti) (12ᵗʰ–13ᵗʰ c.) – Islamic scholar who was born in the city of Barshinkent in southern Kazakhstan

Benedito Spinoza (Baruch Spinoza) (1632–1677) – Dutch philosopher, rationalist, naturalist, one of the prominent representatives of modern philosophy

Berniyaz Kuleyev (1899–1923) – Famous Kazakh poet

Bias of Priene (6ᵗʰ c. BC) – Ancient Greek thinker and public figure, one of the Seven Sages

Buqar zhyrau Qalqamanuly (1668–1781) – Great Kazakh *zhyrau*, poet, advisor of Abylai Khan

Charles Robert Darwin (1809–1882) – British naturalist, traveler, founder of evolutionary theory

Chilon of Sparta (6ᵗʰ c.) – One of the Seven Sages (Chilon, Bias, Pittacus, Thales, Cleobulus, Solon, Periander) from Greece and Sparta

Chinghiz Torequluly Aitmatov (1928–2008) – Great Kyrgyz writer

Cicero (106–43 BC) – Ancient Greek politician and philosopher, prominent orator

Cleobulus (6ᵗʰ c.) – Ancient Greek thinker, one of the Seven Sages

Darius III (381–330 BC) – Persian king from the Achaemenid Empire of Persia

Diogenes Laertius (3ʳᵈ–4ᵗʰ c.) – Historian of ancient antique philosophy

Dospambet (1490–1523) – *Zhyrau*, commander, hero

Dulat zhyrau Babataiuly (1802–1874) – Well-known Kazakh poet

Erich Seligmann Fromm (1900–1980) – German sociologist, philosopher, social psychologist, psychoanalytic

Federico Mayor Zaragoza (1934–) – Spanish scholar, politician, state figure, writer, and poet

Friedrich Wilhelm Nietzsche (1844–1900) – German thinker, classical philologist

Fużūlī (Muhammad bin Suleyman) (1494–1556) – Azerbaijani lyrical poet

George Gordon Byron (1788–1824) – British poet

Gnurus (7ᵗʰ–6ᵗʰ c. BC) – Scythian king

Goethe (Johann Wolfgang (von) Goethe) (1749–1832) – German poet, public figure, thinker, and naturalist

Ḥāfeẓ-e Shams-ud-Dīn (Khwāja Shams-ud-Dīn Muḥammad Ḥāfeẓ-e Shīrāzī) (ca. 1325–1389/1390) – Persian poet

Halel Dosmuhameduly (1883–1939) – Representative of Kazakh intelligentsia, public figure

Herbert Spencer (1820–1903) – British philosopher and sociologist

Hermann Alexander Diels (1848–1922) – German classic philologist

Hermippus (3ʳᵈ c. BC) – Ancient Greek historian

Herodotus (484–425 BC) – Ancient Greek historian

Homer (7ᵗʰ–6ᵗʰ c. BC) – Legendary ancient Greek poet, founder of European literature, exemplar of antique epoch

Honore de Balzak (1799–e French writer, founder of realism in European literature

Ibn Arabi (Abū ʿAbd Allāh Muḥammad ibn ʿAlī ibn Muḥammad ibnʿArabī al-Ḥātimī aṭ-Ṭāʾī) (1165–1240) – Islamic mystic philosopher, thinker, statesman

Idanthyrsus (6ᵗʰ c. BC) – Ruler and commander of Scythian tribe

Ifn Tufail (1110–1185) – Philosopher, physician, astronomer, mathematician, thinker, statesman from Cordoba

Immanuel Kant (1724–1804) – German philosopher

Jāmī (Nur ad-Dīn Abd ar-Rahmān Jāmī) (1414–1492) – Persian philosopher and writer

Jesus Christ (12–4 BC–AD 26–36) – Central figure of Christianity

Joan of Arc (1412–1431) – National hero of Orleans in France

Johann Christoph Friedrich von Schiller (1759–1805) – German poet, philosopher

John Trimingham (1904–1987) – British scholar

John William Draper (1811–1882) – British scholar who studied history, physics, chemistry, and physiology

Karl Marx (1818–1883) – German scholar, philosopher, economist, political journalist, founder of Marxism

Khoja Ahmad Yasawi (1093/94–1166) – Kazakh mystic poet, thinker, Sufi

Lasus of Hermione (550 BC–beginning of 5th c. BC) – Prominent representative of a music school

Qazybek bi Keldibekuly (1665–1765) – Kazakh state and public activist, member of *Biler kengesi* (Soviet judges), famous orator, top judge of middle *zhuz*, one of the founders of the Law Codex called *Zheti zhargi* (Seven laws)

Qorqyt ata (8th–9th c.) – Great thinker of ancient Turkic tribes, flamen, prominent *kui* performer, prophet, philosopher, *zhyrau*, *qobyz* performer, composer

Lucian of Samosata (120–180) – Greek satirist writer

Ludwig Andreas Feuerbach (1804–1872) – Great German philosopher

Luqpan hakim – Fictional character from Eastern folklore

Madjnun (Kais ibn al-Mulavvah) (7th c.) – Persian poet

Maghzhan Bekenuly Zhumabaiev (1893–1938) – Kazakh writer, publicist, pedagogue, one of the founders of the new Kazakh literature

Mahmud Qashqari (11th c.) – Turkic scholar, first Turkic linguist, wrote the first textbook of Turkic language and described its grammar

Maiqy bi (12th–13th c.) – Famous judge, improvisational poet

Mansur al-Hallaj (Abū 'l-Muġīṭ Al-Ḥusayn bin Manṣūr al-Ḥallāğ) (ca. 858–922) – Prominent Sufi scholar who was sentenced for his preachings

Marghasqa zhyrau (17th c.) – Kazakh poet-*zhyrau*

Michel Eyquem de Montaigne (1533–1592) – Famous French writer, political activist, and Renaissance philosopher

Mikhail Bulgakov (1891–1940) – Soviet writer, playwright, and theater director

Mikhail Yuryevich Lermontov (1814–1841) – Famous Russian poet and thinker

Moses – Prophet, son of Amram

Muhamedzhan Seralin (1872–1929) – Kazakh writer, poet, and journalist

Muhammad Haidar Qusayinuly Dughlat (1499–1551) – Famous historian, scholar of literature, author of *Tarikh-i-Rashidi* and *Zhahannama*

Mukhtar Omarkhanuly Auezov (1897–1961) – Famous Kazakh writer, public and science figure, founder of the science on Abai

Myrzhaqyp Dulatuly (1885–1935) – Kazakh poet, writer, one of the leaders of Alash Orda

Myson of Chenae – Ancient Greek philosopher, one of the Seven Sages of the antique world

Nectanebo II (4ᵗʰ c. BC) – Ancient Egyptian pharaoh

Nikita Yakovlevich Bichurin (1777–1853) – Orientalist (scholar of Turkic studies) and diplomat

Nikolai Ivanovich Il'minskii (1822–1891) – Famous Russian missionary, Orientalist, pedagogue, and translator

Nikolay Alexeyevich Nekrasov (1821–1877/1878) – Famous Russian poet, writer, and publicist, well-known world literature classic

Nizami Ganjavi (Jamal ad-Dīn Abū Muḥammad Ilyās ibn-Yūsuf ibn-Zakkī) (1141–1209) – Persian classical poet

Rymghali Nurghalyiev (1940–2011) – Literary scholar, literary critic, writer, academician of the State Science Academy of RK

Nursultan Abishuly Nazarbayev (1940–) – The first president of the Republic of Kazakhstan, academician

Olzhas Suleimenov (1936–) – Kazakh poet, writer, literary scholar, public figure, and political diplomat

Omar Khayyam (Ghiyath al-Din Abu'l-Fath Umar ibn Ibrahim Al-Nisaburi al-Khayyami) (1048–1122) – Persian mathematician, astronomer, poet, philosopher

Pamphilius – Ancient Greek philosopher, pupil of Plato, and teacher of Epicurus

Periander (660–585 BC) – Second Tyrant of Corinth

Philip II (382–336) – Macedonian king

Pittacus (651–569 BC) – Ancient Greek thinker, one of the Seven Sages of the antique world

Plato (437–347 BC) – Ancient Greek philosopher, pupil of Socrates, teacher of Aristotle

Plotinus (204/205–270) – Antique philosopher-idealist, founder of Neo-Platonism

Plutarch (45–127) – Ancient Greek philosopher, biographer, and moralist

Prophet Jesus – Fourth of five Holy Prophets

Prophet Muhammad (p.b.u.h.) (570–632) – Founder of Islam, the first caliph

Protagoras (490–420/485–411 BC) – Ancient Greek philosopher, founder of the sophistic school

Pythagoras of Samoa (570–490 BC) – Ancient Greek philosopher, mathematician, and mystic, founder of the Pythagorean religious philosophical school

Qadırğalï Jalayir (1555–1607/1530–1605) – Kazakh medieval scholar, famous judge

Qadyr Ghinayiatuly Myrzalyiev (Myrza ali) (1935–2011) – Kazakhstan's honored writer, poet, playwright, translator, Laureate of State Prize

Qhumar Qarash (1875–1921) – Prominent representative of Alash, religious poet

Rabguzi (Nasr al-Din Burhan al-Din's son) (13th–14th c) – Turkic speaking writer and thinker from Central Asia

Rābiʿa al-ʿAdawiyya al-Qaysiyya (713–801) – One of the first Sufis, poet

Rashid-al-Din (Rashīd al-Dīn Faḍlullāh Hamadānī, nickname is al-Taib) (1247–1318) – Persian encyclopedic scholar and public activist

Rūmī Jalāl ad-Dīn Muhammad (Mevlânâ Jalāl ad-Dīn Muhammad Balkhī) (1207–1273) – Famous Persian poet

Saadi Shīrāzī (Abū-Muhammad Muslih al-Dīn bin Abdallāh) (1181–1291) – Persian writer and thinker

Saduaqas Musauly Shormanov (1850–1927) – Kazakh poet, public figure, one of the collectors of Kazakh written heritage

Savlius (6th c. BC) – Scythian king, son of Gnur, father of Idanthyrsus

Sergei Vladimiriovich Kisilev (1905–1962) – Soviet historian and archeologist, scholar of the Turkic khanate

Sextus Empiricus (beginning of 2nd c.) – Ancient Greek physicist and philosopher

Shakarim Qudaiberdiuly (Shakarim) (1858–1931) – Great Kazakh poet, philosopher, and thinker

Shalkiiz Tilenshiuly (1456–1560) – Founder of Kazakh *zhyrau* poetry

Shangerei Bokeyev (1847–1920) – Kazakh poet

Shoqan Shingisuly Ualihanov (Muhammed Hanafia) (1835–1865) – Great Kazakh scholar, Orientalist, historian, folklorist, ethnographer, geographer, enlightener, democrat

Shortanbay Qanaiuly (1818–1881) – Kazakh poet

Sigmund Freud (Sigismund Schlomo Freud) (1856–1939) – Australian thinker, psychiatrist, and neurologist, founder of the psychoanalysis school

Socrates (469–399) – Ancient Greek philosopher

Solon (640/635–559) – Athenian politician, lawyer, and poet, one of the Seven Sages of the antique world

Sophocles (496/5–406) – Athenian playwright, tragic

Spandyiar Kopeyev (1878–1956) – Kazakh writer, public activist, honored teacher of Kazakh SSR

Suleiman Baqirghani (Hakim ata) (12th c.) – Kazakh thinker, poet, philosopher

Sultanmahmut Torayghyrov (1893–1920) – Kazakh poet, thinker

Sypyra Zhyrau (14th c.) – Kazak improvisational poet

Thales of Miletus (625–547 BC) – Ancient Greek philosopher and mathematician, founder of Milesian school

Tole bi Alibekuly (1663–1756) – Kazakh state and public activist, member of *Biler kengesi* (Soviet judges), famous orator, top judge of the great *zhuz*, one of the founders of the Law Codex called *Zheti zhargi* (Seven laws)

Vilhelm Ludwig Peter Thomsen (1842–1927) – Dutch historian, linguist

Voltaire (François-Marie Arouet) (1694–1778) – Great French philosopher and enlightener, poet and novelist

Xeniades (5th c. BC) – Ancient Greek philosopher

Xenophanes (580–485 BC) – Ancient Greek philosopher

Ybyrai (Ibrahim) Altynsarin (1841–1889) – Well-known Kazakh enlightener and pedagogue

Yevgeni Bertels (1890–1957) – Soviet Orientalist

Yollug Tigin (7th–8th c.) – Ancient Turkic public figure, ruler of Eastern Turkic Khanate

Yuri Dombrovsky (1909–1978) – Russian poet, literary critic

Yusuf Balasaguni (11th c.) – Turkic thinker, poet, scholar, public figure

Zeuxis (5–4 c. BC) – Ancient Greek artist

Zhamal Qarshi (Abu-Fazl ibn Muhammad) (1230–1315) – Historian, scholar, and writer born in the territory of Semirechye of Kazakhstan

Zhusipbek Aimauytov (1889–1931) – Famous Kazakh writer, playwright, and publicist

Zhyiembet zhyrau Bartoghashuly (1570/1575–1643) – Truly talented Kazakh *zhyrau*, judge, and winner hero

Select List of Publications
by/about Abai Kunanbaiuhli

(Listed in chronological order)

Kazak akini Ibrahim Kunanbaiuhlining ulengderi [*The Kazakh Poet-Sage (Abai) Ibrahim Kunanbaiuhli's Songs*]. 1909. Sankt [Saint] Petersburg, Russia.

Abai termesi [*Songs of Abai*]. 1916. Orinbor, Russia.

Abai Kunanbaiuhlining ulengderi [*Abai Kunanbaiuhli's Songs*]. 1922. Kazan.

Abai Kunanbaiuhlining tangdamali ulengderi [*Select Songs of Abai Kunanbaiuhli*]. 1922. Tashkent, Uzbekistan.

Abai Kunanbaiuhli: Tolik zhinagi [*Abai Kunanbaiuhli: The Complete Collection*]. 1933, Kizilorda, KZ.

Abai Kunanbaiuhlining tangdamali ulengderi [*Select Songs of Abai Kunanbaiuhli*]. 1934, 1936 and 1939. Almaty, KZ.

Abai Kunanbaiuhlining shigarmalari [*The Writings of Abai Kunanbaiuhli*]. Vol 1. 1939. Almaty, KZ.

Abai Kunanbaiuhlining shigarmalari [*The Writings of Abai Kunanbaiuhli*]. Vol 2. 1940. Almaty, KZ.

Abai Kunanbaiuhlining tangdamali ulengderi [*Select Songs of Abai Kunanbaiuhli*]. 1943, 1944. Almaty, KZ.

Abai Kunanbaiuhlining shigarmalarining bir tomdik zhinagi [*The One-Volume Collection of the Writings of Abai Kunanbaiuhli*]. 1945. Almaty, KZ.

Abai Kunanbaiuhlining tangdamali ulengderi [*Select Songs of Abai Kunanbaiuhli*]. 1946. Almaty, KZ.

Abai Kunanbaiuhlining shigarmalarining tolik zhinagi [*The Complete Collection of the Writings of Abai Kunanbaiuhli*]. 1948, 1951. Almaty, KZ.

Abai Kunanbaiuhlining tangdamali ulengderi [*Select Songs of Abai Kunanbaiuhli*]. 1952. Almaty, KZ.

Abai Kunanbaiuhlining shigarmalarining tolik zhinagi [*The Complete Collection of the Writings of Abai Kunanbaiuhli*]. Vols 1-2. 1954. Almaty, KZ.

Abai Kunanbaiuhlining anderi [*Songs of Abai Kunanbaiuhli*]. 1954. Almaty, KZ.

Abai Kunanbaiuhlining shigarmalarining tolik zhinagi [*The Complete Collection of the Writings of Abai Kunanbaiuhli*]. 1955. Almaty, KZ.

Abai Kunanbaiuhlining shigarmalarining tolik zhinagi [*The Complete Collection of the Writings of Abai Kunanbaiuhli*]. 1957. Almaty, KZ.

Zhirenshin, A., ed. 1961. *Abai Kunanbaev: shigarmalarining bir tomdik tolik zhinagi* [*The Complete One-Volume Collection of His Writings*]. Almaty, KZ: Kazakting Memlekettik Korkem Adebiet Baspasi. (Note: This edition alone contains fuller bibliographic info than provided in Akhmetov, Nisanbaev and Shanbai because it was made available via a retired Kazakh scholar in Almaty. It was said by her to be the standard critical edition, though I would suspect that the later 1977, 1986 and 1995 editions have since superceded it; cf. note on the article by Beisenbai below.)

Abai Kunanbaev: shigarmalarining tolik zhinagi [*Abai Kunanbaev: The Complete One-Volume Collection of His Writings*]. Vols 1-2. 1977. Almaty, KZ.

Abai Kunanbaev: shigarmalarining zhinagi [*Abai Kunanbaev: A Collection of His Writings*]. Vols 1-2. 1986. Almaty, KZ.

Abai Kunanbaev: shigarmalarining tolik zhinagi [*The Complete Collection of His Writings*]. Vols 1-2. 1995. Almaty, KZ.

Other works:

Kazakh:

"Абай мұрасының Шығыска қатысы жайлы баспасөзде алғаш жарияланған пікірлер Кәкітай Ысқақов пен «Уақыт» газетіндегі (1908, № 388) мақала еді." ("Абай және Шығыс әдебиеті," http://kazorta.org/abaj-zh-ne-shy-ys-debieti/)

Абай. Шығармаларының екі томдық толық жинағы. Өлеңдер мен аудармалар, поэмалар, қарасөздер. - Алматы: Жазушы, 2002.

Ахмет Байтұрсынұлы. «Абай – қазақтың бас ақыны». «Қазақ» газеті, 1913.

Байғалиев, Бейсенбай. *Абай өмірбаяны архив деректерінде.* Алматы: Арыс, 2001.

Сапар Байжанов. *Абай және архив.* Алматы: «Ғылым», 1995.

Сапар Байжанов. "Абайға Қатысты Кейбір Архив Деректері." Dec 8, 2012, *Abai Instituti* (http://abai-inst.kz/?p=1141)

Әуезов, М.О. *Абайдың өнері һәм қызметі.* 1918.

Әуезов, М.О. *Абай Құнанбаев.* Алматы: «Ғылым», 1967

Әуезов М. *Абайтану дәрістерінің дерек көздері.* - Алматы: Санат, 1997. - 448 б.

Есім Ғарифолла. *Хакім Абай (даналық дүниетанымы).* Бірінші басылым. - Атамұра-Қазақстан. Алматы, 1994. - 198 б. (орыс тілінде, - Алматы «Білім», 1995)

Есім Ғарифолла. *Хакім Абай*. Екінші басылым. - Астана «Фолиант», 2012 (қазақ, орыс тілдерінде).

Есім Ғарифолла. "Абай туралы философиялық трактат." - Алматы «Қазақ университеті», 2004 (орыс тілінде, - Алматы «Қазақ университеті», 2006)

Машанов, Ақжан. *Әл-Фараби және Абай*. Алматы: Kazakhstan, 1994.

Мырзахметов, Мекемтас. Койчубаева, Б. К. Эльконина, Ф. И. *Абай Құнанбаев: библиографиялық көрсеткіш. (Абай Кунанбаев: библиографический указатель)*. Алматы: Қазақстан, 1965.

Мырзахметов М. *Мухтар Әуезов және абайтану проблемалары*. – А., 1982

Мырзахметов М. *Абайтану тарихы*. – А., 1994

Мұхамедханов Қ. *Абай мұрагерлері*. - Алматы: Атамұра, 1995. - 208 б.

Нұрқатов А. *Абайдың ақындық дәстүрі*. - Алматы: Жазушы, 1966. - 345 б.

Бөжеев М. *Абайдың ақындық айналасы*. - Алматы: Жазушы, 1971. - 112 б.

See also:

Beisenbai, Kenzhebaev. "Abai shigarmalarining tekstologialik maseleleri" ["Textual Critical Problems of Abai's Writings"]. In idem. *Turik kaganatinan buginge deiin* [*From the Turkic Kaganate Until Today*]. Almaty, KZ: Anatili, 2004, pp 160-170. (Deals with textual critical problems up through the 1950s; afterwards Zhirenshin's 1961 critical edition of Abai's writings, listed below, was issued.)

Orazalinov, Sultan. *Abai eli* [*The Nation/Land of Abai*]. Almaty, KZ: Oner, 1994.

English:

Auezov, Mukhtar. *Abai: A Novel*. 2 vols. New York: Progress Publishers, 1975. (An abridged version is available in one volume. An English version was published in Moscow in 1960; whether the 1975 U.S. version is a reprint of that or not is unknown.)

Seisenbaev, Rollan, ed. *Abai: Book of Words*. Almaty, KZ: El Bureau, 1995. (Released in Kazakh, Russian and English. English translation by R. McKane and D. Aitkyn).

See also:

Campbell, Ian W. 2017. "The Key to the World's Treasures: 'Russian Science,' Local Knowledge, and the Civilizing Mission on the Siberian Steppe," in *Knowledge and the Ends of Empire: Kazak Intermediaries and Russian Rule on the Steppe, 1731-1917*. Cornell University Press.

Select List of Publications
by Garifolla Yesim

*G. Yesim has published over 300 books, articles, essays, etc, including the following select list given in chronological order:

Sana bolmisi: sayasat pen madeniet turali oilar [*The Essence of Mind: Thoughts Regarding Politics and Culture*]. 10+ vols. Almaty, KZ. (Publishers: Vol 1, 1994, RIMP 'Eksito'-PKP 'Verena'; Vols 2-7, 1996-2002, Gilim; Vols 8-10, 2004-2006, Kazak Universiteti)

Sanadagi tangbalar [*Marks Branded in the Mind*]. Almaty, KZ, 1994.

Abaiding dunietanimi men filosofiasi [*The Worldview and Philosophy of Abai*]. Almaty, KZ: Gilim, 1995. (Co-author)

"Abai." In *Abai: An Encyclopedia*, 332-352. Almaty, KZ: Atamura, 1995.

Falsafa tarihi [*A History of Islamic Philosophy (Falsafa)*]. Almaty, KZ: Gilim, 2000. (2nd edition publ. in 2004 by Raritet)

Proshloe v nastoyashchem [*The Past in the Present*]. Almaty, KZ, 2003.

Adam-zat [*Human-ity*]. Astana, KZ: Foliant, 2003.

Dintanu negizderi / Osnovi religiovedeniya [*Essentials of the Study of Religion*]. Almaty, KZ: Bilim, 2003. (Ed. in chief; Kazakh and Russian editions produced separately)

Filosofia slov [*Philosophy of Words*]. Almaty, KZ: Kazak Universiteti, 2005.

Kazakskaya filosofia: Piramida v stepi, ili filosofia lubvi [*Kazak Philosophy: A Pyramid in the Steppe, or a Philosophy of Love*]. Almaty, KZ: Kazak Universiteti, 2005.

Kazak renessansi [*Kazak Renaissance*]. Almaty, KZ: Kazak Universiteti, 2006.

Sayasi filosofia [*Political Philosophy*]. Almaty, KZ: Kazak Universiteti, 2006.

Printed by BoD™in Norderstedt, Germany